P9-CSC-345

Getting Over Getting Older

ALSO BY LETTY COTTIN POGREBIN

How to Make It in a Man's World

Getting Yours

Growing Up Free

Stories for Free Children (editor)

Family Politics

Among Friends

Deborah, Golda, and Me

Getting Over Getting Older

An Intimate Journey

by

LETTY COTTIN POGREBIN

Little, Brown and Company
Boston New York Toronto London

First Edition

Portions of this book have appeared previously in different forms in *Ms.*, the *New York Times* "Hers" column, and *Family Circle*.

The author is grateful for permission to include the following previously copyrighted material: Letters from Nadine Markova, Phyllis Theroux, Bill Ayers, and Peggy Henretig reprinted by permission of the authors; excerpt from review article by Sandra Pollack from *New Directions for Women*. Copyright © by Sandra Pollack. Reprinted by permission of the author; excerpt from journal by Wendy Orange reprinted by permission of the author; excerpts from *Four Quartets*. Copyright © 1943 by T. S. Eliot; renewed 1971 by Esme Valerie Eliot. Reprinted by permission of Harcourt Brace and Company; excerpts from *Collected Poems 1930–1973* by May Sarton. Copyright © 1974, 1980, 1984, 1988, 1993 by May Sarton. Reprinted by permission of W. W. Norton Company and A. M. Heath and Company; excerpts from "To a Middle-Aged Friend Considering Adultery with a Younger Man" from *Forever Fifty and Other Negotiations* by Judith Viorst; Simon & Schuster. Copyright © 1989 by Judith Viorst. Reprinted by permission of the author; excerpt from "Warning" from *Selected Poems* by Jenny Joseph; Bloodaxe Books. Copyright © 1992 by Jenny Joseph. Reprinted by permission of John Johnson Ltd., London.

Library of Congress Cataloging-in-Publication Data

Pogrebin, Letty Cottin.
Getting over getting older: an intimate journey / by Letty Cottin Pogrebin. — 1st ed.
p. cm.
Includes bibliographical references.
ISBN 0-316-71263-9
1. Middle aged women — United States — Attitudes. 2. Middle aged women — United States — Psychology. 3. Middle aged women — United States — Social conditions. 4. Aging — United States — Psychological aspects. 5. Maturation (Psychology) — United States. 6. Body image — United States. I. Title.
HQ1059.5.U5P65 1996
305.24'4 — dc20 95-44710

10 9 8 7 6 5 4 3 2

MV-NY

Published simultaneously in Canada by Little, Brown & Company (Canada) Limited

Printed in the United States of America

For
Betty and Bernard Miller
who once helped me to grow up
and now teach me how to grow older

Nothing is so dear and precious as time.

— *Rabelais*

Contents

Acknowledgments

I have only myself to blame for the ways in which this book may fall short, but if it succeeds — if it offers new truths about time and aging, and renders the midlife experience in words that touch the reader — then credit must be shared with:

Fredrica Friedman, my editor at Little, Brown, who told me back in 1989 that I had a story to tell and then made sure I told it with more candor and clarity than ever would have been possible without her vision, her patience, and her inspired editorial guidance;

Phyllis Wender, my friend for thirty-five years, now my literary agent, who keeps me growing by asking more of me than I imagine myself capable of giving, and whose loving support and rock-solid loyalty strengthen me in my work and nurture me in my life;

The women at my birthday lunch, who helped me turn fifty;

The board and staff of the MacDowell Colony, who gave me seven precious weeks of care, feeding, workspace, and priceless solitude in Peterborough, New Hampshire — real-life inspiration for *Our Town*, the play that means so much to me;

My walking partners, Barbara Harnick and Gale Robinson, who listened to more of my angst than friends should have to endure, who calmed me down and propped me up during our walks around Saltaire or Central Park and contributed anecdotes and insights that greatly enriched my perspective on aging;

Robin Pogrebin and Abigail Pogrebin, who are always there for me, who read every word of this manuscript, often several times, whose criticisms were smart and tough, but unfailingly sensitive, who save me from my excesses and keep me honest, and who honor me by being my daughters;

David Pogrebin, who offered spirited encouragement, title advice, and the constant reassurance that even though I'm his mother, I'm the youngest fifty-five-year-old woman he knows;

Bert Pogrebin, who lived with my obsessions and agonies, tolerated my writing absences, talked me through the blocked places, vanquished my moods with his tenderness, and gave me laughter when I needed it most; Bert, my husband, who gives me the time of his life, and whose love makes everything possible.

PART I

Facing Age

1

Before We Begin

Do not go gentle into that good night

— Dylan Thomas
(written when he was 38)

"What's it about?" my friends ask when they learn I've started a new book.

"It's about time and aging," I say, by now anticipating the reactions.

"Aging" is all they hear. "Uggh," they groan. "How depressing!" Then they smile and start peppering me with questions: Am I going to write about the insidious body changes, the crazy way time speeds up, the sudden appreciation for small pleasures, the memory lapses, the existential gloom? What about high blood pressure, high cholesterol, high anxiety, and low sex drive? Have I noticed myself gaining weight lately? Have I noticed my husband snoring? And have I noticed that one gets more spiritual with age, less driven, more mellow?

As a matter of fact, I have noticed; noticing is what this book is about. In these pages, I focus on what has been happening to my body, mind, health, psyche, and spirit since I turned fifty, an event disconcerting enough to trigger a maelstrom of soul-searching and a full-scale reassessment of my life. I worry aloud about the things most people over fifty worry about silently — little things like loss, change, weakness, insecurity, illness, and death. I speak of my fears and subterfuges, the struggle to overcome them, and the slogan I've learned to live by — "Feel the fear and do it anyway." I talk about love, sex, and plastic surgery. I try to achieve that delicate balance between accepting age and resisting it, and to explain why I think it so important *not* to accept all the depredations of aging but to draw a line in the sand and fight back in those areas where resistance can be a hedge against despair. In short, this book is an introspective, close-to-the-bone story of one woman watching herself grow older — and trying to grow smarter and stronger in the process. It's about maintaining control in the face of creeping chaos, dignity in the face of the youth cult, and hope in the face of mortality.

The book is divided into four sections: *Facing Age, Keeping Time, Mortal Flesh and Mortal Fears, Rethinking What Matters.* Though filtered through one life and one set of experiences, those themes seem to me to address universal questions about time and aging that bedevil virtually everyone who grapples with the mystery of life. It is my story, I tell my friends, but if I've succeeded, it is also about you.

Clearly, age is on everyone's mind. They want to talk about it; no, they'd rather not. They're coping, or maybe they're going to pieces. Discomfort surrounds them like a fog, and usually they end up muttering, "Write fast; I need this book," or "Can you believe we've come to this?"

Naming the Problem

I've had similar reactions; in fact, I've had every conceivable reaction to aging — from astonishment to anger, from confusion to curiosity, from denial to disgust. Obviously, I am not going gently into this good night. My feminist sisters, Betty Friedan, Carolyn Heilbrun, Gloria Steinem, and others, counsel women to welcome age. They discern nobility and power in the elder female. So do I, but I'm not in a hurry to *be* one. I hated turning fifty, it's as simple as that.

Many of those proud Gray Panther types insist that human beings, like fine wines, get better with age. That sounds like sour grapes to me. I have yet to be persuaded of the so-called gifts of age, since older people seem no more admirable as a group than other mortals, and they have two distinct disadvantages — physical decline and a dwindling future. Why anyone should wax poetic about joining their ranks is beyond me. "Let's face it," said sociologist Chad Gordon. "Aging sucks."

Don't mistake this diatribe for ageism. I'm not saying I dislike old people; I just don't like getting old *myself.* At this writing, more than halfway through my fifties, I continue to resent just about everything that has happened to me in connection with the aging process, including the fact that I stumbled into it with almost no idea of what lay ahead. I would have preferred to be forewarned.

As Gypsy Rose Lee once said, "I have everything I had twenty years ago, only it's all a bit lower." My skin is sagging, my silhouette is drooping, and, if my new toilet habits are any indication, everything that has fallen down is now pressing on my bladder. As if that isn't bad enough, my metabolism has slowed, my anxieties won't stay repressed, my eyes and ears are not what they once were, and my memory is slipping.

Now, where was I?

Ah yes, nothing quite prepares you for this ongoing sideshow of indignity and deterioration, for the way it ambushes you and changes your life from one week to the next. No one warns you that, after decades of sound slumber, you will suddenly find yourself springing out of bed in the dead of night with a nonnegotiable need to go to the bathroom *immediately.* (I expected that to happen in my eighties, not at fifty-one.)

No one tells you that without your spouse at hand, you may find it impossible to achieve total recall of past events, since it often requires two brains to reconstruct one memory. Nobody warns you that suddenly one year, you can't read the print in the telephone book, the next year you're attending your friends' funerals, the next year you have to let out the waistband on every skirt you own, or your shoe size enlarges, or your bra straps leave permanent indentations, or suddenly one morning and every day thereafter, you wake up with sleep creases that make your skin look like crepe paper and require three hours to wear off. And no one warns you that, inexplicably, unpredictably, in the midst of a party, on a beautiful summer afternoon, when your daughter and son-in-law are showing you photographs of their vacation, while you're listening to music, or riding a bike, or clipping a recipe from the newspaper — suddenly, the thought enters your mind that you are going to die.

When I air my complaints to the women in my black-Jewish discussion group (four blacks and four Jews who for ten years have met to talk about issues involving our communities), they instantly put Crown Heights on hold and start to dish about aging.

"The weirdest thing happened last week," announces one of the late-fortyish women in a conspiratorial whisper. "I found a gray pubic hair! I showed it to my husband and we roared, but it made me feel so old. A gray *pubic* hair, can you believe it?"

"That's nothing," I put in. "My pubic hair is falling out!"

We burst out laughing, then another woman admits to the same condition. I feel relieved.

Hearing this story, my daughter Abigail, then twenty-eight, becomes agitated. "Mother, you can't put *that* in the book!" she insists. "You can't write about such private things. Thinning pubic hair is disgusting."

But that's the point. Much of the aging process *is* disgusting, not the least to young people with young bodies, but to those of us who are going through it. And unless we can deal with our shame and fear, and pull the facts out of hiding, unless we can normalize aging by talking about the private things and preparing each other for the worst, it won't be any easier when Abigail is fifty than it is for me and my contemporaries today.

"The age thing is really scary," writes Patricia Bosworth. "Most of my women friends are terrified."

That is no exaggeration. We're all quaking in our Reeboks. Which is what led me to write this book — to rake through the fears we dare not admit to ourselves and certainly won't share with each other, to describe the changes most of us deny, to examine the anxieties of aging in one life observed closely, honestly, and without mercy. Well, a little mercy, perhaps.

Although I have yet to experience heavy-duty decrepitude or serious illness, I see no reason why suffering should be the prerequisite for raging against mortality or why a healthy person must be disqualified from bitching with the best of them about corporeal collapse. Since I tend to count my blessings with clock-like regularity, I am well aware that having been spared a life-threatening illness, financial disaster, and other major crises, I have the luxury of bemoaning the vexations of aging, which are clearly a lower order of concern. But that doesn't negate the fact that, one after another, after another, the vexations add up until together they comprise what we call Life.

Yiddish proverb: "Only a fool does not grow old." Translation: you'd have to be stupid not to notice, so why not get the facts out in the open where we can compare notes.

Comedians have no problem talking about aging in public:

"You know you're getting older when the person you sleep with refers to your water bed as the Dead Sea."

"Middle age is when you finally get it all together, and you can't remember where you put it."

"You know you are middle-aged when: You're on the phone arranging to meet someone and you say, 'I have brown hair . . .' and someone who lives with you laughs."

"Middle age is when you finally have all the answers, but nobody will ask you the questions."

We laugh, we recognize ourselves in the punch lines, but we rarely move from shared laughter to shared intimacies. What little we know about the landscape of aging comes not from each other, but from novels and short stories — Thomas Mann's *Magic Mountain,* John Updike's later *Rabbit* novels, Saul Bellow's *Herzog,* Doris Lessing's *The Summer Before Dark* or *Diary of a Good Neighbor,* Bernard Malamud's *Dubin's Lives* — or from the short fiction of Colette and Grace Paley; the poetry of T. S. Eliot, W. B. Yeats, and Wallace Stevens; the journals and memoirs of May Sarton, M. F. K. Fisher, Jean Rhys, and Edmund Wilson; and a few nonfiction works like Gail Sheehy's *New Passages,* Gloria Steinem's essay "Doing 60," Erica Jong's autobiographical *Fear of Fifty,* Betty Friedan's *The Fountain of Age* (which focuses on the years after 65), and the self-help compendium *Ourselves, Growing Older* (also weighted toward the problems of the later years).

Rich and varied though these works are, when I looked for literary companionship, what I missed was an exploration of the entire process from the inside out — what happens to the whole human being in that enormously eventful period when our physical transformations are more dramatic than any we've known since puberty and our emotions careen between resignation and hysteria. Entering one's fifties is a major turning point, yet we carry on without help or succor, unable to put a mirror to our symptoms, embarrassed by our mutating bodies, mad at our malfunctioning minds, wondering if what's happening to us is happening to anyone else. Left alone with all this lunacy, it's no wonder so many of us are scared.

All of which is to say that I am writing about aging to tame it. I want to expose the whole gruesome ordeal, to open it up and share it, and in the process to make it more manageable and less shameful. I want to tell the truth because I've never read it. "Writers lie out of the best of motives," says Barbara Grizzuti Harrison. ". . . They want to make order out of chaos and bring shape and form to muddle. It is hard to bear witness to the truth and at the same time to shape messy experience in such a way as to make sense of it." But that is exactly what we must do if we choose to steer through life rather than be buffeted about on its waves. And that is why, since my forty-ninth year, I have not only been watching myself age but trying to understand why my generation, which is aging so well, is unable to celebrate its achievement.

Who Are We, and What Are We Thinking?

We are, in fact, the healthiest, fittest, longest-lived people in history. We're an astonishing experiment in species-wide self-improvement, a phenomenal mammal whose life span has nearly tripled in the blink of an evolutionary eye. Let me put it in perspective: according to the National Institute on Aging, in 1900 the average American was dead by age forty-nine; fifty was considered old age, and only one person in ten survived to sixty-five, which was thought of then as *extreme* old age. But today, if you're fifty, you can expect to live an additional thirty-three years (incidentally, thirty-three was just about the whole human life span in 1400), and if you're sixty right now, chances are you have a quarter of a century left. Think how astounding this is. In less than a hundred years, the average life expectancy has increased by well over 50 percent. What's more, in today's world the longevity prognosis for older people is even better than it is for babies. In other words, the longer you live, the longer you *will* live. The average infant born in 1995 has a life expectancy of seventy-five, but those of us who have made it to middle age — and who manage to avoid addictive substances and random gunfire — will more than likely survive well beyond seventy-five (presumably the less fit have already fallen by the wayside). More than 80 percent of American women (only 34 percent of men) reach age sixty in reasonably good health, and a healthy sixty-year-old woman has a better-than-average chance to see her eighty-fifth birthday. Longevity expert Lydia Bronte says the average life span is rapidly inching toward one hundred years.

With this vastly expanded horizon stretching out before us, we have every reason to be grateful. Instead of complaining about age, we ought to be reveling in our good fortune and relishing the extra time — especially since the added years haven't been tacked on to the end of our lives but are ours to enjoy in the middle, while we're in good health. Happily, it is middle age that has widened and lengthened, so that most people's fifties and sixties can be described as an unremarkable, and therefore quite remarkable, continuum of high-energy living. UCLA gerontologist Fernando Torres-Gil "predicts that this generation won't confront 'old age' until well into their 70s," according to *Newsweek.* "The broad concept of middle age is starting later and lasting longer — and looking better than ever before." What is called for next is to reconcile the negative feelings that descend on so many of us at fifty — feelings of being washed up, over the hill, pressed for time, and closer to the end — with this positive new reality; to learn to savor these bonus years and fill them to the brim.

I expect most people reading this book will hail from my own age cohort, some 50 million people born sometime after the Depression and before the end of the Second World War. You might call us "Roosevelt's babies," since our birth dates fall roughly between 1932, when FDR was first elected president, and 1945, when he died, or you might go along with Carolyn Mott Ford, who calls us the "sandwich generation . . . the American cheese melting between two self-important pieces of toast — senior citizens and baby boomers."

"We did not know we were a generation," laments John Updike (born in 1932), but we *are* a generation with distinctive traits, among them our relative invisibility. Our age group accounts for less than 10 percent of the population, "not enough to affect fashions or elections, which gets a generation noticed, but plenty for filling top jobs," says social analyst Wade Green. Despite the attention lavished upon Generation X, baby boomers, and seniors (the first two as attractive to marketing experts as Red Riding Hood was to the wolf, the third a formidable voting bloc), it is my sparse, silent, unnamed generation that now fills the ranks of power. Or some of the men do. For women, the picture is murkier because so many of us changed our lives when the women's movement opened our horizons, and we haven't peaked quite yet.

In point of fact, not much is known about what either sex is up to because, as Roy Blount, Jr. (born in 1941), points out, "People my age are not a media-recognized 'we.'" Roosevelt babies haven't been studied nearly as much as the fortysomethings whose midlife crisis reeks of sex and ego, or the sixty-five plus crowd whose health care issues are front page news. Yet our "we" is quite a remarkable group, a bridge between two worlds, unself-conscious trailblazers who, whether we know it or not, are creating a model of aging that is breaking new ground for the 76 million postWar babies — nearly one-third of the total U.S. population — whose leading edge started turning fifty in 1996. Since January 1, 1996, one of them will turn fifty every seven and a half seconds for the next ten years. As the baby boomers cross the great divide, they may embark upon their journey with less fear and loathing because we have gone before them, reinventing the very essence of age by the way we are living our lives. Our way bears little resemblance to that of our parents, who appeared (and often were) so much older than we are at fifty. And our way is centuries removed from that of our grandparents, who seemed to go directly from flaming youth to dreary dotage, much as women in foreign films age overnight from fiery girls in tight blouses to matrons draped in shapeless black.

Most of the women I know who are in their late forties, fifties, and sixties are in great shape. They're physically active, productive, vigorous, and attractive. The men are all of the above and sometimes more, worldly success having gilded them with the afterglow of male power. These are, to be sure, privileged, middle-class people who, for the most part, do stimulating work, enjoy their leisure, eat nutritious meals, belong to a gym, and have access to excellent health care. They are not working two jobs to make ends meet; they're not getting by on food stamps and four hours' sleep. The women have bodies that are not distended from too much childbearing. They enjoy vastly expanded options, and many are just now realizing their employment potential after years devoted to their families. In short, these women embody a new paradigm of aging. But rather than striding proudly into the future, they don't want to talk about it, they don't want to think about it, they (we) find it too, uggh, ummm, depressing.

You know as well as I how this attitude plays itself out: in terminal denial. Some women lie about their age, some let face-lifts lie for them, or they slather themselves with overpriced wrinkle creams, or starve themselves like teenage anorexics. Their goal is to keep battling gravity and birthdays. Take a week at a spa. Take a lover. Trade in the station wagon for a convertible. Have a massage. A makeover. Finally, the payoff: "You look so young!" And how we preen — but we're still what we are: aging by the minute, inside and out.

If it isn't the appearance of age that torments us, it's the tyranny of the number, especially those landmark birthdays. Numbers can be as haunting as old family photographs seared into the brain like a forecast, or a warning. Somehow, despite all that has revolutionized our world, one thing stays unchanged and unchangeable: our childhood concept of what it means to be forty, fifty, or sixty, and the indelible memory of how our parents looked, dressed, and behaved when they were the age we are now.

Sometimes memory yields nothing but an empty canvas for the simple reason that one's parents didn't survive long enough to leave an image of themselves at an advanced age. My mother died when I was fifteen and she was fifty-three. When I turned fifty-four, I felt a frisson of relief to have passed through that hexed year unscathed. It may well be that I've chosen to write about aging at this point, because at some level, at age fifty-five, I am amazed I'm still here. Maybe I'm writing this book as a way of cherishing the rest of my life, the years I was not sure I would be given, the years my mother never had. Maybe I need to write about these years to force myself to live them more consciously because I am living them for both of us.

Whatever the motivation, the result, I hope, is an honest exploration of *mindful* aging, an account specific and vivid enough to evoke in the reader that shock of recognition that makes the personal universal. Indeed, because this book is so personal, I worry about its being fouled by what Phillip Lopate, editor of *The Art of the Personal Essay,* calls "the stench of ego," an obvious occupational hazard for those who commit their lives to paper. Yet, one takes the risk, he says, knowing that the personal story is important only "insofar as one's example can serve to elucidate a more widespread human trait and make readers feel a little less lonely and freakish." My intent, precisely. And if Lopate is correct, I trust the reader to forgive whatever self-absorption permeates these pages in return for my commitment to candor, and the warranty that I have done, as he puts it, "a fair amount of introspective homework."

Time-Wrestling

In this culture, we rarely get to hear other people's inner thoughts about aging, because whenever the subject comes up — whether in ads, pop culture, or conversations with friends — the focus is on how to turn back the clock, conquer age, beat it, hide it behind a mask. This explains why so many of us are pawns of the $33 billion-a-year diet business, the $20 billion cosmetics business, the $300 million plastic surgery business — industries with a hefty investment in having us peak in our twenties, then buy into the youth quest for the rest of our lives.

The time a fifty-year-old woman spends trying to look thirty (or even forty), is time when she is not fully present in the here and now — not living in the moment but in the longing for something that will be forever beyond her reach. Time squandered in search of youth is time indentured to a myth. It does not belong to us, it belongs to the unattainable. Chasing rainbows, we wander off the main road, meander around in a hopeless maze, up blind alleys, down dead-end streets, all of them detours from the truth.

The truth is, time is all we have. Chunks of time — minutes, hours, days — are the building blocks of being, the containers in which we stuff our pleasures, our pain, our loving and doing, our caring, our meaning. The following chapters will cover many aspects of aging yet keep coming back to the main premise: what really matters in life is not numbers but hours, not age but time. I am saying something as basic as breath: *Time is life.* Use it or lose it. Seize it as if you have every right to it, like air; take it in, hold it, expand it, shape it to your dreams or it will gallop out of control and disappear.

Time is life. It stands to reason, therefore, that people who love life will wish to control time to whatever degree possible; they will try to multiply their actual years on earth by adopting a healthier lifestyle, and they will try to magnify each unit of time by living it more intensely and attentively. Control is a significant leitmotif in this book, partly because I'm a bit of a control freak but largely because I believe there *are* ways to slow time down and prevent the years from racing off with our lives. We can do it by introducing more newness into our lives — more "firsts" of the sort each of us experienced in childhood when everything was happening for the first time and time itself seemed eternal; more challenges and unfamiliar encounters, the surprises that stop time in its tracks; more freshness to keep us in touch with the wonder of youth; more remembering (the nourishments of nostalgia have been underrated); more separable, savored moments; more noticing.

Time is life. We must not let aging distract us from that fundamental truth. We must grasp time while there's still enough of it left to get a grip on. The epigraph from Rabelais in the front of this book bears repeating: "Nothing is so dear and precious as time." Not youth. Not beauty. Not anything.

Since I turned fifty, two things have become crystal clear to me: first, the American obsession with age deflects people, especially women, from the truth of the human condition, which is the diminishment of time and the inevitability of our own death. Second, it is the time/mortality epiphany that lies at the very heart of our fear of aging, though most of us have yet to face the fear or grapple with it. About the fact of his mortality, the psychologist Stanley Jacobson writes, "It is a monstrous boulder of an idea to wrap my mind around, the idea of ceasing to exist in this world. And the more I engage the monster, the more confident I am that working to come to terms with finitude is neither morbid nor eccentric but necessary to good mental health." Yet few of us are willing to take on the task. Daunted by the monster of our own mortality, we turn our attention to aging, the enemy we live with every day, the enemy our culture tells us can be vanquished, at least temporarily.

And so we get sidetracked into the pursuit of eternal youth — a time-consuming, labor-intensive, high-maintenance enterprise that is futile from the start. Some women become so preoccupied with physical aging that they are diverted from all that they might do, contribute, or accomplish. They turn into narcissists too myopic to notice that the world needs their help. They never realize that the time they spend fighting age is the time all of us need most to make our remaining years count.

What good is it to turn fifty with an unwrinkled face if there's no light behind the eyes, no passion in the voice, no new ideas happening inside the head? Why hope to live a long life if we're only going to fill it with self-absorption, body maintenance, and image repair? When we die, do we want people to exclaim, "She looked ten years younger," or do we want them to say, "She lived a great life?" In essence, the choice presented to people over fifty is this: time or aging — which matters most? When time is the target, it changes the way you look at the world. You notice how most people mindlessly squander time and take life for granted. You feel in your teeth and hair and bones how achingly finite everything is. You panic. You make new resolutions. You fall in love with life. You pay attention.

Time is life — and paying attention gives you more of it, which explains why another continuing theme in this book is the profound importance of *mindfulness* as a means of extending life and elongating time. Mindfulness is the term Harvard psychologist Ellen Langer assigns to the state of being conscientiously "alert, in control, and open to life's possibilities." In experimental studies, Langer found that enhanced mindfulness can improve people's health, reverse memory loss, increase brain development, improve eyesight and hearing, reduce depression, increase self-confidence, and lengthen a person's life. All this without any drugs (miracle or hallucinatory). Mindful living asks nothing of us but a commitment to *intentionality*. It requires no effort other than purposeful concentration and the determination to live each day with more aim and awareness. Mindfulness means knowing how to be fully engaged in the present and actively in touch with the past, and in so doing, to trick time into slowing down and delivering more life. Mindfulness is time-wrestling in its most constructive form.

The mindful person doesn't measure life by birthdays or frown lines, but by time lines, the arcs and sequences that mark our existence — those moments on the life span when we notice ourselves in transition from one phase to another and feel a part of ourselves changing. When the American Board of Family Practice asked a random sampling of 1,200 Americans when they think middle age begins, the most popular answers were: when you worry about having enough money for health care; when your last child moves out; and when you don't recognize the names of music groups on the radio anymore. I'm 3 for 3.

"What exactly are we supposed to call them?" asks Judith Viorst about people who are undergoing age-related transformations. "And at what age do we decide that them is us?" Naming ourselves is an issue at this point in life not because of political correctness but because categories tend to be coercive. They create chronological ghettos and transform "us" into "them" just as surely as making sixty-five "retirement age," now prohibited by law, once tracked millions into premature obsolescence. Various polls show that most Americans define middle age as somewhere between forty-five and sixty-five. Since this matches my definition as well, I refer to myself herein as middle-aged or in midlife. You'll find no labels du jour in this book, no gimmicky phrases like "nonaged," "early elders," "young olds," "preseniors," and "the no longer young," and I see no reason to coin yet another neologism for a period that represents vastly different meanings and possibilities for each of us.

Likewise, I haven't focused any laser beams on estate planning, taxes, insurance, demographics, retirement communities, how to make a will, care for aged parents, or other such issues that are adequately addressed by books that you'll find among those listed in the resource section (page 325). What I have tried, instead, is to put into words that which has been experienced but largely unspoken — apprehensions, epiphanies, anger, astonishment, the sadness I've called existential gloom, and the joyful notes that play amongst the blues.

Above all, I have tried to be honest about my deepest fears, because

I've discovered that, however idiosyncratic, and regardless of degree, one's private anxieties rarely differ in kind from those of one's age-mates. So along with my time obsession, you will see me grapple with a lifelong fear of blood, of physical inadequacy, of being out of control, of loss. Rather than surrender to entropy or denial, I've found that one can dive into anxiety the way we force ourselves to plunge into an icy lake on a sweltering summer's day, knowing that no matter how great the shock, we'll feel braced and refreshed once we're in. Having entered our fears, we find, astonishingly, that we are able to speak their name, probe their depths, and come up for air having actually grown stronger just at the point when it seemed we would never breathe again.

Mastering anxiety at this late stage offers a far greater triumph over aging than can be found in any liposuction clinic. If we can reverse the downward slide, if we can turn things around and make ourselves more robust and resilient, then midlife loses some of its terror and becomes a place of promise, a place where time can deliver not just loss and decay, but a flowering of new parts of ourselves.

The other day, I responded to another friend's query, and when I said I was writing about time and aging, she asked: "Is it going to be depressing or uplifting?"

"Both!" I replied, relieved to hear both options. As a matter of fact, aging *is* both depressing and uplifting, disgusting and rewarding, a private experience that is also, like it or not dear Abigail, much in need of public exposure.

Author Grace Paley once was asked, "Do you mind having to get older?" I expected her to say no, like so many stiff-upper-lip Pollyannas, but she surprised me: "I feel great," she replied. "I like my life a lot. It's interesting every day. But it so happens I *do* mind."

It so happens I mind, too, but I'm learning that minding does not have to lead to despair and denial. Minding can lead to mindfulness. Living consciously through these years means learning to live with decay *and* growth, impermanence *and* immutability, losing *and* letting go. Mindfulness can sanctify time. It can force one to distill and synthesize and sort out and see anew that time *is* life, and counting the moments makes time count.

It sounds simple, but it ain't easy. As my favorite T-shirt puts it: AGING IS NOT FOR SISSIES.

2

Feeling Out Fifty

> One day I said to myself: "I'm forty!" By the time I recovered from the shock of that discovery, I had reached fifty.
>
> — *Simone de Beauvoir*

My obsession with my age began in 1989. I know this because I wrote about it while it was happening:

"On June 9, I will be fifty years old," I announced in an essay published in *Ms.* magazine. "I cannot believe it. Fifty is somebody else's age. It's an abstraction. It belongs to my parents' generation. I can't 'relate' to it. I certainly don't feel fifty. What does fifty feel like? What does fifty *mean*? I don't understand any of this. I just know I don't like it."

Many women are ashamed of *being* fifty; I was ashamed of not *enjoying* it. For feminists, age pride is an article of faith. Ordinary females might mourn their passing youth, but any women's movement activist worth her salt — any veteran of consciousness-raising and protest marches — was supposed to have broken free of the orthodoxies of conventional femininity and was expected to stand tall in her ripening self.

Books yet to be written — by Carolyn Heilbrun and Betty Friedan, among others — would eventually give overt expression to a coercive age-positive ideology that bordered on political correctness. Good feminists were supposed to welcome aging because (a) it's important to celebrate women as we really are, and (b) feminism has liberated us from the tyranny of youth and beauty. Or so it was said.

When Gloria Steinem turned forty, a reporter said, "Gee, you don't look forty!" Sensing one of those you're-so-different-from-those-other-Jews compliments that disparage the group while praising one member, she shot back, "This is what forty looks like. We've been lying so long, who would know?" That off-the-cuff comment was repeated by so many women on their own birthdays that it entered the culture — another evidence of our unequal obsession with aging — but soon, the media had dropped her second sentence, making it sound as if Gloria meant that other women should look *like her.* On her fiftieth birthday, she tried a more demographic approach, writing in *Ms.* that women's increased life expectancy, combined with pushing the age barrier, had created a world in which, "Fifty is what forty used to be." Nonetheless, at sixty, she was still explaining that no, she hadn't meant women should look like her — or like anyone but themselves — much less like a stereotype. Even an age-defying comment had been used to create guilt, though it was meant to create a take-it-or-leave-it pride.

Certainly, sixty didn't look like that on my grandmother, an immigrant raising seven children on a grocer's salary, and sixty doesn't look like that on the women who clean offices all night, or who wait table at your local coffee shop, or even on the well-heeled socialites whose hairdressers and skin care specialists are outmatched by the inexorable pull of time, gravity, and genetic predisposition. And sixty won't look anywhere near that good on me.

Actually, the issue of looks has played a somewhat secondary role in my resistance to aging. Although startled and dismayed by the physical changes of the last few years, I had never viewed myself as more than routinely attractive to begin with; heredity had dealt me an oddly girlish aspect, so fading youth wasn't my immediate problem. When I thought about what really was bugging me — which I did incessantly when I was forty-nine — it wasn't loss of looks, it was loss of time. It wasn't my fading youth, it was my fading future.

The View from the Top of the Hill

Suddenly, my orientation to time seemed to shift like the plates in the earth, and I stood on a fault line, feeling the world rearranging itself beneath my feet. When the rumbling stopped, what had been a distant horizon — the possibility of my own death — had drawn much closer, crowding me, pushing forward in time and space and foreshortening what, until now, had been a vast open sky. Clearly, I was more than halfway there, more than halfway to The End, as the storybooks would have it; any way you look at it, the middle was behind me.

We Americans have a well-known habit of placing ourselves in the middle category of whatever attribute is under discussion: whether we resemble Princess Grace or the hunchback of Notre Dame, we call ourselves average-looking; whether we live like Edith Bunker or Brooke Astor, we call ourselves middle class; and whether we're forty or sixty-five, we call ourselves middle-aged. "Fifty is halftime," said Joe Namath when his big birthday rolled around. I appreciate sports metaphors as much as the next guy, but this one won't make the cut. Few fifty-year-olds can expect to play two more full quarters of the game of life. Statistically, the midpoint is about thirty-seven, so at fifty I was closer to three-quarters through. But let's not quibble: the point is, I had fewer years left than I had already lived.

Nevertheless, there *is* a halftime feeling about the midcentury mark, and with it a change in orientation that suggests a physical about-face. Until fifty, most of us imagine ourselves moving onward and upward. At fifty, we see ourselves cresting the hill, standing at the summit, glancing back where we came from, and then tentatively, reluctantly, starting down the other side.

The hill is one of the more enduring clichés of aging. "When you're over the hill, you pick up speed," they say. *It's Better to Be Over the Hill Than Under It,* insists Eda LeShan's book title (though she places the hilltop at sixty). A national group of "mature American skiers who take to the mountain together" call themselves the Over the Hill Gang. And again a T-shirt trumps them all: "Over the hill? What hill? I don't remember any hill."

That message was on a shirt given to me for my fiftieth birthday, and whenever I wear it — an act of willful self-mockery — I love to watch people read my chest and break into a smile, taking obvious pleasure in the paradox that a failing memory, the nemesis of the middle-aged, also lets us forget that we are getting older and the end is getting closer. Pushing fifty, I needed a line like that to help me laugh at myself and my obsessions. I needed anything that might help me accept aging and the time crunch; I needed anyone who could help me understand why this midlife landmark wreaks such havoc and show me how to work through the despair and make the most of the rest of my journey.

"Even if I get another thirty years," I wrote in *Ms.*, "how healthy will I be? And will it be enough time to see how everything turns out: do we finally triumph over the deficit, AIDS, and acid rain? Who will be America's second woman President, Yale's second black president, and the ultimate peacemaker in the Middle East? Can I live long enough to know my grandchildren's lovers? Will thirty years be enough to realize all my dreams: learn Russian, write three novels (the 'promising' first, the 'disappointing' second, and a 'fully realized' third), then maybe win the Pulitzer? Or do I have to accept that nobody gets it all done?"

Missing the finales of the cliff-hangers of my era would be deprivation enough, but the idea that I might not have enough time to get it all done — whatever "it" might be — struck me with the force of a fist. "Not now" used to mean I'll do it when I get around to it, or when I feel like it, or sometime on a sunny someday. But at fifty, I suddenly understood that "not now" is a way of saying "maybe never." Time might actually end for me before I can finish what I want to do and see and be. If someone could guarantee that I'll live to be a healthy, vigorous ninety, I'm not sure I'd have been so upset about turning fifty, but without that assurance I felt vulnerable and pressed for time. Suddenly, death seemed imminent and eminently possible. I'd known many people — family and friends — who died in their fifties. Clearly I could be struck down at any moment, so why hadn't I planned my life more carefully? How should I use the time I have left? Who did I want to be when I grow up? Did I really intend to reach the end of my days with the same baggage I'd been lugging around like an albatross for decades — the same anxieties and fears, the same weaknesses, the same limitations? Had I imagined that someone or something would come along and magically transform me into the new, improved version of myself that I someday hoped to be? Hope? Someday? What was I waiting for? Did I think I was going to live forever?

That I could be galvanized by such questions did not mean I was unaware of how hackneyed they were. Still, every cliché was once an epiphany; some of us just don't "get it" until it happens to us. And, once I got it, I couldn't stop thinking about it; I wanted to talk about it, chew it over, and find out how other people were dealing with it. But while I had begun to live my life with one eye on the clock and the other on the calendar, most of my peers were talking about age without mentioning mortality at all. Death lurked in the corners of their conversations like bad news. But they had no time to think about time.

My men friends were focused on money issues. Whether at the peak of their careers, nursing the wounds of a layoff, or phasing into retirement, most men placed financial matters at center stage, with health and fitness as runners-up.

My less-politicized women friends were talking about wrinkles, weight gain, loneliness, illness, dependent parents, hot flashes, and widowhood.

My feminist friends had their hands full thumbing their noses at the youth cult; they were talking about the politics of age discrimination, sexual invisibility, economic insecurity, the intersection of age and gender stereotypes, and the medicalization of menopause.

When I asked people point-blank how they were dealing with shrinking time and impending mortality, the responses from all quarters were dismissive. Most men maneuvered the discussion back to practical matters, calling my questions "emotional" or "religious." The nonfeminist women seemed to be in denial about age altogether. (I'm thinking of one matron who referred to her fiftieth birthday as the tenth anniversary of her fortieth birthday.) Though actively battling the ravages of time, they found questions about time itself to be abstract and depressing. Most of my women's movement colleagues toed the party line, and the doctrine of age-positive thinking allowed no dissent. Griping about age at all — even if one focused on mortality — was thought to open the door to "age-negativity," an attitude they'd jettisoned along with chin straps and wrinkle concealers. To a feminist, the enemy was patriarchal oppression, not Father Time.

Feminists denying the angst of aging seemed as absurd as traditional women denying the *fact* of aging, yet there it was. Different populations, different motivations, same result: avoidance and denial. While I don't mean to criticize other people's coping mechanisms — each of us wrestles with the angel of age as best we can — I do think that meeting with all that silence explains why, rounding the bend toward fifty, I felt so alone with my obsessions.

Truth or Consequences

After I let some of my thoughts hang out in the pages of *Ms.*, a number of readers wrote to congratulate me for having the courage to admit to being fifty in a world that loses interest in women over thirty. They were so amazed that I had "outed" myself, that is, gone public with my age, that they didn't seem to notice the point of the piece — the mortality part —

or didn't want to, or maybe couldn't afford to. These were women who sheepishly admitted lying about their age for love, money, and vanity; who give fake birthdates and graduation years (though it's illegal for an employer to inquire about either); who understated their children's ages to make themselves sound younger; and who turned fifty in secret if at all.

"I remember how ancient fifty sounded to me when I was in my twenties," wrote one professional woman who said she never tells her age because her younger colleagues would treat her differently if they knew. By leaving the number unspoken, she passes for someone who is old*er* than they are but not *old*.

Another woman, a documentary filmmaker, lies about her birth date "for economic survival." She says she has to compete with young people for temporary work to support herself between film projects, and she's sure she would never be hired if she owned up to her age — or, for that matter, let her gray hair grow out. An actress friend likewise insists her career would be ruined if people knew she was past fifty; her real age would relegate her to grandmother roles, hardly a staple of stage, screen, or television.

"Age is treated as something akin to a fault, a dirty secret," writes Bernice King about the attitude in her family. Women were expected to be literally ageless, to smile their Mona Lisa smile and say, "I'll never tell," or claim to be thirty-nine from the time they were thirty-nine until the day they died. Ideally, no one but a woman's parents should be sure of her date of birth. King and her sister, Jane, obscured their biographical facts so well that even their own sons didn't know their ages. "The deception became ridiculous, self-demeaning," she writes. "So, despite the power of family myth, I finally came out of the closet, dragging sister Jane behind me. Now I find myself in the unique position of being older than my older sister."

The same baroque deception held sway in my mother's circle of friends. Passing the midcentury mark was discussed only in whispers, along with other such verboten topics as menopause, homosexuality, and cancer. At my father's fiftieth birthday party in 1950, I remember the guests kidding that none of them would live long enough to see my mother turn fifty because she was a "much younger woman." As far as I knew, she was three years and nine months younger than my father, but in fact, she was only a year and nine months younger. I learned from her death certificate that she was born in 1901, not 1903 as she'd always claimed. Clearly, those extra two years mattered enough to lie about. In the opening scene of *Three Tall Women* — Edward Albee's Pulitzer Prize–winning play about hope, dreams, and disappointment at three stages of a woman's life — the old woman lies about her age, shaving off a year. She is ninety-two.

In 1879, when Susan B. Anthony became the first woman to celebrate her fiftieth birthday in public, the headline on the *New York Sun* said, "A Brave Old Maid." Some of my single friends can't afford that kind of bravery. They despair of ever attracting a man at this age and, given current heterosexual mores, they may be right. While many women feel obliged by convention to limit themselves to men who are their own age or older, eligible males tend to choose much younger partners, shrinking the pool of potential mates year by year. Romancing younger women is one of the ways men cope with the angst of aging. The May-December relationship, though primarily an expression of male mortality denial, also can be a reciprocal deal: he basks in her youth, she basks in his power; he gives her security, she gives him babies and a new lease on life. In the movie *Moonstruck,* the Olympia Dukakis character says, "Why do men chase women? . . . I think it's because they fear death."

Sadly, not many fifty-year-old women have the wherewithal to barter for younger men, and those who do, risk ridicule — the assumption that the fellow at her side is a gigolo, or that she herself is a "fag hag," a lonely soul who takes young homosexual men to the opera in return for having them as her escort. It's still gossip fodder if a woman is seen on the arm of someone ten years her junior, but few of us bat an eye at a man with a new wife younger than his daughter. I have a female friend who married a twenty-four-year-old man when she was fifty-two. I also have a male friend who, at fifty-two, married a twenty-four-year-old woman. (I'm not making this up.) The fifty-two-year-old man said people are always asking him, "Weren't you afraid of leaving her a widow?" The most-asked question of the fifty-two-year-old woman is, "Weren't you afraid of letting him see your body?"

For a woman to underreport her age to get a date is harmless enough compared, say, to falsifying one's passport — although at this stage of life, it's a rare woman who can shave off more than five or six years and still be credible. But why bother? If it's a boy toy she's after, my sources tell me, a young stud sees scant difference between a woman who says she's forty-five and one who owns up to being fifty. If what she wants is a long-term relationship, one wonders why she would risk losing a man's trust by lying about a fact that is destined for exposure. Should she end up marrying the guy, she'll have to put all her cards on the table eventually, and in retrospect, the lie will look like a snare. Meanwhile, how does she explain those children who visit every Sunday and keep calling her Grandma?

I sometimes think it would solve a host of evils if we had to paint our ages on our foreheads. This would provide instant proof that people over fifty are as varied as people under thirty, and some of them are positively spectacular. It would be as plain as the foreheads on their faces that the woman who trounced you at tennis is fifty-eight, that sexy guy with the Zapata moustache is fifty-one, the man in the movie line with the marvelous sense of humor is sixty-four, and the woman you sat next to at dinner, the brilliant one who cleared the cobwebs off quantum theory, is seventy. By the same token, a quick forehead check would prove that people in their twenties and thirties can be awkward and absentminded just like us.

Am I going too far? Then would you agree instead to take one small step for yourself, one giant leap for womankind, and announce your age wherever you are and as often as you can? If every woman did it, there would be no way for employers to discriminate against masses of midlife women without setting off alarms, and just think how quickly we would demystify the far reaches of the life span and normalize the image of the aging woman in her infinite variety. Proclaiming her age could be as radical an act for the average woman as coming out of the closet is for a lesbian or gay man — and just as liberating.

Those who doubt the power of example to alter even the most rigid preconceptions need only consider what Ronald Reagan did for septuagenarians. Without evaluating his stewardship or addressing the rumors that he regularly fell asleep in Cabinet meetings, one can agree that by being president for two terms, he pushed back the threshold of "old." And because every American knew his age, any man in his seventies was able to say, "If Reagan could do it, I can do it," and be believed — and believe it himself. What women need in this land of fibbers and face-lifts is not just one but thousands of middle-aged women to "out" themselves and serve as reality checks to demonstrate how fifty, sixty, or seventy really looks, acts, and feels; and to prove, by what they are doing every day, that older women can do anything.

Gripes and Grievances

Admittedly, when I was facing down fifty, I wasn't coping with job discrimination or sexual ageism, I was just feeling fragile, curmudgeonly, and out of sync with everything that being fifty stood for. I had no interest in repudiating my age, only in challenging much of what I associated with the phrase "a woman in her fifties," associations that had little relevance to me or my life. Why should this birthday, this number, be allowed to redefine a woman or alter her place in the world? Futhermore, what's so admirable about "accepting" one's age, and who's to say acceptance is always the healthiest attitude? Some forms of acceptance are indistinguishable from resignation, which is the last feeling anyone needs at this stage of life. It makes more sense to me to steer a course between acceptance and resistance, that is, to make a conscious distinction between those aspects of aging that I would learn to live with and those I would fight tooth and nail to prove to myself (and anyone else who cared to notice) that there's lots more life in the old girl yet.

In the meantime, I would *not* roll with the punches, go with the flow, look on the bright side, or abide wisecracks about aging that aren't funny. "I can't figure out if I've lost my sense of humor," writes Judith Viorst. "Or if, after fifty, it just gets harder to laugh." For me it was both. I was ready to administer an overdose of Geritol to the next person who offered up one of those trite bromides as if it might possibly be comforting. To wit:

"You're not getting older, you're getting better." Better at what? Better than whom?

"Age doesn't matter unless you are a cheese." Please don't remind me: even Roquefort rots.

"Aging gracefully." Clearly an oxymoron, not to mention a dubious behavioral prescription. If anything, I was aging disgracefully, sour as a pickle, bitching and moaning every step of the way.

"If you don't like growing older, consider the alternative." Forced to take my comfort cold, I preferred Dorothy Parker's icy, "People ought to be one of two things: Young or dead." Okay, the choice was clear; now what?

"Fifty isn't old for a tree." Verrry funny.

"Older but wiser" also fell on deaf ears (more on hearing loss later). I felt no wiser at fifty than I did at fifteen, only more experienced.

One thing experience had taught me was that, regardless of her chronological age, every woman has an *internal* age, a year that feels most authentically, organically in tune with who she is. For no apparent reason, mine is thirty-six. From the inside out, I am perennially, immutably thirty-six, but from the outside in, certain changes had come to my attention that confirmed the calendar.

For instance, I used to be treated like a wunderkind. But at fifty, when you do something clever no one is surprised. By now you're *supposed* to be competent — if not now, when?

Another thing: I had noticed that, more often than not, I was the oldest person in the room. Physically, if you didn't look too closely, I might blend in with those in their late thirties or early forties, but then some telltale gaffe would give me away and it would become clear that I was the only one in the crowd who thought Bon Jovi was a cheese. Or I'd mention something I assumed *everyone* knows about — like Oxydol or Davy Crockett hats — only to be greeted by blank stares. Rather than lapse into the role of old geezer and give my listeners a guided tour down memory lane, I started censoring myself: why compare someone to Baby Snooks if you have to spend five minutes explaining who she was? (A 1940s radio character played by Fanny Brice. *Please* don't ask me who Fanny Brice was.)

The most upsetting physical changes were the subtle ones. At forty-nine, I wasn't turning gray or developing a dowager's hump but I noticed that people had stopped telling me I looked like my daughters' sister, and the construction workers' whistles had dwindled to a paltry tweet or two per year — hardly a feminist measure of self-esteem but one that couldn't be missed by any woman who walks the streets of Manhattan.

The assault on my vanity was nothing compared to the toll age was beginning to take on my senses. Worse than the crow's-feet at the corners of my eyes or the circles under them was the failure of the eyes themselves. "It's getting so bad I need glasses for sex," said Woody Allen, and this time I had to laugh.

I also had to concentrate a lot harder to hear voices at certain registers. It's one thing to listen to French with every fiber of your being in order to translate word by word, and quite another thing to have to expend the same effort to decode English. My taste buds, too, were taking time off; everything needed more salt and I had a hunch it wasn't the cooks' fault. As for memory loss, forget it — which is often what I did. We're talking hard-core deterioration here: if my mind wasn't out to sea trying to dredge up an evasive name, or trolling for a long-lost couplet, my mouth was spewing words that had drifted far from their moorings.

"We have lots of congressional singing at my synagogue," I heard myself say when it certainly wasn't what I meant. "Most low-birth-weight babies are born to poor women who had no prenuptial care," I declared another time to the muffled giggles of my audience. But I didn't find myself funny. Of all the signs of aging, memory lapses and involuntary malapropisms scared me most. My whole life, I'd thought of speech as strength. It had been the keystone of my I-may-not-be-beautiful-but-at-least-I've-got-brains self-image. What would become of me if the mind failed and the words got garbled for good? What would I have left? I didn't realize it then, but that was only the beginning.

Before I could cope with the sometimes frightening, always unpredictable, physical and mental symptoms of midlife, I had to do something about my attitude. I had to work on my head, decode my preconceptions, and figure out why I was so belligerent about turning fifty.

It's Only a Number

The button helped a little.

Amidst a thirty-year collection of political buttons displayed on a corkboard in my kitchen — anachronisms with in-your-face slogans like "Bring the Troops Home Now," "1963 March on Washington," "The Moral Majority Is Neither," "I Believe Anita Hill," and "George Bush Reminds Every Woman of Her First Husband" — is one button, a party favor I think, that simply says, "It's Only a Number." As I prepared to turn fifty, I found this slogan as reassuring as the voice on my portable radio during the blackout of 1977. I took it as my mantra: "It's *only* a number," I said before I went to bed. "It's only a *number!*" I repeated as I watched the calendar close in on my birthday, June 9. *"It's only a number."*

Who was I kidding? Who is anybody kidding? If it's only a number, why did the magazine *50-Plus* change its name to *New Choices?*

Emerson wrote, "You do not count a person's years unless there is nothing else to count," which just goes to prove he wasn't always right. We count our years when we have a full life and want more years to enjoy it. We count them the way a ship captain checks fathoms or a pilot checks altitude: to get our bearings and figure out exactly where we are.

"I imagine fifty as some sort of a gate," writes Paula Gunn Allen; "the door is going to open and I'm going to be somebody else." Turning fifty, I held the same life-changing / boundary-crossing / turning-point / sort of view, but I was certain the "someone else" I was about to become wasn't anyone I particularly wanted to be. My birthday was coming up fast, anxiety had begotten depression, depression had begotten misery, and I was beginning to wonder how I was ever going to get myself over the hump.

Rationally, I knew that I wouldn't be significantly older or closer to death at fifty than I was at forty-nine or would be at fifty-one. But not every number registers on the psyche in the same neutral way; some bear a greater symbolic weight than others. November 22 is not just a number; it's a motorcade in Dallas. The fifteenth of April isn't just a number, it's a deadline. The number seven elicits a tumble of associations — seven seas, days of creation, pillars of wisdom, lively arts, deadly sins. Similarly, tribes, disciples, and jurors give the number twelve more resonance than that possessed by, say, eleven or fourteen. And, of course, ten brings to mind Commandments, plagues, the top slot of the rating system, Bo Derek, decimals, the rounded number. No wonder those birthdays that end in zero pack an extra wallop. Few of us are aware of growing older between age twenty-four and twenty-five, or thirty-seven and thirty-eight; but traversing from twenty-nine to thirty, or thirty-nine to forty, demands our full attention, and transporting ourselves from forty-nine to fifty requires a bridge across the Rubicon.

I once saw a needlepoint pillow that said, "AGE IS A NUMBER AND MINE IS UNLISTED." Well, mine had been publicly listed in that article in *Ms.*, but telling the truth didn't make it any easier to take the leap. I may have accomplished something by revealing that I was turning fifty, maybe taking the onus off it for someone else, but since my problem was time more than aging, telling my age did nothing to save me from my own cosmic sludge. Then, one morning four months before my birthday — and not a minute too soon — I opened the Science section of the *New York Times* and discovered that, silence and denial notwithstanding, I was not alone after all.

"For Many, Turmoil of Aging Erupts in the 50s, Studies Find," blared the headline on a story that, to my great relief, revealed how other fifty-somethings were dealing with the key issue that had been driving me nuts for months — not the economic or the physical but the temporal.

The article cited studies by Bernice Neugarten of the University of Chicago that validated my new time orientation to the letter. "Even though people in their 50's don't see themselves as old, there's a reversal of the direction of time," she said. "You count the number of birthdays left instead of how many you've reached. . . . It's a time of taking stock and increased reflection."

The people quoted in these studies described a familiar cognitive dissonance: they knew they were no longer young but still couldn't quite believe it. They saw themselves existing in some vague middle ground where youth was clearly behind them but old age was nowhere in sight. Looking ahead, they thought they might begin to be "old" somewhere around seventy, although it wasn't so much a specific age as the onset of illness or disability or topping out in their careers or being treated differently by others that seemed, in their eyes, to change a person from aging to old.

"Old," to me, was always twenty years older than whatever age I happened to be. I remember thinking in my twenties that the book *Life Begins at 40* had to be a joke. At thirty, I looked at colleagues in their fifties as if they lived in another world. Now, of course, my formula has been disproved by the many vigorous seventy-year-olds in my life. A Yankelovich survey of American women, commissioned by Clinique, found that the average age that women believe to be the "end of youth" is fifty-four. This sounds reasonable, even reassuring, but as with all averages it masks the very different views held by each age group: women under thirty consider forty-three the "end of youth," while women over fifty think a person stops being young at sixty-five. The other day, discussing age relativity with my twin daughters, for whom fifty seems as distant as Mars, I reminded them that at that very moment — midway in their twenty-ninth year — fifty was exactly as far away from them in one direction as nine was in the other. "Do you remember being nine?" I asked. "Was that *so* long ago?" If I'm not mistaken, they blanched. They remember their childhoods just as vividly as I remember myself at thirty; the difference between us is not in the clarity of our hindsight but in our view of the *next* twenty years. I was afraid of my future; my daughters, quite naturally, were relishing theirs. Ahead of me lay infirmity, loss, endings; ahead of them (I pray), years of growth, possibility, and new beginnings.

"While any number of people anguish over their thirtieth birthday and try to hide their fortieth," Boston College sociologist David Karp told the *New York Times,* "it is in their fifties that most people first think of their lives in terms of how much time is left rather than how much has passed." Many of those he interviewed said they've been taking a good, hard look at the activities they were involved in and questioning whether they could reasonably expect to complete them in their lifetimes and whether the projects are even worth pursuing in their remaining years.

"The fifties is a kind of fulcrum decade," said Karp, "a turning point in the aging process during which people, more sharply than before, are made to feel their age."

Well, if it's such a bloody fulcrum, why haven't we heard more about it? Where have the experts been until now? And why aren't we fiftysomethings talking to each other? The *Times* hadn't a clue: "Despite its significance," the paper said, "the 50's are a relatively unknown decade, little discussed, and even less studied."

While researchers have been tripping over one another studying babies who are too young to understand the results, college students who are too busy to care, and the very old who may be too far along to benefit, my age group has been roundly neglected and thus cheated of usable science. "It's the last uncharted territory in human development," said MacArthur Foundation president Adele Simmons when she announced a $10 million grant to fund an eight-year research project on middle age. But in the meantime, the fifty-to-sixty-five age group, a clearly identifiable segment of the population with particular needs and problems, are largely unseen, and except for studies on menopause and early retirement, those fifteen uncharted years of the human life span remain a virtual mystery. No wonder I'd been feeling as if I had dropped into a deep, dark well with nothing but platitudes to cushion the fall.

The late Daniel Levinson, author of *The Seasons of a Man's Life,* the classic study of male aging, said he used to believe the mid-forties were tough on men, but recent studies had persuaded him that the most intense and painful self-questioning happens in the mid-fifties, which is why most men of this age observe a kind of taboo against talking honestly about what they are going through. It is in the fifties, said Levinson, that people question the very essence of their existence, the meaning of their lives and commitments, the condition of their marriages and careers, their fear of becoming irrelevant, and their sense of shrinking life options.

Taking in this story with my coffee and toast, I felt the same satisfaction a patient feels when, after months of dismissing her complaints, the doctors finally concede that something is really wrong with her. I still had the angst but somehow, once it was acknowledged by experts and other people in their fifties, it became easier to bear.

Changing Aging

Undoubtedly, such acknowledgment will happen on a grand scale as more and more baby boomers cross the Rubicon. By the year 2000, close to one in three Americans will be over fifty. This immense and powerful constituency won't stand for coyness or obfuscation; they're going to expect detailed maps of this new frontier and everything associated with it. Their hunger for information will be well served by the social sciences and the media, who will study them to a fare-thee-well, invent a more upbeat vocabulary to describe aging, and polish the image of every fifty-year-old in public view until the zeitgeist expands to make room for Madonna at midcentury.

There's a change in the wind already. In 1992, *Newsweek* ran a cover story on "The New Middle Age" illustrated by a drawing of a woman moaning, "Oh God . . . I'm really turning 50!" After noting the American tendency to deny the reality of aging, the story concluded, "The funny thing about denial is that sometimes it works. Boomers will look, act and feel younger at fifty than previous generations did."

If that prediction is borne out, it won't be individual acts of denial that turn the trick, it will be the result of a systematic media effort to endow age with glamour. The campaign has already begun, with the rich and famous of my generation leading the way. The glittering nabobs of the 1990s have not been permitted a private segue into their fifties; they've taken the trip in full view of Oprah and Sally Jessy, Leno and Letterman, *People* magazine and "Saturday Night Live."

It's a reciprocal deal. Superstars like Mick Jagger, Lauren Hutton, Barbra Streisand, Paul McCartney, Michael Douglas, and Rod Stewart could turn fifty in the public eye because the great postwar population bulge coming up behind them needs its pop royalty to make it safe for everyone else to turn fifty in their own backyards. And the celebrities need us, their publics, to witness them doing it so they can be reassured that we still love them even after we know the truth. It's a safe bet that, over the next decade, more and more of America's cultural icons will celebrate their fiftieth birthdays out in the open where we can hear them tell us how great it feels, because there's a huge silence to be filled and seventy-six million boomers waiting to be told that there's life, sex, and sex appeal after fifty.

Age and Identity

Though it can happen on any birthday, the fiftieth is the twenty-one-gun wake-up call, the moment when most of us take stock of our place in the universe and intensify the midlife quest for self-knowledge and authenticity. Given our position on the timeline, age is germane to our identity, yet some people have trouble accepting the very fact of their age, as if it were an ill-fitting garment that they had been sewn into while they weren't looking. "You find yourself saying, 'I'm fifty-one,' and thinking, '*What?* I'm *what?*'" writes Roy Blount, Jr., who calls the very fact of his age one of the "fantastic surprises" of midlife.

In a recent national survey, a large sample of men and women aged fifty and over said they felt an average of fourteen years younger than their actual ages and guessed that they look six years younger. If nothing else, this proves that Americans have definite expectations as to how a particular chronological age is "supposed" to feel and look, and that most of us have concluded we do not match the norm. Friends of mine say that they often stare at other people their age and think, "Can I possibly look as old to them as they do to me?" Others say they feel spiritually and physically younger than almost everyone else in their age group. I wonder why we bother to number our years if the sum doesn't add up to anything anyone can identify with. Surely the *meaning* of age is up for grabs if the number we answer when asked how old we are has no reliable markers, no universal definition, and no useful application.

When he was a mere thirty-two, Isiah Thomas, the point guard for the Detroit Pistons, was asked how he felt about getting older. He reassured himself and his fans with, "Age isn't what it used to be." Quite so, but then what is? For basketball players and ballet dancers, age is a subject of economic concern, since they inevitably reach a point when they become too old to make a living with their bodies; but the rest of us have few tangible measures of the impact of age upon our lives. Even if we did, I'm not sure we could explain what transforms aging from a fact to a state of mind.

The singer Bonnie Raitt released an album called "Nick of Time," in which she deals with her feelings about growing older and running out of time. She made the record when she was only thirty-nine. A male music reviewer showed uncommon sensitivity to Raitt's early angst when he wrote that "American popular culture is hard on women who are too old to be ingenues and too young to be dowagers." For most of our lives, women are neither, yet there is barely enough space between the two stereotypes for us to slip into an identity that feels comfortable.

I'm still having problems with my own ill-fitting garment. On June 9, my daughter Abigail called to report that I had finally made it into the big time — a wire service item reporting on the birthdays of public personalities: "Former World Bank President and Defense Secretary Robert S. McNamara is 78. Broadcast journalist Marvin Kalb is 64. Author Letty Cottin Pogrebin is 55. Baseball player Dave Parker is 43. Actor Michael J. Fox is 33." While it's true June 9 is my birthday, I felt misperceived.

"That's not me in that lineup," I thought. "There must be some mistake."

In 1970, when big hair first came into vogue, I bought a wig to camouflage my baby-fine hair and had occasion to see myself in a magazine photograph wearing it. The person in the picture was clearly me but it wasn't *me,* if you know what I mean. In the same sense, I was the person in the wire service item, yet I couldn't recognize myself; my name attached to the number 55 was as strange as my face had been attached to a wild mane of hair. It can't be me, I thought, because fifty-five sounds so *old* — and I didn't invent that perception, I got it from five decades of age-negative brainwashing. How could fifty-five not sound old when one reads in the newspaper that an "elderly" woman had been murdered and it turns out she was sixty? Or when a story about a violent carjacking describes the victims, aged sixty-two and sixty-four, as "an elderly couple"? Even feminist Carolyn Heilbrun seemed to equate oldness and the fifties when she opined, "It is perhaps only in old age, certainly past fifty, that women can stop being female impersonators. . . ."

If Raitt is feeling her age at thirty-nine, and people in their early sixties are defined as elderly, what does that make me? And if Heilbrun is equating "old age" with "past fifty," where's the hope?

You should have heard me when I got my recruitment letter from the AARP. I went bananas, and I've since learned that nobody on the receiving end of this pro forma invitation is merely nonplussed. "The letters sent by the American Association of Retired Persons to potential members when they turn 50 produce a degree of hyperventilation comparable to a draft notice or a tax audit," noted the *New York Times* in an editorial commenting on how "Americans by and large dislike being reminded of advancing age." Furthermore, many people take exception to an organization ostensibly concerned with "retired persons" trying to recruit those of us who are in our occupational primes or have embarked on new careers. Being fifty is bad enough; we don't like the assumption that we're ready to be put out to pasture.

Likewise, people in their fifties and sixties do not like being lumped with the seniors "market." The perks of seniority are not without emotional cost, as anyone knows who has ever wished she could exchange an over-fifty discount for a feeling of being more welcome at a disco. In our culture, the flip side of privilege is ageism. It's nice when one's age is an entry ticket, but all too often the ticket also buys status with a stigma.

Discovering this, the purveyors of tours, travel books, and housing that is meant to appeal to older people have learned to use words like "travel easy" or "mature traveler" to connote destinations with certain amenities. Retirement communities call themselves leisure villages. An airline gives its age-specific promotion package the spunky title "The Get Up-and-Go Passport." At a large discount store, the card that entitles people over fifty-five to an extra 10 percent discount every Tuesday is called the "Special Privilege Card."

A friend in her sixties says, "It shakes you up when you go to the movies with your granddaughter and she pays full price and you pay half." A sixty-something man insists on remitting the full subway fare. He buys movie tickets at the seniors price only when no one else is standing near the box office. During a trip abroad, he discovered that in England, the senior citizen category starts at fifty, so he availed himself of museum discounts and special tour buses because he could imagine himself to be passing for fifty-one. But in New York, he says, it isn't worth saving a few cents on the subway fare if it means he has to admit to being a senior before he is internally ready for it. He would rather waive the discounts and privileges than admit to himself that he has become "them."

None of us wants our age to subsume our entire identity. We don't want to *be* our age, we want to be ourselves. My age remains an abstraction to me; it has never been a description of who I am, and though I admitted to turning fifty and I admit to being fifty-five now, I honestly believe that the number — whether stripped of meaning or freighted with bad vibes — has nothing to do with me.

When we're young, we internalize dreadful ideas about old people, and let's face it, to a kid, fifty is *old.* Then, when we ourselves enter the middle years, we inherit by default all the depressing images that were calcified in our minds long before we ever conceived of ourselves as potential members of this club. No wonder so many of us don't think well of our age group even when we're in it. The psychologist Ellen Langer says that when she constructed consciousness-raising experiments to improve the physical and mental capacities of elderly people, the greatest obstacles she had to overcome, both in the old people themselves and everyone around them, "were the premature cognitive commitments about old age that people make in their youth. Even when corrected, so much else has been built on this foundation that a new attitude is difficult to form."

Those "premature cognitive commitments" lock into place very early. The AARP did a study of children aged six to eleven in which the kids were asked to draw pictures of a young person and an old person and then to discuss the drawings and their own aging. The older children's drawings were more negative — frowns, wrinkles, wheelchairs — and these children revealed more antipathy toward aging than did kids in the younger age group, suggesting that anti-age attitudes start young and get worse fast. When a ten-year-old was asked how she would feel when she was old, she answered, "Sad, tired, and mean." Jim Thompson, an AARP gerontologist, says the negative images of old people held by children and ultimately the rest of society can become self-fulfilling prophecies when old people themselves start thinking, "If the public thinks I'm sexless or senile or whatever, that's how I'm going to feel." By the same token, if we recognize that the negativity associated with age is not *intrinsic* but is based on misconceptions formed in earlier experiences, then we also might realize that we can change it.

I own up to my age because I think public acknowledgment helps dilute the stigma, but I don't own my age in my heart because I cannot accept, and don't want to internalize, what it stands for in this culture. Undoubtedly, I wouldn't be so pugnacious if aging had a different value in America or if I lived in the Far East, where older people are subjects of veneration. You don't have to be an anthropologist to know that being fifty in Nanjing is not the same as being fifty in New York, for age is neither a neutral nor a universal concept. The meaning of age is socially constructed: human beings create it and human beings can change it if we choose to. Until we help children to view older people as nice, peppy, and pleasant, instead of sad, tired, and mean; and until more of us are able to recognize ourselves in the popular images of the over-fifty age group, it will remain difficult to embrace our years in the same organic way that we claim other aspects of our identity, such as being female or male, tall or short, a Puerto Rican, a parent, or a Presbyterian.

The psychological dislocation born of this age-distancing impulse is not strictly a private matter. When large numbers of people refuse to acknowledge one essential component of their identity, there may well be political and social ramifications. Feeling detached from our age keeps us alienated from our age group and less able to make common cause with them on issues of mutual concern. When we say, "It's irrelevant that I'm fifty because I'm not like those other fifty-year-olds" — the equivalent of Clarence Thomas claiming it's irrelevant that he is black — we opt out of the evolutionary social change process that might redefine what fifty-year-olds are really like. Then, by our absence, we lessen the power of our own natural constituency. Meanwhile, people over sixty-five are acting in solidarity and we're not. If you and I refuse to join forces with the fifty-plus community, that community will never reflect the spirit and concerns of people like us, and we will continue to be represented in the public square, as is the case today, by purported spokespersons who actually speak from a much older or much younger perspective. For this reason, if no other, I think it important for each of us to claim our age, incorporate it into our identity, and speak in our true voice, a voice of authority, whether we feel it or not. By virtue of being who we are at fifty, and doing what we do, and looking like we look, if we simply found a place for ourselves under the big tent, we would contribute to the transformation of the concept "fifty" and help to dilute its stigma.

For me, chronology has always outrun identity; I've watched my body and mind age while my inner self is stuck somewhere in arrested development trying to figure out who she is. I'll never forget the morning I turned the page of my 1989 calendar and stared in disbelief at the question of the day: "When did you 'grow up' and what do you think that really means?" It was as if I'd found a quote from Albert Camus on my bubblegum wrapper or a fortune cookie with my home phone number in it. Questions like that had been hounding me for weeks: What exactly is a grown-up? How old is old? What does it mean to "act your age?" How can age be a fact if each of us shapes it differently? Is it possible to feel at home in a fifty-year-old body if you feel like a kid inside, or if you see yourself as fourteen years younger, at least? How do we "accept" the aging process if we don't feel our age — and what does it *feel* like to feel it?

At fifty I knew I wasn't young anymore, but I wasn't old, either; so what was I? I must be a grown-up, I thought, and if I could figure out exactly what that means, I'd embrace the identity gladly, because feeling adult is obviously preferable to feeling old. Some cultures even consider it a status worth claiming. In the Native American tradition, a person is not considered fully grown until age fifty-one. In parts of India, a woman becomes a free agent only after she finishes raising her children and stops menstruating. I must be a grown-up, I told myself, I've just started menopause.

Yet, just as we complain that our numerical age doesn't fit, so, too, the shoes of a grown-up may seem like hard-to-fill hand-me-downs passed along to us too soon. My idea of a grown-up is my mother, sitting in a straight-backed chair at the rear of my fourth grade classroom on Open School Day, wearing a fashionable but decidedly matronly print dress and sensible shoes with thick, stumpy heels. My mother embodied age as Other. When she was forty-eight, I was nine. When I was forty-eight, my twin daughters were out of college, my son had graduated from high school, and I was wearing jeans and sneakers like the rest of the world. But my image of age forty-eight, my sense of "forty-eightness," remains personified by that grown-up in the back of my fourth grade classroom, and because my mother set the standard and I never met it, I never felt forty-eight. I've been forty-eight, but I've never felt like a grown-up.

Another thing: I cannot recall a single instance when either of my parents got down on the floor to play with me. It would have been unseemly, no, unthinkable, for them to squat or sit cross-legged over a game of jacks. Their unwillingness to stoop to ground level says more about the unsupple otherness of that generation than any measure of their years, and what it left with me is an image of maturity symbolized by an adult sitting properly in a chair. To this day, when I'm down on the floor, I feel like a child. It's confusing, this sense of dislocation, knowing that what one is bears little resemblance to how one feels.

"How did I *get* to be a grown-up?" asks Erica Jong in *Fear of Fifty*. "At times I find myself still sitting on the hillside, plotting revenge against the adult world. I still say 'Mom' when I am scared. . . ."

Tom Brokaw also had problems adjusting to the big five-oh: "It's not that I am angry or melancholy," he writes in a column in the *New York Times Magazine*. "It's more an irritation. Sort of a chronic low-level virus." Noting that many of his former classmates and old girlfriends are grandparents, and the icons of his generation, like Jack Nicklaus, now are eligible for the senior circuit, Brokaw tries to reach the same conclusion I've been seeking. "It's finally time to be a real grown-up," he writes, then quickly backpedals: "Not true. If I still wore mittens, I'd still lose them."

Christopher Lehmann-Haupt, a book critic, had several "unconscious criteria of becoming a grown-up" — wearing a bathrobe, drinking coffee, and above all "developing enough command of my time to arrive at a film at the beginning." Although self-discipline always seemed to him a measure of adulthood, he now questions whether achieving it is worth the price: "You wonder if you have really grown up by getting to the movies on time. Or, as with so many other aspects of getting older, whether you have simply cheated yourself out of another richer apprehension of experience."

Intrigued by this speculation, I was thrown back to my own childhood preference to enter the movie house whenever I happened to arrive without regard for the projection schedule. I had complete confidence in my ability to follow the plot in progress or piece it together backward. "Here's where we came in," my friends and I would say and traipse out once the fragmented experience had been made whole, the puzzle solved. Of course, I don't come in in the middle of movies anymore. I'm too grown up, but I'm not sure whether the insistence on perceiving things in sequence is the mark of an adult or of a mind grown slack and lazy with age.

I digress to prove that I'm not the only one ruminating about what it means to be a grown-up. Still, if ever a temperament was suited to a task, mine is suited to this one. I can hardly recall a time when I haven't been studying people older than myself, noticing how they behave, who's in charge, where the power is. I think I've been trying to define adulthood all my life, yet I could never imagine *myself* at fifty. When I tried, the screen went blank. It's not that I didn't have older women in my life, some of whom I loved a lot; it's that I had never known a fifty-year-old woman I wanted to *be*.

Just before my big birthday, I attended a seminar on aging where dozens of successful midlife women were asked to respond to this question: "When you were twenty-five, what did you imagine you'd be like at fifty?" One woman said that at twenty-five she had absolutely no image of being fifty because girls were taught not to plan ahead: "You had to be flexible enough to accommodate to whomever you married." Another said she thought all her dreams would be realized by fifty and she'd be well taken care of; but the dreams were always vague. Other replies were equally telling:

"I never thought I'd *live* to be fifty."

"All I knew for sure was that I didn't want to be what my mother was at fifty."

"I never wanted to leave my teens because I never saw older women having any fun."

"I knew I'd be married and have children and that's *all* I knew."

Unlike most men of comparable age, who spent their boyhoods imagining their grown-up glory, anything beyond Happily Ever After was a blur to girls of my era. We weren't trained to become adults, we were trained to become *women,* and the two were far from synonymous. In a 1970 study that remains a classic in its field, psychologist Inge K. Broverman and several colleagues asked mental health professionals to choose attributes that described a healthy man, then attributes that described a healthy woman, and finally, attributes of a healthy "person," gender unspecified. Regardless of the sex or age of the respondent, the answers were pure stereotypes: A mentally healthy woman was defined as submissive, dependent, subjective, and suggestible. A mentally healthy man was seen as aggressive, independent, objective, and autonomous. What made the results significant was the finding that the mentally healthy *person* was described in the same terms as a healthy man, which betrayed not just a double standard for mental health but the prevalence of a deep-seated belief that a fully grown woman is expected to have the character traits of a child, and to behave like a perpetual child — innocent, helpless, dependent, and cute. No wonder I had trouble defining what it meant to be a grown-up. Grown-ups were men.

But it took me a while to figure that out. Or to notice that all the representatives of wisdom, maturity, and "good" aging were men — commander, leader, inventor, explorer, judge, counselor, adviser, adventurer, hero, guru, professor; each word conjured the image of a male, often one who was older, bearded, kindly, and sage (and Caucasian). For women, all the good words and praiseworthy images sprang from the brief and transient moment of youth — princess, maiden, nymph, sprite, lass, coed, virgin.

"What do you want to be when you grow up, dear?"

"Young," answered the smart little girl because there was no other answer. People name their daughters after the spring months, the young months — April, May, and June. The language yields few meritorious metaphors for the older woman. Grandmother? Kind but rarely sage. Good Witch? A granter of wishes, but still a witch. Dowager Queen? Elegant and beautiful maybe, but packing a poison apple. Not much to aspire to; not much to work into daydreams; not much to fire the imagination of a young girl trying to see herself at fifty.

Who's the Grown-up Here?

In a sense, I've been waiting all my life for something to happen that would make me feel like a grown-up. Surely I'll feel adult when I finally get my period, I thought, in my early teens, but menstruation gave me more cramps than status. Through the years, many milestones promised that adult sensation, but as each one passed — driver's license, first job, legal drinking age, college graduation, first checking account, first apartment — I couldn't remember why such ordinary events had loomed so large. They came, they went, leaving the child within.

I can only guess that, like everything else, this state of mind has something to do with an early trauma. For many years, I was the youngest person in whatever category I happened to find myself, which meant others were the grown-ups and I wasn't, and they wouldn't let me forget it. Then, too, for much of my adult life, I looked ridiculously young and was often treated accordingly.

"How *old* are you?" colleagues would demand, and, loathing the question, I nonetheless had to answer. (I wasn't old enough for my mother's Mona Lisa smile.)

"Gee, you look like a kid," people said again and again, until I came to cringe and steel myself against those words. At fifty-five, that remark is a gift; at twenty-five or thirty-five, when you're trying to be taken seriously, it's a crusher. So maybe I got crushed for good. In the long run, I've found looking young to be a mixed blessing — a disadvantage in the early years, a boon in midlife, then finally, when the youthful illusion goes, a rude fall from grace. Whatever pleasure one gets from people's shocked reaction only compounds the pain felt when the reaction stops, which of course, it must. Eventually, Dorian Gray catches up with his picture in the attic. And, needless to say, looking young doesn't change the number of years one has left to live. Like the lemon in a used-car lot, the body can mislead, it's the engine that counts.

Philip Roth writes, "Adult life began for me, as it often has for American young men during these last forty years, when I was discharged from the Army." Without the military to mark their coming-of-age, most girls of my generation expected their wedding day to herald the beginning of adult life. It didn't work for me. Between age twenty-four and twenty-nine, I married and had three children, but deep inside I often felt like I was playing house. In 1969, I turned thirty just as the chant of choice was "Don't trust anyone over thirty." It didn't stop me from identifying with the younger set, even with the three kids in tow. You'd think I'd have felt like a full-fledged adult in the 1970s when my first three books were published, but a writer's natural state is vulnerable and insecure, very much like that of a child. Nancy Mairs says, "As the author of two books, I am a writer and therefore must be grown-up. This state scares me a good deal. It's easier to be the dreamy child than the active adult, responsible for her own well-being."

In the 1980s, when my kids left to live on their own, the mantle of Parent Emeritus didn't sit any more firmly on my shoulders than Parent had, for I'm convinced that mothering is a role we play by ear, never feeling like an expert, always susceptible to the imposter syndrome. And finally, menopause didn't do the job, either; knowing I could no longer get pregnant made me feel free and therefore, in a sense, young again.

Everyone has a theory about what finally delivers that elusive grown-up feeling: a woman I know told me quite emphatically that the true mark of adulthood is owning a house — and then proceeded to describe the experience in the words of a six-year-old: "I have a wonderful new house and it's my Barbie doll and I want to change its clothes and play with its accessories."

Ethel Barrymore once said, "You grow up the day you have your first real laugh — at yourself."

Journalist Sydney J. Harris insists, "We have not passed that subtle line between childhood and adulthood until we move from the passive voice to the active voice — that is, until we have stopped saying, 'It got lost,' and say, 'I lost it.''

Glen Elder, a sociologist at the University of North Carolina, sees the retirement of a mentor as a major transition point because "You have to think about yourself playing that role."

Many people believe we only come into our own when both of our parents are dead. "It's a terrible thing to say, but it's true," writes May Sarton:

I shall not be a daughter any more,
But through this final parting, all stripped down,
Launched on the tide of love, go out full grown.

Losing my mother at fifteen made me prematurely self-sufficient but far from full-grown, and by the time my father died nearly thirty years later, I had long since felt orphaned by his absence. With both parents and all twelve of their siblings gone, I have suddenly become the older generation. Ask me, "Who's the grown-up here?" and I will answer, "I am," but without much conviction, no doubt because of a disinclination to stand exposed, unshielded by the layer of elders who, until now, had stood between me and death. If they're gone, I'm next in line. Maybe that's what it means to be a grown-up — and why I've been in no hurry to be one.

Two more possibilities seem plausible:

My reluctance to claim adult status may be my way of dodging responsibility for what I cannot control. By deferring to others, the ones in charge, those vague, distant authority figures who are supposed to know what to do and how to fix it, I don't have to confront my own powerlessness to repair what I consider a violent, unjust world. Someone else will take care of it, someone who is the grown-up that I have yet to become.

For the last quarter-century, I've devoted myself to feminism, interethnic relations, sexism in Judaism, and Middle East peace — and not one of these causes has enjoyed firm, lasting success. Despite women's strides, we're experiencing a virulent backlash, poor women are worse off than ever, and gender violence has reached epidemic proportions. Despite efforts at rapprochement, ethnic and racial tensions have become more explosive. Despite a more liberalized Judaism, in many quarters women are still second-class Jews. And despite the handshake on the White House lawn, hatred and terrorism still plague the Middle East.

So many battles won, lost, then needing to be fought again. Could it be that I have chosen to waive adult status as a means of protecting myself from accountability for all this backsliding? At some level, of course, I'm aware that the man behind the curtain is not a real wizard, and there are no saints or saviors in high places who can solve these problems with a flick of the wrist. There are only other mortals like me, scared, well-meaning citizens of the world who are muddling through, and doing the best they can. We are all responsible now. "And it will not hurt us to learn," writes Leon Wieseltier, "that leaders and teachers are always rattled, and improvising, and anxious for the understanding of those who come after them (that is, after us)." My generation has come of age, dragging me with it.

The final possibility is this: maybe I've been confusing adult with *old.* Maybe I still harbor the child's view of a grown-up as a finished product, fully formed and all-knowing — and I'm not ready for that kind of closure. At eighty-eight, William Fulbright, former chair of the Senate Foreign Affairs Committee and founder of the Fulbright Fellowships, went to work every day, led an active social life, and wore a button that read, "Aged to Perfection." I'd like to be able to make that claim someday. But since I am not finished growing, logic tells me I am not a grown-up; I'm a work in progress. A Beaujolais, not a vintage cabernet.

By the time I finished contemplating the issue, two conclusions seemed obvious: first, feeling like a grown-up is not as important as believing there is still room to grow and taking the time to do it. And second, when you're fifty, you can't pass the buck; regardless of how you see yourself, you're a grown-up in the eyes of the world, and the buck stops with you.

The Wisdom of Women

Through the many meanderings of my fiftieth birthday crisis, I was lucky to find some wise cartographers to help me explore the rough and rocky terrain of aging. Women who had their big birthdays the same year as I became my guides and coconspirators, widened my perspective on time and change, and helped me navigate the last bend of the road. There was, for instance, this letter from my friend Nadine Markova, a professional photographer who has lived in Mexico City for the last twenty years (she is also a wife and mother of a grown daughter). Nadine turned fifty six months before I did, and when my turn came, her unsanctimonious candor freed me to think impolite thoughts:

> Yes, we are going to be 50. How are you adjusting? I haven't gotten over the shock of turning 40. I've been fat and I've been thin but this is the first time I've been old. Men do not make passes at women who wear bifocals. I don't like aging. I guess I hate the glasses the most. Before I had them I couldn't see the wrinkles.
>
> Last week, I was shooting photographs from a small clipper and I noticed that the fat under my upper arm was flapping in the wind. I almost threw myself out of the plane. Others say I look good. What they mean is, "she's alive and she's not sick." At 50, this is sexy. I'm thinking I'm starting to smell old. Even Mexican men, not known for discriminating tastes, limit their filthy murmuring to younger women. I haven't been *Pssst* at for five years. I used to hate it. Now I miss it. I want to be a sex object again. . . .

Of all the unmentionables among aging feminists, yearning to be a sex object had to be among the top ten. You could decry men's leering and notice when it stopped, but you couldn't *miss* it. Nadine's matter-offactness pushed me to confront my own ambivalence about sexual radar, something I had deplored on those rare occasions when I aroused a leer from a stranger and now — miracle of miracles — something I also missed. Was my feminism a fraud because I had noticed myself noticing — and lamenting — the retreat of the male gaze?

A disability rights activist — a survivor of childhood polio who spends her waking hours in a wheelchair — once told me how desperately she wished to be treated as a sex object just once in her life. What must it feel like, she mused, to be the focus of someone's desire? And how intoxicating to have the power to decide whether or not you will respond to it. I thought of her when I realized that I, no great beauty, had nonetheless — since I was fourteen or fifteen — taken for granted the male glance and the choice to disdain it. No woman wants to be eroticized in nonsexual contexts, like school or work, or to feel objectified or unsafe on the street, but those demands do not preclude the admission that sensing the self as magnetically female is one of many wellsprings of self-esteem. Consciously or not, I had drawn some small portion of confidence from that magnetic field for the past thirty-five years, and now I felt it trickling away.

When I put down Nadine's letter, I checked for loose skin on my upper arms. I wondered if I, too, were starting to smell old. I passed the line of construction workers sitting on the sidewalk eating their sandwiches, and I waited to see what they would tell me about myself. They never looked up from their lunch.

Shortly after my big birthday, in the summer of my discontent, I received a letter from the writer Phyllis Theroux that I must have reread a dozen times:

> Your 50th birthday and mine came the same year. It is pretty horrible because it's then we realize how much creatures of the culture we are. 50 and androgyny seem synonymous. I've just stopped waking up each morning, rushing to the mirror and saying "50? No way." On the plus side, I do feel a bit more entitled to speak my mind and am finding that I am far more detached from some of the needs and wants that used to tip me over. Oddly, now that I don't need and want so much, I seem to have more choice and opportunity to fill the old empty places that now don't feel so empty. That's a metaphorical way of saying that I am more in the

> driver's seat, both with men and myself. Where were they when I was 38 and needed a husband and father? They were waiting for my children to leave home I've decided. . . .
>
> But I feel full of life, as opposed to dread, as if I am on the brink of diving into something important to do. In the meantime, I've found myself led to very non-verbal activities, like painting, sculpting and one way or the other re-connecting with the basics of life. . . . I've got a bicycle, a typewriter, a bag of clay and all kinds of wonderful people who read Browning to me, and lead free, penniless lives and I am content and grateful for everything.

What would it mean for me to be in the driver's seat, I thought? If I'm not there, who's stopping me? And if no one is stopping me, why am I not there? Why have I always resisted "nonverbal activities," and what am I missing out on? Isn't it high time to stop living my life from the neck up? I, too, have "all kinds of wonderful people" in my life, so why don't I see more of them? I, too, "am content and grateful for everything," so why do I keep letting small vexations overwhelm me? Why do I feel so depressed about getting older? And why has it taken me so long to get around to this soul-searching?

A fifty-two-year-old writer named Sandra Pollack was smart enough to figure out while still in her forties that time is a slippery toad:

> When I was 44 years old, I had a strong sense that I was at the midpoint of my life. A perpetual list maker, I made a list of all the things I wanted to do in the second half of my life — write another book, do more political organizing around lesbian issues, be in a committed relationship, buy a house, spend more quality time with myself. Now eight years later, I find I often refer back to that list and am surprised at how many of those goals I have been able to achieve — and how many of the remaining ones still seem both important to me and within the possibility of accomplishment.

At the countdown to my fiftieth birthday, I didn't have a list and I needed one badly. Did I honestly want to spend three or four years learning Russian? Was it realistic to think I would produce even one novel? Come *on*. What book *did* I care about writing before I die? What field of study is worth years of hard work at this stage of my life? If I were serious about becoming physically fit, why hadn't I done anything about it? What was I waiting for? I'd been cruising along as if I had forever, profligate daughter, squandering time the way we sometimes let the water run in the shower while we answer the phone. I needed a list. I needed to know my priorities, because no one gets it all done.

I once read that when people between eighty and ninety-five years old were asked what age they would want to be if they could choose any age at all, most said they'd like to go back to being fifty or fifty-five. From the vantage point of a very long life, they judged *this* time, *my* time, to have been the best time. Would I have to wait thirty years to realize how marvelous it was to be in my fifties? Would I need hindsight before I could see what is before my eyes today?

Christopher Robin said, "Now I am six," and felt good about it. I would find a way to say, "Now I am fifty," and feel just fine. I would figure out what it means to be a grown-up. I would learn to cherish where I've been and look forward to what's ahead. I would change myself without reproaching those who stay the same. I would grow the stunted parts of me. I would change the meaning of age by getting physically stronger, making time my ally in personal betterment. I would value what I have while I have it, and when it fades, I would let it go, because I would have learned how to put something else, something new, in its place.

If I did all that, I told myself, I would get through this birthday and all the rest, and at sixty, seventy, or eighty, I would look back and wonder why I made such a fuss about turning fifty when, clearly, it marked the start of the most well-lived, fully savored years of my life.

3

Happy Birthday to Me

I celebrate myself and sing myself,
And what I assume you shall assume.

— *Walt Whitman*

I was in my early forties when a friend showed me a button that had been given to guests at a fiftieth birthday party the night before. The huge lapel pin proclaimed, "Fifty Never Looked So Nifty!" and the fine-looking woman pictured above the caption confirmed the claim. "She looks terrific," I said to my friend, "Why would she want to advertise that she's fifty?" Since I've always admitted my age, I couldn't believe my reaction, but there it was.

A few years later, a similarly retrograde response overtook me when my husband, Bert, and I went to a journalist friend's fiftieth birthday party given by her husband at an outdoor restaurant in Central Park. It was a beautiful evening, but I remember having to stifle the distinctly distressing thought that my friend's career might suffer as a result of her age being publicized in such a big way.

Shortly before I turned fifty, it happened again, this time at a fiftieth birthday lunch for Selma Shapiro, my close friend and former college roommate. All the women at the table were between forty-five and fifty-five except for Selma's secretary and assistant, who were in their late twenties. To them, I remarked that, not long ago, just *having* a fiftieth birthday party out in the open would have been unthinkable for a woman because this milestone was too doleful to be acknowledged. I said how glad I was that we had progressed to the point where a woman can be publicly feted on her fiftieth birthday and feel good about it. One of the twentysomethings kindly responded that she was glad women like us existed to be role models of proud, assertive aging. We elders preened, but a few beats later, I started wondering whether making a fuss about fifty was such a good idea after all. Maybe it was drawing too much attention to Selma's age. What if these kids started thinking of their boss as proudly and assertively *old?* Would they start treating her differently? Would she regret this? Eventually, I calmed myself down and enjoyed watching Selma luxuriate in everyone's love — but the cloud had crossed my mind.

I used to anticipate my childhood birthday parties as if each were an annual coronation. Like most kids, I loved sitting at the head of the table with a crown on my head. In recent years, however, birthdays have been more like medical checkups — no fun at all but necessary if one intends to stay alive from year to year. The idea of "celebrating" the march of time was unthinkable; I couldn't even bear the thought of the first birthday card purporting to congratulate me for achieving my august age.

Just because you finally hit the
Big 5-0 doesn't mean your life is over . . .
Sex is over. But life
will probably go on.

If you want to feel good about turning fifty, don't expect help from Hallmark. The greeting card manufacturers make a fortune tweaking us while we're down, and some tweaks are worse than others:

As you turn 50, you must begin to ask yourself several
nagging, sometimes painful, questions:
Which hemorrhoid treatment works best —
cream or suppositories.

Getting one of these cards in the mail is about as heartening as finding a foreclosure notice tacked to your door, yet people send them by the millions, putting the burden on the recipient to greet the greeting with a sense of humor or whatever else might dull the pain.

But nothing compares to the ordeal of the midlife birthday party. When we're young, a party is an unambiguously joyous event, because kids welcome the arrival of each new year as a measure of their growth toward independence. In the twenties, birthdays are still as cheerful as childhood, but when we turn thirty, some of us begin to detect a note of disharmony in the Happy Birthday song — a kind of uh-oh drumbeat under the melody line — while others consider this leap into adult society well worth celebrating (depending on where they are in terms of self-predictions and expectations.)

Once past forty, it's the rare person who doesn't hear the song with a certain dismay; "Happy" Birthday seems more prescriptive than descriptive. At this point, the toasts begin to turn smarmy, the "downhill" jokes proliferate, and when the party's over, we sometimes wish we'd skipped the whole thing.

At fifty, the negative subtext is overt and the beat is decidedly down. Attempts at revelry often come off as forced mirth, as if the crowd were whistling past a cemetery to calm their jitters. When the champagne wears off, the fiftieth birthday party reveals itself to be an exercise in communal consolation, a three- or four-hour distraction from the eternal light at the end of the tunnel. We can't kid ourselves anymore; birthday parties no longer celebrate growth or progress, they simply celebrate survival.

Of course, survival ought to be enough. Not being sick or dead is a miracle worth celebrating every day of the year, but most of us don't notice ourselves enduring, we notice ourselves aging, and as I've noted, in this culture, aging bears no fruits and brings no homage. "When my friends threw a surprise party on my sixtieth birthday, I could have killed them all," reports Betty Friedan at the beginning of *The Fountain of Age*. "Their toasts seemed hostile . . . pushing me out of life . . . out of the race." All of which raises the question: Who needs it? Why mark a midlife birthday with a public ritual when everyone's attention is focused on the dread ahead and the guest of honor may well experience the supposed festivities as a medieval water torture?

Party Time

A typical fiftieth birthday bash starts off with a gag about her age spots. *Drip.* Or some breezy reminiscing about the good old days when he had hair on his head and an unobstructed view of his feet. *Drip.* Then he can't blow out all fifty candles in one breath, which reminds someone of a friend who died from emphysema. *Drip.* And she can't eat her butter-cream birthday cake, which inspires a discussion of fatty foods and breast cancer. *Drip.* Her "humorous" birthday presents include a tube of denture cream and a book on adult incontinence; just for laughs, he gets a subscription to the *Journal of Gerontology* and a pamphlet entitled "Warning Signs of Prostate Disease." Ha. Ha. *Drip. Drip.* Aw, c'mon, it's all in fun.

Why do people assume that every fifty-year-old is a masochist?

My Dallas cousins tell me that Texans celebrate their midlife birthdays with "black balloon parties" — a flat-out parody of a funeral. The party invitation is bordered in black. The party room is decorated with black crepe, funeral wreaths, and black balloons bearing such messages as "We Mourn the Passing of Your Youth," "Dead-End Day," "Down the Drain," and "Over the Hill" (that old hill again). Other "fun" birthday gifts include canes, crutches, hearing aids, and a voodoo doll with the number 50 on its chest and enough pins for the whole crowd. The man who has everything is presented with a pair of permanently creased undershorts imprinted, "Of course it's wrinkled; I'm old," and the lucky woman gets an "Over the Hill Bra" that proclaims across both cups, "They've fallen down and they can't get up."

This is not my idea of fun. Who in her right mind would want a dirge at a time like this? For a party to be a celebration, I would have to check my black balloon mentality at the door, not an easy task given the fact that I grew up in the 1950s and was raised with the notion that, for a woman, passing the midcentury mark is the end of the game.

What's to Celebrate?

When Gloria Swanson starred in Billy Wilder's film version of *Sunset Boulevard,* she was a fifty-year-old actress playing a fifty-year-old actress, the reclusive silent-film star Norma Desmond, who desperately wants to make a comeback. Back then, a fifty-year-old was a pitiable has-been. Today, Barbra Streisand is perhaps the biggest name in show business and at this writing she is fifty-three. In 1993, at the premiere of his musical version of *Sunset Boulevard,* composer Andrew Lloyd Webber had this to say about the changes in American women's attitude toward age since Swanson's era. "My wife went to a birthday lunch with all the Hollywood wives, and they said, 'We're all fifty and we're all beautiful.' Today fifty is nothing, but in those days, it was shocking."

While I wouldn't say fifty is "nothing" nowadays, describing it as "shocking" back in the 1940s and 1950s is no exaggeration. Then, women believed the midlife birthday party should be banned as a mental health hazard. I cannot remember my mother, aunts, their friends, or any of my friends' mothers ever actually partying on their fiftieth birthdays, or on *any* birthdays for that matter. At most, they acknowledged the date to their husbands, went out to dinner, and received their gifts in a quiet presentation attended only by the immediate family.

In my time as well, the only things a woman celebrated openly were youth and marriage. Lucky girls got a Sweet Sixteen party, wealthy girls got a coming-out party, betrothed girls got an engagement shower, and brides got a wedding — the first two events established the girl's availability, and the last two rewarded her achievement. That was *it* for parties. One didn't surprise a grown woman with a birthday bash for the simple reason that such a party had an uncanny way of raising the subject of age.

Although I've always told people how old I am, at an unconscious level I must have been fighting this early conditioning because every so often — usually in connection with a birthday party — the shame factor popped to the surface.

Rites of Passage

"Neither for men nor for women do we anywhere find initiation ceremonies that confirm the status of being an elder," wrote Simone de Beauvoir. Thanks to the women's movement's campaign against ageism, that's no longer true. If I've ultimately triumphed over the shame factor, it is due, in large part, to my recent exposure to some of the new coming-of-age ceremonies created by feminists to celebrate older women and transform the once painful ordeal of turning fifty (or forty or sixty) into a ritual of renewal as powerful in its way as the life cycle ceremonies surrounding birth and marriage.

Calling one of these new rites of passage a birthday party would be like describing baptism as bathtime, or *kiddush* as a drinking song. Still, I'm not sure what else to call them, since New Age rhetoric has an unfortunate way of reducing meaningful spiritual endeavors to touchy-feely psychobabble that makes everything sound like coffee talk for codependents. I had to gag my Rationalist Censor before I could begin to appreciate what's been going on among feminist ritual-makers for the last decade or more. Yes, the coming-of-age ceremonies *are* touchy-feely, but that's because they are authentically touching and full of feeling. They are also creative, aesthetic, playful, improvisational, cathartic, and intensely personal. Unlike those awful birthday cards, they acknowledge age but don't fixate on the number. They use poetry, art, biography, prayer, tree planting, and naming rituals as a means of accepting, affirming, even glorifying this pivotal point in a woman's life.

When women create their own aging ceremonies, a surprising number choose the crone as the muse of liberation. Hearing about "The Crowning of the Crone" ritual for the first time, I'll admit, I cringed. That the word conjures up the unloveliest images of womenkind is not my fault. The *Random House Dictionary* defines a crone as "an ugly, withered old woman," Webster's has crone as "a withered hag," and both authorities omit the historical meaning of the term. Originally, it meant either a "survivor of the burning times" or a "wise woman, teacher, postmenopausal woman with long experience and the time to reflect upon it." (One can only deduce that *pre*menopausal women were too busy with offspring and incessant pregnancies to do much reflecting; or they died in childbirth at an appalling rate; or maybe nobody noticed women's wisdom until there was little else to notice.)

What today's ritualists have done is simply to reclaim the original definition of the noun and transform it into a verb. "Croning" is now an established female coming-of-age ceremony, part of a grassroots movement to appropriate the positive attributes of age — wisdom, knowledge, experience, caring — and fashion them into a status to which a woman might actually *aspire*. Those who've been "croned" say it's a rite of passage as powerful in its way as the puberty rituals that initiate young people into their culture at the other end of the life span.

Mina Hamilton, a yoga therapist and writer, has devised a deeply cathartic croning ceremony in which women sit in a circle and write on small pieces of notepaper everything about aging that makes them afraid or ashamed: Loneliness. Illness. Infirmity. Dryness. Economic insecurity. Regrets about the past. Loss of sexual energy. Fear of change. Fear of death. Then they throw their notes into a large fireproof bowl, set them aflame, and watch the terrors of aging turn to ash.

Lillian Rand, a screenwriter, describes a "Crowning of the Crone" celebration that borrows from the classical Wiccan, or women's spiritualist, tradition (though strict Wiccans won't crone a woman until she's fifty-six). Rand had expected a room full of middle-aged Wonder Women, but when she first saw the group that had gathered in the Grange Hall for the croning ceremony, she says she "felt a twinge of revulsion. Did I really want to align myself with a bunch of older women, genteel Yankee ladies with courteous smiles, little makeup and neat grey curls?"

During the course of the evening, however, these ordinary Yankee ladies did extraordinary things. They created sacred space; they chanted, drummed, purified the air with burning cedar and sage, invited nature's energizing forces to join their circle and give them strength. They read aloud from women's writings about midlife. They talked of particular women who had touched their lives — mothers, grandmothers, friends, teachers, mentors — and lit candles of gratitude to honor them. And then each aspiring crone came forward to be crowned. Rand writes of the home-made crowns:

> Some were comical with long, dark feathers sticking up; others were whimsical, with tinsel and silver stars; still others were romantic and freewheeling with wreaths of wild flowers and oversized fruits. One looked like a Valkyrie helmet.

It would be easy to ridicule a ritual in which, one at a time, women sit on a makeshift red throne, get topped with a silly-looking headpiece, and then march three times around a circle proclaiming that they have claimed "the power and wisdom of the Crone." But such a ceremony is no more ridiculous *on its face* than one in which Catholics take communion or Jews perform ritual circumcision. Ceremonies carry the meaning that a community endows them with, and, as Rand retells it, the "Crowning of the Crone" ceremony carries transcendent meaning and beauty for the community of midlife women who give themselves to it. As one of the new "cronies" said:

> When women get together this way, it's a powerful antidote to society's dismissiveness. Secetly, I had accepted a negative image of middle age. It robbed me of self-love and alienated me from my aging body. But by the end of the ceremony, I had seen another dimension. What a joyful surprise, like seeing snow for the first time.

In *The Wise Woman: A Celebration* and *Midlife: A Rite of Passage,* Irene Fine writes about life-cycle ceremonies from a Jewish-feminist perspective, but the premises underlying her ideas can easily be adapted to other spiritual traditions or can be secularized entirely. Fine's two-part ceremony begins with a renaming rite in which the honoree changes her name to symbolize her changed status. What's in a name? Everything. The feminist canon gives great weight to the prerogative to name, a power largely reserved to men, whether it was Adam naming the animals in Eden or Sigmund Freud naming women's supposed neuroses. If kings and popes receive a new name upon ascending their thrones, why shouldn't we?

Long before I came to feminism, I learned at my mother's knee that a new name can transform a person, and even save a life. A short while after she arrived in America, she changed her name from Sarah to Cyral and then to Ceil, in effect performing her own naturalization ceremony in a land where she thought Sarah might mark her as a "greenhorn." She and my grandmother also believed that if you change the name of someone who is gravely ill, you can outwit the Evil Eye — the Devil who prowls the earth looking for vulnerable mortals to cart off to the netherworld. The alias throws the Evil Eye off course, giving the sick person time to regain his or her strength.

The renaming ritual makes particular sense in the case of the typical fifty-year-old woman who has been carrying a given name chosen by her parents, a nickname dubbed her by her childhood friends, and the surname of her father or of the man she married (and perhaps divorced). But the name she chooses in her coming-of-age ceremony is hers alone, and in choosing it, *she* defines herself.

The second part of Fine's rite of passage is the covenant ceremony, a ritual in which women can renegotiate their relationship with God and their community. One woman borrowed from the original Biblical covenant (which established the rite of circumcision for Jewish males), and devised a ribbon-cutting as her covenantal ceremony. She cut several lengths of ribbon and asked her friends to retie the ends together, symbolizing the renewal of her attachment to her beliefs and her community on her fiftieth birthday.

Bonnie Feinman's rite of passage, witnessed by eighty friends and relatives, included songs, blessings, a ritual of purification — washing the hands in water symbolizing "the purity and sanctity of this ceremony" — as well as a renaming and a covenantal ceremony. Feinman chose to renew her personal covenant with the "God of my mothers and fathers" by cutting in half an apple (signifying the beauty of nature, sweetness, Eve, knowledge), and placing between its two halves a candle whose light represented hope and blessings, and whose fire symbolized both warmth and fear.

In the croning ritual devised by Savina Teubal, the guest of honor wears a *kittel,* a soft robe made of the finest white linen, which is meant to enfold her at this and other ceremonial occasions and eventually to serve as her shroud. "It is symbolic of an acceptance, in the larger scheme of things, of the cycle of life and death," says Teubal, who ends her ritual with the planting of a tree.

Marcia Cohn Spiegal, a well-known ceremonialist, wore a kittel and planted a tree when she became a crone at sixty. Before a group of 120 celebrants in Rolling Hills, California, Spiegel spoke about the "fragility of life," about her losses, her adventures, her mentors, her family. Then, standing under her grandfather's outstretched *tallit* (prayer shawl), she and three friends said the traditional prayer for healing. The new name Marcia chose for herself was Miriam, after the prophet who was Moses' sister and who led her people into the Red Sea with timbrel, song, and dance: "I will strive to be a Miriam," Spiegal said, "to be a leader, a healer; to lead in joy as well as in sorrow; to possess her wisdom and integrity; to love and be loved."

E. M. Broner is a longtime inventor of rituals, many of which are described in her book *From Me to You to the World: Ceremonies to Come; Ceremonies to Go.* "Like midwives, we help each other into the coming decade," Broner wrote ten years ago in *Ms.* magazine, where she first reported on new celebrations for women's midlife birthdays. "Harriet Berg, dance teacher and choreographer, gave herself a tea dance. . . . Her invitations are printed dance cards with five sets of dances, beginning with "As Time Goes By." To congratulate her or chat with her, Harriet's guests had to dance with her — "the jitterbug, cha-cha, hustle, twist, waltz, Charleston, tango, miserlou, polka, conga, rhumba, and the finale, the fox trot."

Teresa Bernardez, a psychiatrist at Michigan State, gathered friends, colleagues, and former patients for a rebirth-day party, at which they formed a tent-shaped tunnel with their legs, a midlife birth canal through which Teresa could symbolically traverse from her past to her present. "At the end of this tunnel of friendship," writes Broner, "Teresa falls onto a receiving blanket and is proclaimed a Wise Woman."

How else to celebrate becoming fifty? Let me count the ways. California actress Naomi Newman gave herself a party she called, "A Spirit-lift Instead of a Face-lift." Marleen Brasefield dispensed "Salty Old Woman Awards" to friends who met her criteria:

> The ageless Salty Old Woman is made not born: You are one if you (1) switched careers in midlife, (2) express your opinion in public even when outnumbered, (3) are always learning something new, and (4) wake up every morning wondering what's going to happen and look forward to it.

Bea Kreloff, a lifelong social activist, gave herself a sixtieth birthday party at a Manhattan disco and turned it into a benefit for Kitchen Table: Women of Color Press, a small publishing house that showcases minority authors.

Without reference to a particular birthday, Eleanor J. Piazza organizes a yearly ceremony to honor Women of the Fourteenth Moon, so-called because "if there are thirteen full moons in a given year, a woman who has not had a period for a year will begin a new phase in her life upon the fourteenth full moon without bleeding."

Piazza writes: "Every year we flesh it out differently, and every year we learn from the ceremony itself . . . and it teaches us about power and control, about giving and receiving, about humility, self-esteem, appreciation, friendship, community, and much, more more. Each woman who attends, attends her own unique ceremony. Surely this is magic."

Man-Made Revelry

Of course, devising unique ways to celebrate one's most meaningful birthdays is not strictly the province of women. The author John Stoltenberg chose to forego a party for his fiftieth, but instead asked his friends to contribute whatever they would have spent on a present to "New York City's financially stretched rape-crisis hotline BWARE . . . or some other good cause of your choice."

I'm not suggesting that everyone must repudiate birthday presents in favor of charitable donations. In fact, I could probably make the case that if ever there was a time for sybaritic self-indulgence — for doing something entirely pleasurable with the people who matter most — one's fiftieth birthday is that time, especially for women. It is still unusual for the average woman to be feted and fussed over rather than be the organizer and enabler of the fete and the fuss, and rather than be taken for granted by her family. Husbands and other men who want to honor a woman at midlife do not necessarily have a clue about what to do or how to do it — which is why I was so moved when my friend Nadine, the photographer in Mexico, described how her husband, Larry, made her fiftieth a fiesta of adoration that continued into the following month:

> Larry and Marissa [their daughter] showered me with presents. They served me chocolate cake in bed for breakfast. In the evening, Larry took us to Las Mananitas, an outdoor restaurant in

Cuernavaca where I was serenaded by strolling musicians as I marveled at the purple-bloomed trees in the lush, tropical garden and the fountains full of red poinsettias. I was elated when one of the wandering peacocks who inhabit the grounds spread his feathers in a birthday salute.

Larry kept his hand on my thigh all evening and assured me that I was the most beautiful and youngest-looking 50-year-old he had ever seen. Naturally I don't believe a word he says. The hunt for a plastic surgeon is on.

It is a week into January and I am still celebrating. Yesterday, we drove into the mountains to drink a bottle of French champagne at the foot of two snow-capped volcanos. The wind was as cold as the bubbly. And our tuna fish sandwiches tasted like caviar.

A few other men I know also have pulled out all the stops for the woman in their life: Jerry Isenberg gave his wife, Carole, an alfresco fiftieth birthday party with the theme "A Midsummer Night's Dream," for which he hired a local theater group to perform scenes from Shakespeare's comedy. After dinner the party guests — who'd been asked to wear fantasy summer outfits — presented a skit recapitulating Carole's life. In the opening scene, Carole, who was born in Brooklyn, is shown as a baby in heaven begging to be born in Paris.

Mentioning the skit reminds me of the Paris trip that the actor-director Alan Alda planned as a birthday surprise for his wife, Arlene. In secret, he managed to buy the tickets, make the hotel reservations, and plan the whole itinerary but, most remarkable of all, he packed her suitcase for her — something few men I know could manage — and spirited it into the trunk of their car the night before they left. (He told her they were driving to the airport to meet a friend's flight.)

The Perfect Gift

Like lox with bagels, presents go with birthdays, but in those landmark years when feelings are raw and everything takes on added symbolism, choosing a gift can be hazardous. Just as no respectable Tooth Fairy would put a bottle of cod liver oil under a child's pillow, certain birthday presents are a bad idea regardless of whether they're good for us, and other presents are a great idea because they're perfect for that particular person and that particular landmark.

At her croning ceremony, Ruth Driker Kroll's friends inscribed their memories of her onto a handmade scroll, a long sheet of butcher paper glued onto wooden dowels, wrapped in a velvet casing and tied with a golden ribbon. In addition, reports Esther Broner, people gave her store-bought gifts with special significance — "luggage to carry Ruth far afield; *Love, Anarchy, and Emma Goldman,* by Candace Falk, for activism and eroticism, whatever the age; a volume of letters by Virginia Woolf, to honor women in our literature of correspondence."

When I turned forty, some friends organized a small surprise party to which everyone brought a present that embodied a message they thought I needed to hear. The blue football jersey with my name on the front and the number 40 on the back told me I was still "in the game." The milky hunk of raw crystal glowing atop a light-box signified both durability and the illumination of age. The silver wine caddy was meant as a permanent reminder that I must keep toasting life. But the pièce de résistance was a collection of recordings of classical pieces written *after* each composer was forty — such titanic works as Beethoven's Ninth Symphony, Tchaikovsky's Fifth, Bach's *Goldberg Variations,* and Vivaldi's *Four Seasons* — each composition offering listenable proof that sometimes the best is yet to come.

Handmade gifts add even more meaning to a big birthday; for instance, the patchwork quilt assembled for Marcia Cohn Spiegel by her grown-up children.

> Secretly they gathered honors, awards, certificates, and old family photos: my grandparents, my parents, my baby pictures, important events in my life, their pictures, my grandchildren. These were photographed and printed on fabric which was sewn into a quilt of memory. Embroidered on the quilt were the words from my service [her Wise Woman ceremony] and from a special song written for that service and all of their names. When I said I would treasure it and hang it on the wall for everyone to see, they said, "No, it was meant to keep you warm. Don't hang it, use it." And so I do, wrapping myself in their love.

Shortly before Bernardine Dohrn's big day, her friends received this letter from her husband, Bill Ayers:

> While Bernardine has organized a group of women turning fifty, and has created a fascinating study / discussion group around the theme "Women Coming of Age," several of us have been struggling with an inspired gift to mark this momentous occasion. We now have an idea and we'd like your help.
>
> We want to give Bernardine a scrapbook that would include photographs, artifacts, and biographical fragments from her life. We want her friends to reflect briefly on her life and times, what she has taught us and why we love her and honor her at this milestone in her remarkable life.
>
> Here's what we'd like you to do: write something (a letter, poem, sketch, recollection, whatever) for this collection and send it along with any artifacts you want included (photos, clippings, old letters, postcards). DO NOT MENTION THIS TO HER — THIS IS A SURPRISE! We will then assemble it all and create a beautiful and unique book from all of us.

Counting down to my fiftieth, I decided to give *myself* a present, a coming-of-age ceremony to suit my particular needs — a birthday lunch that would preempt the possibility of a funeral parody, or a vodka-soaked cocktail bash, or even an elegant dinner party, however well intentioned. I was about to depart from a sweet, verdant land and enter a place of uncertainty and fear. I needed an escort, nothing fancy, just a group of friends ready to do the labor of love: I wanted help turning fifty.

Not Your Ordinary Ladies' Lunch

The activities I had in mind for my birthday lunch would demand the truth, the whole truth, and nothing but the truth, so I decided to invite only women. Not because there are no honest men in my life, but because I'd learned that women are more candid about feelings and experiences — especially when they're in a single-sex group — and I needed some of that sisterly self-disclosure as an antidote to my impacted agony about aging.

I chose to limit my invitees to friends who were either forty-nine-going-on-fifty or in their fiftieth year, because I felt I needed to be surrounded by women who were exactly where I was right then — feeling the midcentury sensation to the core. I didn't want the wisdom of hindsight: women in their mid-fifties and sixties tend to look back at fifty as young;

their perspective would help me someday but not now. As for women in their forties, I didn't want to put any antififty ideas in their heads — and I wasn't in the mood to envy them.

Despite my exacting criteria, I instantly came up with seven friends who fit the description perfectly — Annie, my downstairs neighbor, who's a stockbroker; Ene, a TV producer whom I've known since we were in a consciousness-raising group together in the early seventies; Harriet, an editor and journalist who for many years was a colleague of mine at *Ms.* magazine; Wendy, a respected literary agent; Anne, a lawyer who is now a theatrical producer; Judy, a singer and writer; and Fredi, a book editor whose early interest in my aging obsessions gave rise to the volume you are now reading. Eventually, after culling the names in my address book, I expanded the guest list to fourteen women who were the right age, and a few days before the event, I sent them an assignment:

> Please be prepared to talk for a couple of minutes, extemporaneously, about how you feel about being 49-going-on-50, or having recently turned 50. Just for the fun of it, please bring:
>
> 1. An inexpensive grab bag present. (Choose something you think will comfort the recipient, be instructive, or make her laugh about aging.)
> 2. A photograph of yourself as a baby, a teenager, or whatever age most embodied your inner self.

June 1 was one of those gorgeous spring days that make Manhattan feel like a city in your dreams. I filled the apartment with fresh flowers, opened the windows wide, and welcomed each guest as though greeting my own deliverance. Since everyone knew the criteria for attendance, each woman knew that all the others were exactly her age; some of them even knew each other. Still, one guest seemed genuinely surprised when another woman walked in the door. "Annie!" she burst out. "I always thought you were younger than I!"

Not only is it rare for an adult to be in a situation where she knows the age of everyone in the room, but this was probably the first time since kindergarten that any of us had been gathered in one place simply *because* of the year we were born. Chronological age seems so important when we're young, before it is eclipsed by other attributes, before people start sorting us by race, class, or beauty — whether we like it or not — and before aging makes age important again for all the wrong reasons. But here in my living room, we were back in kindergarten, where date of birth was what mattered and being fifty was as relevant as being five was then.

I looked around the group and asked: "Why do I think our mothers looked so much older when they were our age?"

"Because they did!" was the answering chorus. Feeling pleased with ourselves and sorry for our mothers, we discussed the phenomenon: women of previous generations were older-looking because they led hard-scrabble lives or were more sedentary, ate bad foods, and wore matronly clothes, but also because of how they thought and acted and carried themselves in the world.

Almost surreptitiously, like an adolescent stealing glances at her friends' progress toward puberty, we studied each other's faces and figures. One woman spoke the words I was thinking: "We're not just younger-looking than our mothers were at our age, we really look *young*." Feminists aren't supposed to care about looks, yet we — declared feminists all — admitted that we had noticed the attractiveness of the group and no one seemed the least bit embarrassed about it. I suspect this is because we were reacting out of a purely positive impulse, an impulse supposedly uncharacteristic of women: rather than feeling jealous or competitive, we were taking pleasure in each other's appearance. Only a few were conventionally pretty, but the life force emanating from every woman in the room was so palpable it seemed to galvanize into a kind of beauty, a radiance that language labels "young-looking" because the culture yields no other vocabulary to describe it. In our collective image we saw dramatic confirmation that something extraordinary was happening to our age group. It couldn't be all bad if *these* were my peers, I thought. Just looking at these vivid, spirited, attractive women made me feel better about being fifty. My birthday lunch was paying off already.

After we'd eaten our fill and settled comfortably around the living room, each woman introduced herself with a brief biographical sketch. Out of fifteen women (myself included), seven were married, four to our original husbands; eight were single — of whom six were divorced, one widowed, one never married. Most of the singles were heterosexuals living in committed relationships; one was in a long-term union with a woman. Three of the fifteen had no children. The oldest offspring was Roxanne's thirty-year-old; Anne had the youngest child, nine, and the oldest stepchild, thirty-four. Judy, the singer, was our only grandmother. "She's twenty months old but I don't call her my grandchild," said Judy, smiling. "I call her my son's daughter."

Everyone was amused to discover halfway through the go-around that four of us had dated the same man when we were young and single, but only one of us had married, and divorced, him. "I saved three women in this room from a terrible fate," said Sally, the ex-wife. "Don't I get some thanks from you guys?"

Two of the women were students, everyone else was employed, not necessarily nine to five, but earning a living. Several worked in publishing as editors, agents, consultants. A lawyer, stockbroker, placement director, news documentary producer, and professional singer made up the balance.

Our names were as fascinating as anything else. There was Anne, Annie, and Ene (pronounced Eh-na, Estonian for Ann), and there were two Judys — testimony to Judy Garland's popularity in 1939, when we were born, and *The Wizard of Oz* was everyone's favorite film. We had the exotic (Roxanne) and the lofty (Fredrica), but for the most part my friends bore the commonplace names of the 1930s — Judy, Sally, Harriet, Carol, Helen, Wendy, and Jane — with nary a Melissa, Stacey, or Jessica in the bunch.

A woman might lie about her age and never realize it's her name that dates her. A name may not be as reliable as a carbon-dated fossil, but it is a fair clue to the era that spawned us. Early in the twentieth century, most-favored-names-status was given to Mollie, Sophie, and Charlotte, names that are making a comeback today, but in my era, they were considered embarrassingly old-fashioned. In the 1930s and 1940s, when Shirley Temple movies were on American screens, there were Shirleys in American cribs; by the 1950s, Shirleys dwindled. Comedian Mark Russell reminds us that the baby boomers are bound to get old like other mortals, which means one day we'll actually have people in nursing homes named Heather and Debbie.

My given name was Loretta. My parents told me I was named after my father's late mother, Yetta, but it can't be accidental that my mother's favorite actress was Loretta Young. When I was in the third grade, an immigrant English girl joined our class and summarily dubbed me Letty, which she said was the proper diminutive of my name; it stuck because I liked it.

After the women finished their introductions, I launched into my spiel: "As you know, I convened this lunch with the most selfish motive: to make myself feel better about turning fifty, which has been depressing me terribly for the last eleven months."

"Only eleven months?" a voice piped up.

"I'm not complaining for the same reasons our mothers did," I continued. "I'm not weeping over my empty nest or wondering what I have left to live for. My problem is that I have *so* much to live for and so much yet to do, and I hate watching the time go. I hate the mortality part."

"We can't help you with the mortality part," said Jane, deadpan, as it were.

I explained that I wanted to know from the fifty-year-olds how they had weathered the milestone and from the forty-nine-year-olds how they'd been preparing for it. I wanted to check my angst against everyone else's, and learn their secrets for emotional survival: "I invited you here the week before my actual birthday so I could benefit from your advice in time to put myself in a more positive frame of mind," I concluded. "So please tell me — tell us — how you feel about aging and how you see yourself and your future at this point in your life."

I'm glad I asked.

Stories as Celebration

Over the next three hours, they told their stories, tales of self-discovery and suffering, stories about life-threatening illnesses, a double mastectomy, rancorous divorces, the discovery that a husband was a closet homosexual, the trauma of early widowhood, the death of three close family members within a year, perilous finances, troubled children, lost jobs, lost homes, lost loves. With all this, each woman in her way had managed to beat down adversity and move forward. Each had been able to dig out of the mess or the misery and construct a life of meaning that brought her to this moment feeling stronger at fifty than she'd been at forty or even thirty.

Looking back on the scene, I find myself recalling May Sarton's journal description of the friends who came to salute her on her seventieth birthday:

> It was marvelous to see this galaxy gathered together. . . . And as I looked around the table, what struck me hard was that, none of us young, we had all managed to become our true selves, that none of it had been easy, and that all of it has been built on dedication and on love.

The same could be said of our little group. Almost everyone had undergone a dramatic change in circumstances, a search for a more authentic self, a time of questioning, of love and of growth — a blossoming.

Two of the women had returned to school, including Helen, who was just finishing her freshman year in college:

"I had a real hard time being fifty. The first thing I thought was that I couldn't dream anymore. Then I realized that it was time to look at my list of dreams, cross things off, and turn the rest of the dream list into a To Do list.

"When I was eighteen, my parents said I couldn't go to college. For years, I was always thinking, why didn't they let me go? why didn't I go? I should have gone. This year, I said to myself, look, you're fifty, just do it, already. So I took a test, got a scholarship, and just completed my first course — and it's an honors class.

"It was a monumental step for me to push through the rage and do this. I used to hang out in the background when I was with my college-educated friends. But now that I'm in school, I've realized, Gee, I'm smart. You don't have to go to college to be a smart person. My teacher tells me I'm a fabulous writer and I should do something with it. I said, 'I'm fifty years old! I'm taking three credits a year, and you're talking about my writing career?' I don't know what I'll do next. I've owned a flower shop, and before that I was a fabric designer. I'm not sure my onion has shed its last layer yet."

Helen laughed, then turned to me and said, "You've talked about wanting to write novels and learn Russian. Well, stop looking at what you're not doing and ask yourself, 'Am I going to leave this item on the To Do list or what?'"

Roxanne was rounding the last stretch of a long journey. "I wanted to find my own name," she said. "I wanted to move away from being defined by everyone else around me, not just my husband, but my children, parents, background." Roxanne's ex-husband and the father of her three children is a famous political figure. She was raised in a family that maintained a strict definition of woman's role. Now she was literally reinventing herself.

"It all started when I was thirty-eight. I was feeling anxious and lonely and I decided to find out what I really needed and wanted before I turned forty. Today, coming to grips with fifty is the fruition of the anxieties I felt at forty.

"I started college as a freshman at forty-two. I registered in my own name. It's not my Dad's name, it's mine. But I didn't know if I could be just me. I didn't know who me was. I'd been Mrs. Famous Politician for so long and gotten a lot of mileage out of it. It was hard, but I've grown comfortable with just being Roxanne. I've found that she has a lot of strengths, and I get to pull them out now and take some chances.

"When I look back at this incredible decade of change, I see that it was filled with such godawful things. My marriage has taken forever to break up, but it's the way I had to go through it. I've done it on my own terms. I've begun doing everything on my own terms in my own time. It doesn't matter that I started college at forty-two, it only matters that I'm now well on my way toward a Ph.D. I just have to finish my dissertation. I also have to come to peace with my parents the way I'm at peace with other aspects of my life. And I'm looking ahead to a new kind of relationship with my kids where I can allow them to go through their pain without my feeling responsible for it or thinking I can do something about it — or that it's Mom's job to make everything right for everyone. I don't want to do that anymore."

Though a luminous, natural beauty, Roxanne concluded her remarks with a comment about her looks: "I hate my neck and I hate my chin and I can't do anything about them except hold my head higher when I talk to people. Otherwise, I feel okay about being fifty. The last ten years have shown me that I can survive incredible stress and that I get stronger every day. I look ahead, now. And I try not to do two things: feel guilty or be fearful."

Anne identified with a lot that Roxanne said. Though not a household name like Roxanne's ex, Anne's husband is a prominent lawyer whose name she admitted she "traded on." Anne went to law school for the same reason Roxanne started college — to become her own person. She had just started lawyering again after years of full-time motherhood. "I'm working for the Children's Rights Project of the ACLU, although my little one says, 'Mom, you don't know *anything* about children's rights.'"

Anne, who could easily be Julia Roberts's older sister, touched on the perils and pleasures of looking younger than one's years: "When I was first married, people used to say, are you Howard's daughter? I'd rush home and tell him, the poor man. But that never happens any more. Suddenly, people have stopped exclaiming, 'Oh, you couldn't possibly be that age." It's not a big problem as problems go, but you notice it when it stops."

"I was never invested in being young and pretty," said one of the Judys, "so I haven't paid attention to the physical changes of growing older. And I don't share Letty's view that age means mortality, because if you've had friends and relatives who've died in their twenties, thirties, and forties, you don't think of death as a function of age, but of life. [This Judy lost her first husband at a very young age.] In my late forties, after a decade of various losses, I started feeling a sense of entitlement — to enjoy more, to trust my instincts, to pursue my interests — so fifty hasn't hit me as a major setback or a time of privation."

"I wasn't invested in being young or beautiful, either," said Jane. "I never even thought about my appearance until I suddenly realized that it might be gravitating away. I'm not reconciled to that and don't expect to become reconciled to it.

"I have a photograph of my mother holding my daughter as a baby; my mother must have been fifty then because she's twenty-five years older than I am, and I was twenty-five when that baby was born. It's odd to look at the photograph and consider that she was as old as I am now, and twenty-five years from now I'll be as old as she is now. Mortality marches on.

"I've had, as we all have, a lot of pain in my life and a lot of joy. In the past year, I've been at the top of the Karakoram Mountains, sixteen thousand feet above the world, and I've been in the depths of despair. If you're not open to risk, you're not living. I've leaned on the support of my friends and family, especially family; this year reminded me how significant they are. My children are a source of enormous pleasure to me. I love my work. But, Letty, there's no way to avoid what you call existential terror. We all have to live with it."

The second Judy, the singer, sounded a fatalistic note, which wasn't surprising given all she's been through: "My teens were rotten, my twenties were ugh-ugh, and my thirties were terrible because, although I had a successful professional career, I had absolutely no idea what I was doing in my work. I also had a lot of physical problems. I'm an alcoholic and I didn't know the first thing about it then, so I was drinking throughout that time. My forties have been about learning how to fill my own shoes, and accumulating a lot of information I'd need because I knew I'd be a late bloomer. I've worked in my profession for thirty years. I've been in a great relationship with the man I live with. His energy and mine are very balanced, very compatible. Also, my family is important to me; they've always mattered but now even more so.

"I'm a singer who wants to grow up to be a writer, and a writer who wants to grow up to be an artist. I don't want to do anything in the same way I did it before. I know it is going to be a lifetime process, but my desire to be the best of whatever I am is more intense than ever.

"I don't think I can save the world anymore. I know I'll keep trying, because I've tried all my life, but I don't think it's why I'm here. Which is a big relief.

"I know that any time I do something creative or tough, I do it not only for myself but for others and for the future. I have a concept of universal timelessness. If people hadn't been talking so much about my being fifty, I wouldn't have paused long enough to think about aging, because I see it as an organic part of the process. I know I can't reach eighty, or ninety, or one hundred, without being fifty first. I have to move through it. Besides, I don't believe this life is all there is. Buddha lived eighty years before he achieved Nirvana. I can't wait to see what's next."

Harriet, a veteran of the 1970s consciousness-raising groups, opened with, "It's been fifteen years since I've sat with perfect strangers that I know this well.

"I turned fifty last Monday, and I've been partying like a banshee," she continued, explaining that my lunch was her fourth celebration; the first was with childhood friends, the second with current friends and colleagues, and the third with her daughter's pals, who had also become *her* friends. Then Harriet focused on her work frustrations and her lingering regret at having left the magazine eight years ago.

"Being an editor at *Ms.* was the most meaningful work I've ever done. It's difficult to realize that something is behind you that you might never be able to recapture. It took me a long time to make peace with that. And I'm out there now [at a newspaper] where there aren't those same support systems and the same caring or values we had at the magazine.

"After twenty-nine years as a journalist, I still have the hots for it. But I worry that I won't have the fuel to match the intensity or to carry me through what I want to do. So that gap is scary. But right now, I feel very confident and very good."

Sally, widowed in her second marriage, described a cannonade of crises that made the perils of Pauline look like a bad hair day. "I'm just so pleased to be among the living. I'm grateful to be part of the middle class and to be working. Five years ago, my husband died of a heart attack. His family saw no more need of me. His estate sold our apartment. I had two kids from my first marriage and I had no place to live, no support from the children's father, and no job, because I'd given up my business to take care of my husband when he got sick. I was totally abandoned by everyone and everything. Terrible things have happened to me and I have survived. Now it's five years later and here I am. I have a wonderful job as a placement director. And, knock wood, my children are okay. I've dragged them through every kind of adversity — the ups and downs of fortune, had money, didn't have money, married, not married, in and out of schools — but they're really okay.

"By the way, I'm thrilled not to be the mother of young children anymore," Sally confided, and several of her listeners nodded in agreement. "I was the W. C. Fields of mothers. I didn't like small children. I kept looking at them and thinking GROW, GROW, GROW! I'm so happy they're finally adults. I feel like a survivor. The fact that I'm fifty is totally incidental."

She paused, and I turned my attention to the next woman, but then, just as Roxanne had done, Sally, who appeared so confident and well-put-together, cried out with frustration, "Inside of me is a fat person struggling daily to get out. It takes me ten times as long to look half as good. I go to the gym. I pound myself. I don't eat. The physical plant requires lots of maintenance. But I'm a lot smarter than I was before and I don't make the same stupid mistakes that I used to. I've been given a second, third, or fourth lease on life. I'll be fifty on June seventeenth. I'm happy to be here."

Annie also focused on the high-maintenance problem. "The biggest change in my life is that I can no longer look the way I want to look when I leave the house — which I could always do before. I don't mean I was pretty, but I could stand in front of a mirror and get myself to look the way I wanted and I can't do that anymore and it's driving me crazy. Believe it or not, I sometimes leave the house in a rage.

"I talked to my mother about it and at first she was very sympathetic. She said, 'It's a stage; you'll get over it.' But when I kept complaining about how hard it is to look decent now that I'm older, she blurted out, 'Well, make an effort! And by the way, tell your daughter to make an effort too.' That moment, I realized that my daughter is going through adolescence and I'm going through menopause and we're not enemies; we're companions. Both of us are mad at our bodies. It was a major epiphany and very helpful."

Ene, the only never-married woman in the group, was also the only "refugee" (her word, not mine): "I was born in a little town in Estonia. When the war started, we fled; we just walked out of our house; we didn't even lock the door, we got into a boat and went to Sweden. Yet, here I am. I'm in New York. I'm fifty. I'm working. It took me a long time to sort all this out — being displaced, a refugee, and a foreigner."

A network television producer, Ene finds a useful paradigm for aging in her work: "I was thinking about the process of editing on film. I do a story, get ten hours of rushes, and I'm just swimming in dailies. All the footage blurs together. Then the moment comes when I see the emotional line of the piece and about fifty percent of the material just falls away and the rest begins to select itself. I've become so good at it that instead of worrying about what I don't have on film, I begin to look for the rhapsodic solution.

"I feel I'm at that same point in my life that I get to in the editing process. And it's very exciting because a lot of the unimportant stuff has just fallen away. It's just gone. I don't think about it anymore. I'm looking for the rhapsodic solution. It's thrilling but it's frightening, too.

"I was listening to the women here talk about marriage and family and that's something I didn't do and something I really want." Ene's voice turned soft and sad. "I want the warmth. I look at children on the streets. I get lost in looking at children. A couple I know have just had a baby and I wonder if I should adopt. I have all these thoughts, but I know I either have to do it or forget about it. The clock is ticking and I can't just postpone things anymore. That's the hard part." Then she brightened: "But I think I've made peace with my choices. Life is a work in progress and you go on."

"I never had a baby, either," said Wendy, "but a friend of mine who has several children told me, 'Don't think that just because someone has had a baby, she outgrows this longing to have a baby. There's nothing quite like an adorable baby.'"

Wendy was moved by the realization that she'd known half the women in my living room for nearly thirty years. "Either we met in college or at the start of our careers, and now three decades have passed and it's great to be able to say I've known someone for thirty years, but it's also part of the shock of being fifty.

"This year, I've felt an ending to a part of my life, an end to almost ten solid years of sickness and death in my family and my own illness. As an agent, my job involves keeping a lot of things in the air at the same time, but when I was sick, I was incapable of that sort of concentration. I thought my ambition was gone for good, but as I got better, it came back. Now I'm experiencing a lot of new beginnings — a new marriage, new stepchildren, a new business — and the thing that saves me in tough times is the knowledge that nothing stays the same. Things evaporate, and get destroyed, and new things grow. Life is about change."

Fredi was struck by how much had changed in her life and yet how much has stayed the same. Executive editor of a large book publishing firm, she was juggling a demanding career, a marriage, and two grown children. "My life has gotten more stressful trying to maintain all three parts in balance. I have to keep asking myself, 'Where should my energies go? Am I making my decisions or are they being made for me? I've done more than I ever expected, and I think the women's movement gave me a sense of empowerment that I would never have otherwise had, but I am often confused.

"When I was nineteen, I remember asking myself, Who am I, what am I doing, where am I going? Now I'm about to be fifty and I'm asking the same questions."

Carol was the "oldest" woman in the room: fifty and eleven months. When I invited her to the lunch, she told me she had nothing to contribute because she'd given so little thought to aging, but by June 1, she'd reached a few conclusions. "I remember coming out of the shower on my fiftieth birthday and finding that my family had put up a patchwork of computer graphics that said '50, 50, 50, 50' all across the room. I looked at all those numbers and sat down and wept. I wasn't crying about being fifty. I like the life I've made for myself *finally.* I like who I am, and what I do, and how I look. What horrified me was how quickly the years had flown and how little time is left. Neither of my parents lived beyond seventy.

"When I was twenty, I thought I was magical. I thought I could do anything and have anything and any man if I put my mind to it. I got married at twenty-eight and if you had asked me at thirty what the rest of my life was going to be like, I'd have said it was going to be great.

"By the time I was forty, I'd learned my husband was gay, I was two years divorced, my parents had died, I had no other family, I had two tiny children to raise — and I was absolutely terrified. I'd just started a new career, and I thought if I made one misstep, the three of us would all fall over the precipice.

"Now that I'm fifty, I look back and realize how much I've accomplished. I have terrific kids, eighteen and nineteen years old. I have a good career. I have a happy life. But I see now that so much of what I did was in response to others. I didn't choose a lot of my life. So the years that I have left are really for me. And I feel liberated, not depressed. And I'm already thinking, okay, let's see what sixty is like."

"Should we all get together then?" someone asked.

"Let's not wait ten years!"

"Let's do it at fifty-one!"

Pictures and Presents

The iced tea had turned watery-pale. The wine was history. It was time for show and tell. How would these friends interpret my request that they bring a photograph of themselves, an old one or one that most embodied their inner selves?

Roxanne had chosen a picture of herself when she was six. "That's me," she said pointing to the little blonde girl in a party dress, looking prim in her glasses and wavy golden bangs. "This was taken in 1945, right after V-J Day. I remember Mother fixing my hair and putting me all together to go the naval base to meet Dad, who'd been gone in the South Pacific all during the war. It was my first trip out of the small town where I was born, and I knew then that it would not be my last."

Roxanne's was the only childhood picture, but several women had brought snapshots from their teen years.

Ene's photograph showed her at her fifteenth birthday party, all dolled up in lipstick, high heels, and a Veronica Lake hairdo that fell like a curtain across one side of her face. Standing with two girlfriends, she looked nothing at all like a refugee, yet she introduced her snapshot with, "This was taken three years after we left Estonia" — as if all time for her was measured from the point of exile.

One of the Judys had brought a picture taken in her grandmother's rose garden in 1952. "The most horrible time in my life," she said. "I look like Anne Frank, a nice thirteen-year-old Jewish girl in a black dress with white trim. But there's something about this dress. . . . If I saw it today, I'd buy it."

Carol had brought two photographs, one from her early twenties, "when I was supremely confident based on not knowing anything about the world," and one showing her "looking scared" at forty-two, after the gay husband had split and she was raising two kids alone.

Sally's picture captured her playing her guitar in the midst of the Cambridge folk music scene in the early sixties, eons before the miserable first marriage, the small children who wouldn't GROW, and the second husband who wouldn't stay alive.

Not surprisingly, Harriet's photograph dated from her halcyon days at *Ms.* "It was taken in the mid-seventies when I was doing exactly what I wanted and I was making a living. No matter how much I make now, I'm poor."

The rest of us had brought more recent pictures capturing more recent pleasures, but Wendy's photo was the most up to date. "I got my husband to take this shot this morning because now is the best time and this is my best self."

The stories I heard at my birthday lunch had little to do with me and everything to do with me. The details varied, but each was, in essence, a parable of change, the tale of a woman who had battled her demons, taken control of her life and made *more* of it than before. Even the less epic accounts were about gaining something — wisdom, autonomy, freedom. Though they spoke of the death of their loved ones, no one had tackled her own mortality head on, but the subtext of every tale was the evanescence of time, and the words that filled the room — *grow, learn, expand, extend, more, better, best* — were words that helped keep mortality at bay.

I'd been to countless ladies' lunches in my time, but nothing like this. I loved listening to women who felt excited about the future. I loved that everyone was building on the past, not clinging to it — as opposed to many men our age who have to reach back to their youth to find their best years. I loved the fact that, in their distinctive voices, out of their very different lives, each woman was trying to send me the same nourishing message. Their lives had taught them what a difference a day makes, or a year, or a decade. They weren't afraid of time because time had served them well; time had cradled them in crisis and led them to a new place. They gave me my first inkling that new beginnings might still lie ahead.

All that remained to complete this birthday ritual was the distribution of the grab bag presents. A few women had brought predictable body-critical gifts — Porcelana Medicated Face Cream "to help lighten and prevent age spots;" a pumice stone "for the rough areas;" color gel hair color "to wash away the gray." But now, after all we'd heard, these objects seemed out of place, throwbacks to negative thinking, while the more positive gifts, however modest, were so clearly life-affirming. There was a cassette of hit songs from "The Unforgettable Fifties," a book of women's poetry, a white silk pillow "for your daily nap," an address book with the instruction to "fill it with ten new friends a month," a cloth-bound journal with blank pages on which "to record all your wise thoughts," a five-dollar bill "to spend toward a ticket to see the feminist comedy team Kathy and Mo, and a delicious cucumber body lotion that made no promises about wrinkles.

When it was my turn at the grab bag, I pulled out a twofer — a "diet spoon" with a dime-size hole in the middle of its bowl, and a black satin sleep mask, accompanied by an explanation: "These gifts address the most prevalent problems of aging (I've been told) — eating too much and sleeping too little."

Finally, it was time for the party favors. I passed around a bowl containing the fifteen cloisonné rings I'd bought for all of us as mementos of the day. Each woman found a ring that fit in a color she liked, and swore like a child to wear it forever.

It's been said that "Christians leave and never say good-bye, while Jews say good-bye and never leave." I can't vouch for Christians, but whoever conceived that ethnic joke certainly knew the sort of Jewish people I know; we bid our farewells, then spend an hour hanging around at the door. "How long did you stay after you left?" is my friend J.J.'s way of putting it. My lunch group included Christians and Jews, but this time *everyone* stayed until past three o'clock; it was a workday but they stayed, they talked, they compared grab bag gifts, they exchanged phone numbers, then they lingered some more, as if leaving would break the spell.

These women weren't my closest friends or my oldest friends, but they had come through for me and I would have been happy to hang out with them all week. Once they'd gone, though, and I was alone with the dirty glasses and leftover lemon squares, I had the surest sensation that they were still there. I kept hearing their voices. I kept replaying their stories and seeing the faces in their photographs. For days afterward, they stayed with me — not like a memory, more like a mirage. And when I awoke on the actual morning of my birthday, a week later, I could have sworn I saw them standing around my bed singing "Happy Birthday," laughing, and clapping their hands, their cloisonné rings gleaming in the sun.

PART II

Keeping Time

4

Time Is All There Is

> As we advance in life, we acquire a keener sense of the value of time. Nothing else, indeed, seems of any consequence; and we become misers in this respect.
>
> — *William Hazlitt*

Every now and then, I leave my watch at home and try not to steal glances at bank clocks or other people's wrists, but rather to live in time more organically, sensitive to its natural ebb and flow, aware of the changing light of day, and the changing pulse of the city. The experiment lets me tune in to the larger rhythms of life, and I'd like to report that I've been liberated by it, but the truth is, I usually feel lost, disoriented, like a referee trying to run a game without a stopwatch. When we cannot keep time, time keeps us. When I can't keep time, I lose control of my life. Keeping time, measuring it, tracking it, are things anyone can do; understanding it is harder. Here is St. Augustine on the subject, and though his words may seem impenetrable at first, on second reading the passage becomes quite clear and stunningly provocative:

> But if the present were always present, and would not pass into the past, it would no longer be time, but eternity. Therefore, if the present, so as to be time, must be so constituted that it passes into the past, how can we say that it is, since the cause of its being is the fact that it will cease to be? Does it not follow that we can truly say that it is time, only because it tends toward nonbeing? . . . How, then, can . . . the past and the future be, when the past no longer is and the future as yet does not be?

From Augustine to Immanuel Kant, from Ernst Mach to Einstein to Stephen Hawking, great thinkers have argued that time unfolds in several dimensions, which is more than most of us can handle. I'm already having enough trouble understanding the cosmology of historical time and the conundrum of eternal time, boundless, infinite, everlasting, and essentially unfathomable. Dealing with yet another dimension would send me around the bend.

Children live in eternal time until adults initiate them into historical time. We want them to know they are heirs to a particular past and have a duty to believe in the future even though it contains their own death. In Edward Albee's play *Three Tall Women,* a fifty-two-year-old with a sharp tongue and a cynical outlook says, "I'd like to see children learn it — have a six-year-old say, 'I'm dying' and know what it means. . . . Start in young; make 'em aware they've got only a little time. Make 'em aware that they're dying from the minute they're alive."

We teach our children to tell time but not what to tell it. We show them how to measure time but not how to use it. We give them a watch but don't warn them that watching doesn't help. I used to notice time because it loitered. Now I notice it because it's breathing down my neck.

Despite much-improved longevity predictions, it's a pretty safe bet that fewer years lie ahead of me than behind and the years to come are unlikely to be as healthy or vigorous as those gone by. Illness lies in wait, as do infirmity, further deterioration, loss, and the Grim Reaper. What a downer.

On the other hand, I could be around for a while. I could last another thirty years, which is as long as some of my children have been alive. If thirty years was enough time to grow a highly complex human being from scratch, then the next thirty years deserve my respectful attention. What am I going to do with them? How can I appreciate the time of my life while I have it? Instead of just worrying about time's passage and rushing to get everything in, dare I dally long enough to penetrate the soul of time, make it an ally, see beyond the hands of the clock into that place where the power of perception and mindfulness can stretch time and give the Reaper a run for his money? That, in a nutshell, was my quest.

Time Defined, Time Refined

More has been written about time than about any other subject, except perhaps love. Millennia before William Hazlitt penned the words at the top of this chapter, Ecclesiastes declared there is "a time to be born and a time to die"; Horace cautioned, "Seize now and here the hour that is, nor trust some later day"; Plutarch advised, "Be ruled by time, the wisest counselor of all"; Diogenes deduced, "Time is the image of eternity"; and Manilius made the gloomy observation "As soon as we are born we begin to die."

Millions of words have been written about the brevity of life, and time's swift flight, its relentlessness, its evanescence — and all of them are as true today as the day they were put to paper or parchment. Andrew Marvell's plaintive "Had we but world enough, and time," written 350 years ago, is a plea for the ages. And no one who has known death could improve upon Keats's gentle "Life is but a day; a fragile dew-drop on its perilous way." The message is plain. Time waits for no one. *Use it or lose it.*

Use it or lose it.

Time talks out of both sides of its mouth. It brings decay and growth; it rots but also heals; it is at once our adversary and our treasure; it flies and drags and even stands still. Wildly different metaphors express these paradoxes of perception and reality. Depending on which poet you read, time is a "thief" or "a kind friend"; "a liar" but also "a great legalizer"; a "playmate" and a "peddler"; "a great teacher" and an "aged nurse." "Time runs" and yet "is stalactite." "Time is money" and "time is broke."

Well worn in the literary canon, the subject also has had its share of quotable expositors in the pop tradition: "I've been on a calendar, but never on time," said Marilyn Monroe, or maybe the studio said it for her. "There's a time in every man's life," declared Casey Stengel, "and I've had plenty of them."

Human beings have been tracking time for more than 3,000 years, starting with the Egyptian shadow stick, which measured the passage of the day by the progess of a shadow thrown across set markers, followed by the water clock, the sundial, the nocturnal star dial (oriented to the North Star), the hourglass, and the Anglo-Saxon candle clock, a taper marked at regular intervals. In the Middle Ages, the first mechanical clocks appeared, driven first by falling weights and later, springs. These were not precise instruments meant to measure time in any absolute sense but were for the most part used in monasteries to divide the day into equal parts so as to determine the times for prayers. In the mid-seventeenth century, the Dutch scientist Christian Huygens, acknowledging the influence of Galileo, perfected the swinging pendulum and the balance spring, which, though adversely affected by temperature changes, improved clock functions considerably, What we would call complete accuracy in time measurement was not achieved until jewels were introduced as bearings in the mid-eighteenth century, and from then on, whoever owned a watch could know the time almost to the second, which was not necessarily to everyone's liking.

After the eighteenth-century philosopher Jean Jacques Rousseau wrote his *Discourse on the Moral Effects of the Arts and Sciences,* in which he blames technical advances for the corruption of modern life, he retreated from "civilization" into the world of nature, where he was determined to live day by day without time and the corrupt institutions it had spawned. "Thank heavens! I shall no longer need to know what time it is!" he exclaimed, and, since he considered it the fundamental instrument of modern mechanized society, he sold his watch.

No one has brought more intellectual muscle to the time-defining enterprise than T. S. Eliot but even he admits that

> . . . to apprehend
> The point of intersection of the timeless With
> time, is an occupation for the saint.

So why do I have the chutzpah to add to the din? Because, I can't help myself. Because no one can age mindfully and ignore time's role in human consciousness. Because I'm haunted by my mother's meager years. And because, though everything's been said, not everyone has said it. I'm only taking my turn.

For most of my adult life, I was reading about time and mortality with the eyes of an English Lit. major, not with the heart and mind of someone who had confronted her own perishability. The wisdom of the ages didn't really register on me until, approaching fifty, I suddenly felt time picking up steam, until I looked back and realized I had clear memories of things that happened forty years ago — forty years! — and then looked ahead and panicked.

Psychologists say that one's "time orientation" — the way a person relates to the past, present, and future — reveals key elements of her or his personality. Obviously, those who live only for the moment have a very different concept of time than those who can project themselves far ahead. Research shows that younger people tend to have a more present-centered perspective (wanting it *now*), whereas older people are more future-oriented — better at meeting deadlines and postponing gratification in the interest of later rewards. People's time orientation also seems to correlate with their income: the middle class is more future-oriented than the poor, who tend to be present-centered and fatalistic. (That's logical: If you don't have the money to see you past Saturday night, it's hard to think to Sunday.)

When I stumbled on time orientation research in my late forties, I had trouble placing myself. I fit the economic and age profile of a future-oriented type and was well schooled at postponing gratification, yet I saw the future as threatening, and change, its carrier, as a disturber of the peace. The past remained an interesting place to me and I enjoyed thinking about long-ago pleasures, but, unlike the past-oriented people in the research, I didn't prefer yesterday to today. By a process of elimination, therefore, I decided the present was my favorite place. I wanted life to stay just as it was. I didn't want more, just more of the same. I'd finally gotten some of the important things figured out and the unimportant things running fairly smoothly; now I wanted everything to last. I didn't want to be younger, just not any older.

Why fear the future? For one thing, because I shared most Americans' view of aging as a downward spiral and was in no hurry to experience my own decline. For another, the future was freighted with too many unknowns. I'd lost faith in uninterrupted progress and in the essentially benign operation of human intelligence. I no longer believed that the world is on a steady course toward better things. I'd lost my youthful trust in technology, in society's capacity to alleviate human misery or to resolve conflict without violence, in "civilization" itself, which, since the Holocaust, has become a debatable concept. I come from a people that has seen *everything* get worse, a people for whom change often bodes danger. With such a legacy, it's no wonder I favored the present. "Anxiety is the natural state of the Jews," wrote Martin Buber. We prefer the devil we know to the devil we don't. I'm fifty-five years old and there is a lot about this age that I don't particularly like, but at least I know where I stand. As long as nothing changes, I'm safe. But in the future, who knows. . . .

Betty Friedan says most people do not see the "strong face of age," they see only disengagement and decay; they perceive aging as a series of descents rather than challenging transitions. In my case, descent seemed inevitable, since I considered my limitations congenital and my flaws beyond redemption; all I could imagine were turns for the worse. However, in the last few years — after I turned fifty, locked horns with time, and felt inspired to attack some of my deficiencies head-on — I began to entertain a different possibility: that I might actually *develop* through the years, not just age. With the help of friends, and the succor of books, and the heavy lifting I did in the weight room of my own worries, I realized that change could be time's blessing, not just its curse. In other words, if I could create compensatory gains to offset the losses of aging that are beyond my control — if I could use the time of my life as a container in which to cause positive changes to happen — I could soften the blow of aging and maybe give myself a midlife boost, to boot. For example, my eyesight, hearing, and skin elasticity were losing ground, no question about it, and there wasn't too much I could do to reverse the damage, but, it turns out, there *was* something I could do about my ebbing physical strength. I could increase my stamina, build a few new muscles, and speed up my metabolism. To think time might yield such changes for the better, to anticipate pleasant surprises and not just bad news, to imagine that I could keep growing — stronger, more competent, happier — not just older, gave me the first clue that this arrested midlife crisis seemed to boil down to the issue of control. Some developments, obviously, were beyond my control — disease, accidents, natural disasters; they would happen and I would have to cope when they did. But other changes, the good ones, I would have to bring about myself, and I would need time to do the job. If I were ever going to make my peace with time, I had to learn to put as much trust in the future as I'd been investing in the present.

Change, even good change, must situate itself in real time, and there's the rub. As if there wasn't already too little time, the older we get, the faster it moves. When we were young, it seemed to take a year to get from Labor Day to Christmas but now life seems stuck on the fast forward speed; now, we hardly finish sweeping up the New Year's confetti when the fireworks go off on the Fourth of July.

Stretching Time

If you are as fixated on time as I am, life experience has already taught you some of the more obvious braking mechanisms. Suffering slows time down. So does waiting. People who have survived extreme privations describe the agony of waiting for deliverance, for relief, for the cover of darkness or the break of dawn, for a loaf of bread. In the land of the Good

Humor man and the Sparkle Plenty doll, I experienced the American child's version of suffering — waiting for childhood to end.

These days, what I'm usually waiting for is the check in the mail or people who come late to meetings, but when I was small, I waited for time itself. I waited for time and age to bring the skills and milestones I thought would never come: learning to tie my own shoelaces, riding a two-wheeler, starting school. While time took its time, I daydreamed, or studied the grown-ups, or chronicled my uneventful life in a green leather diary with a tiny brass lock, or pasted snapshots and favorite sayings in an oversized album I called my "Things 'n Stuff." During the school year, time moved like cold molasses. My friends and I were always staring at the big wall clock over the blackboard and pushing the minute hand along with our eyes. Carved into my desktop at Jamaica High was a drawing of a tombstone that said, "Here lies a student who died waiting for the bell to ring." Sometimes, I, too, felt moribund back then, but now the days whip by and the bells are always ringing before I'm ready. In my teens, I waited for my breasts to grow, for my period to start, for the phone to ring, for a boy to ask me out, for my parents to stop fighting. Then I waited for my mother to return home from the doctor, the hospital, the cancer treatment center; waited for her pain to subside and when it wouldn't, waited for her to die.

Suffering elongates time, yes, but so does bliss. That's why July and August always seemed to last twice as long as the whole school year. In the summers of my childhood, when life was new, time stretched out like an open field and days were slow and lazy with reluctant twilights and endless nights filled with adult murmurings and the promise of tomorrow. I remember spending a long, languid vacation at my cousin's house in the Catskill Mountains only to discover much later that the visit lasted just two weeks.

The class reunion, known as a splendid opportunity to check out how we're doing in comparison to our age peers, is less often acknowledged for its temporal impact — for being a stark reminder of time's relativity. Returning for a reunion, we hear the same chorus of bedeviled reactions. "Can you believe it's been a quarter of a century?" "Where has the time gone!" "It seems like yesterday!" The decades since graduation have raced by like a jet stream, sucking us along and depositing us in the present before we realized what was happening. But the four years when we were in school were as leisurely as a stroll; they ambled, they meandered, they distinguished themselves one from the other — freshman year, sophomore, junior, senior — as if each were a separate country, and we a different person every year.

Maybe time moves more slowly when we're young because at five, a year is a full 20 percent of one's life, while at fifty, a year is a mere 1/50th. It's only natural for such a sliver of time to zip by in a trice. I'm more inclined to think we perceive time in slow motion during childhood because that's when we do and see so many things for the first time. Faced with the unfamiliar — whether you're a child with a new toy or a fifty-year-old with a giant tortoise in your tent — human beings tend to become hyperalert. The tenth time we see the toy or the tortoise, its features will have become predictable, even prosaic, but the first time, we behold every detail as if illuminated by a floodlight, and time seems to stand still while we do it. Riveted by the intensity of our concentration, time stops long enough for us to take in what we must and figure out how to deal with it.

"Most of us lose our ability to observe the world this directly along with our roller skates and baseball gloves," says Ralph Keyes in *The Courage to Write*. "The older we grow, the harder it gets to see our surroundings in detail. This has less to do with declining eyesight than with the security zones so many of us create to protect ourselves from surprises. The ability to muffle anxiety feels like a perk of adulthood. We cut a Faustian deal: in return for not being so anxious all the time, we agree to tune down our whole nervous system. As a result, our powers of observation decline along with our sense of smell, taste, and hearing. This is partly a function of dulled senses, partly due to the fact that we're seeing so little that's surprising."

Unfortunately, the greater portion of life's surprises belong to childhood, as does most of its newness, its noticing, and its slow-moving time, all of which would come in handy in middle age. Since fear slows things down, and children — who are more vulnerable and faced with more unknowns — harbor more fears than adults, it makes sense that youth breeds a slower perception of time, a perception compounded by frequent bouts with terror. Some adults try to recreate the conditions of childhood, when all trails led to unknown destinations; they do it by courting risk in the form of daredevil exploits, wilderness treks, fast cars, dangerous drugs, seeking to match the stomach-churning thrill of a child's first night alone in the dark, first ride on a swing, first sight of a large animal, first dive off the high board. I'm sure they do it not just for the excitement of the thing itself but for the sharper, slower, more intoxicating relationship to time that only fresh, new fears can produce.

"Fear flushes clogged pores of perception," says Keyes. "Ears listening for the crunch of bears' paws, eyes scanning the horizon for enemy soldiers, and noses sniffing the air for the smell of fire have heightened awareness. . . . Intense stress illuminates everything in sight when we feel frightened."

We all know this. People who have lived through childbirth or a car accident will tell you that while it was happening, time played peculiar tricks: a millisecond was a minute, an hour seemed a day. At one level, things seemed to be happening in slow motion, at another level, life flashed before our eyes like a film, yet we saw everything with utter clarity and calm.

Something similar, though rather more pleasant, happens on vacation. Exotic locales elicit the same sharpened focus and childlike concentration as did all of life when we first encountered it, when everything was new and worthy of notice. In travel, as in childhood, we look and listen harder, we sit at the edge of a fountain watching the spray, we look up, down, and around instead of straight ahead to our destination. My friend Selma says she learned "to see" when she was walking in Monte Verde, the Costa Rican cloud forest. In regular life, we look without seeing; the eye takes in the wide-angle shot, passing over the details because the details are not always as important as "the big picture." But, in a dense rain forest, when one is looking for tiny hummingbirds or resplendent quetzals amidst a tumult of trees, one either learns to see or misses everything. On vacation, when we look and see more mindfully, time is distended; a week in a new place always seems to have many more days than a week at home, and when we return, we're surprised that our friends are surprised to see us back so soon. For everyone else, time has whizzed by in a blur of routines. For us, time was too full to fly.

I've taken an obvious lesson from this: to unhurry time and extend the future, to prevent the years from racing off with our lives, what we need is more firsts and more freshness. More separable moments, observed and savored. More noticing. And we need to start now before the dullness sets in. Short of taking a vacation once a month or changing jobs regularly, we can give ourselves fresh experiences as simple as walking to work by an unfamiliar route, or reading a different newspaper than we're used to, or programming into each day whatever newnesses are likely to perk up our perceptions, shake up our assumptions, and keep us alert as we age. (More about mindfulness training in the next chapter.)

The cellist Pablo Casals discovered his freshness within the familiar, always making time for the daily ritual that enabled him to see life anew:

> For the past eighty years I have started each day in the same manner. It is not a mechanical routine but something essential to my daily life. I go to the piano, and I play two preludes and fugues of Bach. I cannot think of doing otherwise. It is a sort of benediction on the house. But that is not its only meaning for me. It is a rediscovery of the world which I have the joy of being a part. It fills me with awareness of the wonder of life, with a feeling of the incredible marvel of being a human being. The music is never the same for me, never. Each day it is something new, fantastic and unbelievable.

Others have proposed rather different ideas for slowing time and noticing life. Mark Twain suggested that people addicted to smoking should quit: "They won't live longer but it will seem longer." Albert Einstein applied his theory of relativity to practical matters by guaranteeing every man that a minute spent sitting on a hot stove will make that minute seem like an hour, while an hour spent watching a beautiful woman will make that hour pass like a minute. Dunbar, the character in Joseph Heller's *Catch-22*, went out of his way to cultivate boredom so life would feel interminable. Imagining the dilemma of having only six months to live and wanting his time to go both pleasantly and slowly, the essayist Joseph Epstein says he "would eat chocolate-covered orange peels, which seems to take no time at all, but only at Laundromats, where time hangs so heavily." Newton Minow recalls that a student once told him if she had only one hour left to spend on this earth, she'd like it to be in Minow's class. Flattered, the professor asked why, and she replied, "Because your class makes an hour seem like eternity."

Rationing Time

The time famine is spreading. According to a nationwide survey taken in the late 1980s, one-third of the population feels rushed, while only a quarter said they felt that way twenty-five years ago. Other surveys have indicated that one out of two Americans is getting too little sleep. People are working 160 hours more per year than they were twenty years ago. Nearly one in four of us has no time to take a vacation. Half of all U.S. workers say they would trade a day's pay for a day's time. Working couples find only twelve minutes to talk to one another during the average weekday. One in two fathers, one in eight mothers, and one in three single parents said they regularly work more than forty hours a week. Almost 60 percent of parents feel they're not able to spend enough time with their children. People who used to give time to good works and charitable causes now give money instead; or, in the words of the philosopher-environmentalist Arthur Waskow, money is "congealed time." And, though they may be rationalizing their behavior, one-third of Americans say they have no time to vote. Or to pray, it seems, or meditate, or do anything spiritual that requires intense, single-minded, uninterrupted time. Writing about spirituality and concentration, Marian Henriquez Neudel says most people are so busy that they have to become "multi-taskers," doing two or three things at once just to keep their heads above water. "They dictate memos while they drive, put on makeup as they ride the train, eat lunch in the doctor's waiting room, do laundry while cooking dinner and supervising the children's homework, do their tax returns while waiting for the mechanic to do the brake job, and so on. In this kind of life, any spiritual path based on doing one thing at a time is almost doomed to fail."

To those who don't have enough money, it may seem frivolous to worry about not having enough time, yet most people worry about both and try not to waste either. And to those who yearn for more time, the idea of wasting it may seem like an unimaginable luxury, yet most people have both wasted it and worried about it — and written about it as well.

"I wasted time and now doth time waste me," wrote Shakespeare in *Richard III*. Benjamin Franklin warned, "Dost thou love life? Then do not squander time, for that is the stuff life is made of." And from T. S. Eliot,

> Ridiculous the waste sad time
> Stretching before and after.

Elie Wiesel, the Nobel laureate, who lost his youth in Auschwitz, puts it as unartfully as the simple truth, "The main thing is not to waste time."

What meager power humanity has over time is the power not to squander it. Admittedly, what I define as wasting time, others might call fun, and what I see as time well spent, some people have been known to label compulsive productivity. Still, there's no denying that millions of people waste trillions of hours doing things that are neither productive nor pleasurable. From birth to death, the average American spends five years standing in line, four years washing dishes, mopping floors, and vacuuming (which sex, I wonder?), two years trying to return the phone calls of people who never seem to be in, one year looking for misplaced objects such as eyeglasses or dry-cleaning receipts, eight months opening junk mail, and five months waiting for red lights to turn green. Add to this the six years we spend eating, fun though that is, plus the great blocks of time devoted to work or sleep, and there isn't a whole lot left to argue about. Whether in an automobile or on foot, each of us waits in line for a half hour a day, which means the whole population hands over 37 billion hours a year to these killer queues. Many of us will choose one bank, restaurant, or supermarket over another just to avoid lines — voting with our feet because we don't have time to spare.

Americans' leisure time has shrunk by 37 percent since 1973, but despite all the complaints about time pressure, most people spend 33 percent of whatever free time they have watching television. (Socializing and reading are a far-distant second and third.) So the real issue is not how much extra time one has, but how one spends and values it.

While shooting a movie in Morocco, the actor Sean Connery was being driven to the film's location when he noticed an old man walking along the side of the road carrying twigs and a sheaf of rough paper.

"The twigs he'll make into charcoal," explained Connery's driver. "He is an artist and he's walking from the Atlas Mountains to Marrakesh to sell his drawings."

At day's end, the actor's car passed the man again, slowly wending his way to market. "Walking will take days; we can get him there in forty minutes," said Connery, instructing the driver to pull over and offer the man a lift. But no matter how much the driver coaxed him, the artist refused to accept a ride.

"What the problem?" asked Connery.

"He says he won't know what to do with his time when he gets there."

At the end of the day, each of us must live within our own relationship to time and no one else's. Mine happens to be extremely intense and closely observed. In the words of T. S. Eliot's J. Alfred Prufrock, "I have measured out my life with coffee spoons." I hoard time and appreciate every extra minute that comes my way, which is why I love the Saturday night in autumn when we set our clocks back and gain an hour; all day Sunday, I feel that twenty-fifth hour making space for me, giving me room to move and time to breathe. Once, I crossed the International Date Line and, overjoyed, picked up a whole day and actually lived December 1 *twice.* Flying home, of course I had to give the day back and felt the loss. Whenever my watch has stopped and I realize it's really much later than I'd thought, I experience the time loss like a theft. (It occurs to me that I own a wind-up watch, not a battery-operated one, so maybe I *want* time to stop.) I try not to spend more than an hour a day reading the *New York Times,* a time bandit if ever there was one. I feel cheated if I've spent a half hour on a movie line only to reach the box office and be told that this showing is sold out. I hate being put on hold.

Am I crazy to ration time this way or is everyone else crazy to let it fritter away? No need to answer that — but I will say I felt less alone when a woman I know said she and her husband instituted a new system a couple of years ago to ensure that they have more quality time with their children: "We bathe and dress them the night before and they sleep in their clothes. In the morning all they have to do is brush their teeth and put on their shoes. It's been great, because we can really enjoy our breakfasts together without all the bedlam we used to have when they were rushing to get ready for school and all of us were grouchy."

I was similarly comforted when I heard an acquaintance in his sixties say, "Statistically, I only have another five hundred or six hundred weekends left in my life, so I'll be damned if I'm going to waste one of them." And you can imagine my relief when I met my match in print: Joseph Epstein, editor of *American Scholar,* whose essay "Time on My Hands, Me in My Arms" could be an addendum to this book. I have never met Mr. Epstein, but clearly, he is the male me, or I am the female he — both of us, in our mid-fifties, obsessing over time and mortality, worrying over whether we have produced enough work to earn our leisure, busily gathering evidence that we're not the only lunatics who harbor "this feeling that time seems out of control, whirring by, regardless of all attempts to make the best of it." Compared to Mr. Epstein, as a matter of fact, I'm a laggard and a sloth: "Any day that I sleep past 6:00 A.M. I consider very near a lost day," he writes. ". . . I am one of those people who think digital clocks a swell invention, because I like to know to the minute what time it is when I awake at night." He hears (predigitally) "the tickings, the endless tickings, of a clock in my head. . . ." And he notes with frustration, "eating and sleeping also take time — and how I admire those fortunate people who need only four or five hours of sleep each night!"

Though a pretty fair clock-watcher in my own right, and guilty of occasional sleep deprivation in the interest of gaining a few extra hours, I do not want to leave you with the impression that I'm incapable of having fun. In fact, I'm no stranger to spontaneity, enjoy myself with reasonable regularity, and don't begrudge myself the pleasure. The trouble is that, later, when the fun is over, it wouldn't be unlike me to ponder how little time is left for more such enjoyments — a thought process that is arguably neurotic.

Now and then, believe it or not, I even give myself open-ended time with no particular agenda. I just let myself sit still and stare out the window, knowing that, in the Zen sense, doing nothing can clear the mind and refresh the spirit, though I confess that even when my mind is at rest, I'm usually doing something else with my body — walking along the beach, bathing, cooking, or staring out the window of a bus while en route to a planned destination.

For all my neuroses, I did draw the line at something called the "Personal Life Clock." According to its advertising copy, this high-tech wonder "reminds you to live life to the fullest by displaying the time and the actual hours, minutes and seconds remaining in your statistical lifetime." The manufacturer claims the average life lasts only 683,280 hours but promises to set your personal clock to your exact actuarial profile so the future you watch disappear with digital accuracy is your own. Though this product might seem right up my alley, I decided not to buy it. For one thing, the manufacturer's ninety-day warranty didn't augur well for a clock meant to measure a lifetime. For another, I don't want to know how many hours I have left. It would only make things worse.

Treasuring Time

While trying to illuminate this place called time, my main literary beacons have been *Four Quartets,* the poetic ruminations of T. S. Eliot which, though replete with Christian symbolism, speak to my Jewish soul; *The Sabbath,* a meditation on sacred time by Abraham Joshua Heschel; and *Our Town,* the play by Thornton Wilder, which unfailingly brings me to tears.

The plot of *Our Town* is simple. A narrator, called the Stage Manager, takes the audience into the turn-of-the-century world of Grover's Corners, a small New Hampshire town, where we see ordinary people going about their business on a couple of ordinary days: the doctor has just delivered a baby, the editor is about to go to work at his newspaper, women make breakfast and conversation, kids bicker and do their homework. Eventually, the story zeroes in on two of the young folks, Emily and George, next-door neighbors who spend the first two acts growing up, falling in love, and settling down together in the community.

In the third act, we learn what the dead know and the living rarely see — how precious it all is, even the ordinary; no, *especially* the ordinary.

The setting is the cemetery where the deceased townspeople of Grover's Corners are talking with Emily, now twenty-six, who has just died in childbirth. Gazing longingly at the living, Emily asks the dead if she can return to reexperience one day in her past. Everyone tries to dissuade her. Too painful, they warn, but she insists. She will choose a happy day, she says.

"No! At least choose an unimportant day," one of the dead protests. "Choose the least important day in your life. It will be important enough."

So she returns to relive a Tuesday of fourteen years before, but this time around she notices how beautiful everything is — Mr. Morgan's drugstore, the livery stable, the white fence around her house, the idle talk in the kitchen on a cold winter's morning. As her mother fusses at her to chew her bacon, the dead Emily is overwhelmed by how offhandedly the two of them address each other. She knows the tragedies that will befall them in the next fourteen years, and she cannot bear to watch them take each other and their contentment for granted.

"Mama," she says in a voice her mother cannot hear, "just for a moment we're happy. *Let's look at one another.*"

But they don't; they live the day as most of us do, without noticing it, without stopping to appreciate our lives.

"It goes so fast," says Emily, distraught. "We don't have time to look at one another. I didn't realize. So all that was going on and we never noticed. . . ."

"Now you know!" chides one of the dead. "That's what it was to be alive. To move about in a cloud of ignorance. . . . To spend and waste time as though you had a million years . . . that's the happy existence you wanted to go back to. Ignorance and blindness."

I think I cry over this play because of my mother — because we didn't have enough time to look at one another, and because I know all the ordinary, wonderful things she missed by dying young. Or maybe I cry because of my children — because their childhood passed so quickly and I took so much of it for granted. Or I could be crying for myself and my husband because one day death will separate us, and if the statistics bear me out, it is I who will be left alone. I can already imagine everything about him that I'll miss, even though he is right here right now.

I think I already know what the dead know, but I also know how hard it is to realize life while we live it. Eliot again:

> For most of us, there is only the unattended
>   Moment, the moment in and out of time,
> The distraction fit, lost in a shaft of
>   sunlight,
> The wild thyme unseen, or the winter lighting
> Or the waterfall, or music heard so deeply
> That it is not heard at all . . .

Attentiveness is no more natural than good posture. We have to work at it, or else consciousness slips and slides and wanders off forgetting its mission. To keep mindful, we need the urgency of Thomas Mann's admonition (complete with exclamation points): "Hold fast the time! Guard it, watch over it, every hour, every minute! Unregarded it slips away, like a lizard, smooth, slippery, faithless. . . . Hold every moment sacred. Give each clarity and meaning, each the weight of thine awareness, each its true and due fulfilment."

But how? The only moments I know that are measured so precisely and lived so watchfully are musical moments — that instant when the timpani must enter or the cymbals clash — or the attenuated ten-second count in a boxing match, or the suspenseful final seconds in a close basketball game when time seems to pass into a different dimension.

If human destiny were to swing back and forth as precipitously as the score of a basketball game, we, too, might tune in to every second with rapt attention. Otherwise, it's impossible, if not insane, to attempt such vigilance as would be required to heed Mann's words and "give each moment the weight of thine awareness." By the same token, it's unrealistic to hope to live each day with the "unambiguous happiness" that the author Robert Hine felt when he emerged from years of blindness, regained his sight, and beheld the world in all its glory, the same world the rest of us hardly notice when we wake up to it every morning. Short of returning from death or darkness, how can we see more clearly what we have while we have it?

I find my answer, not *the* answer, in the Jewish view of time, a concept that is easily transportable to secular life. Every culture seems to apprehend time differently, and Judaism's inordinate preoccupation with it is discernable throughout our texts and traditions. The Hebrew Bible opens with "In the Beginning," and the Talmud with the words "From when?" — both designations of time that suggest, says Professor Debbie Weissman, that the main purpose of these books "is to teach us how to spend our limited time on earth wisely." Time consciousness is woven into the fabric of Jewish life and Jewish death. (The traditional year of mourning is divided into fixed time segments, each of which makes different demands on the bereaved.) The Jewish day is delineated by a schedule of prayers; the Jewish year is freighted with time-bound obligations — six days to fast, eight days to eat unleavened bread on Passover, eight days to light candles on Hanukkah, seven weeks to "count the omer," enumerating the days between the Israelites' liberation from slavery in Egypt and the giving of the law on Mount Sinai. Counting is a way of noticing and anticipating: it reminds us that a day counts or it doesn't. Counting imputes meaning; we rarely count what we do not value.

Given my upbringing, I am heir to this heightened sense of time, absorbed through ethnic osmosis if not actual study, yet since I am not religiously observant, I've been surprised by how much my relationship to time has been shaped by a book called *The Sabbath*. The author, twentieth-century philosopher and rabbi Abraham Joshua Heschel, asserts that most people look at time as a "slick treacherous monster with a jaw like a furnace, incinerating every moment of our lives." Recoiling in fear from its fierce appetites and its foreshadowing of our mortality, we turn our backs on time and take refuge in what Heschel calls "thinghood," substances that occupy space.

Indeed, I spend much of my life producing *things* — magazine articles, vegetable soup, political petitions — things I can see, touch, read; things I can measure as the product of my waking hours. As long as I have some*thing* to show for my time, I can tell myself I know where the time went and what it was for; I feel I master time by using it. But, insists Heschel, "One can only master time in time." (An uncanny echo of Eliot's "Only through time is time conquered.")

You don't have to be Jewish to see the paradox. While most of us try to control our time by using it to produce things that have a real presence in physical space, we miss experiencing time as a thing unto itself. *Time as time* can only be mastered in its own realm while we are inside it, attending to it, at peace with it, moving *with* it, not against it, and appreciating it for being in our lives at all. As Heschel conceptualizes the Sabbath, it is *pure* time: "The hours of the seventh day are significant in themselves," he writes; "their significance and beauty do not depend on any work, profit or progress we may achieve." On that one day, we are supposed to enter time's realm, a creation as miraculous as life itself, and to treasure it for its own sake. This I had never done. Forget about for a full day — I'd never done it for an hour. I had never treasured time as time, I had always viewed it as something to be trapped and utilized to produced thinghood, ultimately a poor substitute.

Though I remain incapable of the rigors of religious observance, I have often envied those who, as the expression goes, "keep the Sabbath." I function in a milieu where time-trapping and time-keeping is the way of the world, but those who keep the Sabbath are keeping time in a much more profound and deeper sense; they are spending one-seventh of the week within the very essence of time. The novelist Mary Gordon once interviewed Alice Shalvi, a prominent Israeli feminist who also happens to be an Orthodox Jew, a professor of English literature, mother of six, and grandmother of fifteen.

"How do you do it all?" asked Gordon.

The answer, said Shalvi, is the Sabbath. "How many women do you know who have twenty-four hours a week when they are not on call, [but are] forced to reflect and to be quiet?"

Though as fully engaged in worldly pursuits as anyone, Alice Shalvi has something in her life that most of us are missing — "a palace in time," Heschel calls it, ". . . not a date but an atmosphere . . . *a sanctuary in time* . . . the opportunity to sanctify time, to raise the good to the level of the holy."

When I gave a talk before the Harvard-Radcliffe Jewish Students' Organization, I ventured that, had I been raised with the concept of sacred time instead of the shoulds and shouldn'ts of the Sabbaths of my childhood, I might have been a different person with a different life. Instead of rushing from one project to another, wondering which activity should be today's priority, I might have kept myself in better balance. I might have learned respect for the fullness of empty time.

A young graduate student in my audience seemed genuinely puzzled by my statement. "How have you been able to distinguish the holy from the rest?" she asked. "When I had mononucleosis, I slept constantly. The weeks ran together, and for a month I was too sick to keep the Sabbath. Every day was the same. Without the Sabbath, all of life is like day after day of sleep."

Such blissful certitude is beyond me, but with some effort — a leap of consciousness, if not faith — I've been able to construct a vastly scaled down version of the palace in time. I am learning to set aside moments of pure-time serenity, a way of being quietly but intensely mindful of the present as it is unfolding, whether in peace and stillness or excitement and wonder. I haven't lost my need to produce "thinghood," and I cannot hold *every* moment sacred as Thomas Mann would have it — nor even every Sabbath as Heschel and my ancestors would wish — but I have found that I can stop running long enough to enter those moments in time, ordinary or sublime, that seem to me deserving of elevation "to the level of the holy."

Sacred Moments

Observant Jews have a different blessing for all the ordinary acts of daily life — waking up, washing, breaking bread, drinking wine, studying texts, doing a good deed, even going to the bathroom. "The sages who constructed these blessings some two thousand years ago saw them as a way to focus a person's attention on the miracles of existence," David Elcott explains in *A Sacred Journey*. "Nothing is too mundane to be elevated by and seen as a blessing. Even the most basic biological functions . . . demand that a person stop and reflect on the significance of the human body and the wonder of being alive." This premise, when you stop to think about it, is not so different from the theory underlying Ellen Langer's work with mindfulness training. Like mindfulness exercises, speaking a blessing is a way of noticing things that might otherwise be done mechanically, without inner meaning.

I have always been especially moved by one blessing in particular, the *sheheheyanu,* which is said at the start of a holiday, or upon doing or seeing something for the first time, something that gives one inordinate happiness. It is a brief sentence that simply thanks God for having sustained us and enabled us to live long enough to reach this special moment. It is also known as the blessing over time.

I've taken to saying this blessing, silently but mindfully, in situations that overwhelm me with wonder and gratitude — moments of transcendent joy, love, humility, or peace, in which doing and being, an act and its meaning, are one and the same. Such moments deserve a palace, a small sanctuary in time, for they bring me as close as I have ever come to the realm of the sacred. The least I can do is to stop and say thank you.

"Take care of the minutes," Lord Chesterfield advised, "for the hours will take care of themselves." I like to think I'm taking better care of the minutes than I used to but the hours still slip away from me. I'm always rushing around and then rationalizing that being in a hurry is one of the tributes I pay to life, for I'm only trying to get more of it into the time that is allotted me — the perfect defense of an incurable compulsive. I want more time so badly that I've fantasized a science fiction world in which one could buy the time rights that other people don't use, much as real estate developers buy air rights from the property owner next door. The books piled high at my bedside remind me that I need more time to read. The bulging folders remind me that I need more time to write. The continuing-education catalogues remind me that I need more time to study. The travel magazines remind me I need more time to see the world. But perhaps free time, like other kinds of freedom, is something we want but don't necessarily know how to use. Maybe, like the Moroccan twig-bearer, I wouldn't know what to do with more time if I had it. Or maybe there is no such thing as *enough* time for those who want it. Even Queen Elizabeth I, who had wealth and power to spare, was moved to cry, "All my possessions for a moment of time." They were the last words she uttered before her death.

It's impossible to think about time without bumping into the "D" word. With all my talk of stretching time, and my ardent desire to be here long enough to improve with age, I am not trying to wish away the tragedy of being human. We grow old and we die. And the knowledge that death lies at the end of our journey is what makes great art and poetry. It's why people plant gardens and have babies. It's what makes sunrise so sweet and sunset so poignant. I don't want death to disappear. But I do want the fact that we die to serve as a reminder that time is not just an enemy or a treasure; *time is all there is.* That's what Emily was saying when she gazed back at life in Grover's Corners. That's what a friend of mine was talking about when she said, "Cherish life as if you were going to die tomorrow, but enjoy life as if you were going to live forever." That is the answer my fifties have given me to guide the rest of my days.

A lesser-known nineteenth-century poet named Henry Austin Dobson summed it all up in the space of a haiku:

Time goes, you say? Ah, no!
Alas, Time stays, we go.

But at fifty-five and counting, it's not enough to acknowledge mortality and the speed of time. I am learning, finally, to take time in and also to enter it; to make it tangible and to let it go; to prize its sacred moments and also its more modest ones. As May Sarton put it:

Now there is time and Time is young.
O, in this single hour I live
All of myself and do not move.
I, the pursued, who madly ran,
Stand still, stand still, and stop the sun.

5

Forgetting and Remembering

> The time is close when you shall forget all things and be by all forgotten.
>
> — *Marcus Aurelius*

A friend got undressed the other night and threw her underwear in the garbarge pail. Another drew a blank on his brother's phone number. Last week, I went to the hardware store and, for the life of me, couldn't remember what I needed when I got there. "At this age," says Gloria Steinem, "being able to remember something is as good as an orgasm."

The mind is the Bermuda Triangle of aging. You never know when a shipshape fragment of knowledge — someone's name, a movie title, a simple word — will sail into treacherous waters and disappear without a trace, or when a raft of information given up for lost will suddenly wash up on the shores of memory.

Forgetting and remembering are critical issues of aging, partly because any sign of mental slippage triggers our fears of gerontic dementia, and partly because memory is the pathway to personal history wherein lies proof that we have lived and loved and made a difference in the world. Without access to that history — not just the lived life but the daydreams of it — we can almost feel ourselves disappear. In that sense, midlife forgetfulness is much more than a practical annoyance; it is a self-inflicted preview of the way we ourselves will be forgotten when we die, a subtle reminder of the destiny we fear. ("This is probably why so many people want to be famous," says the humorist Russell Baker: "so they will be remembered after they are gone.") If the innocuous moment of forgetfulness can seem like an early-warning symptom of one's death and obliteration, so, too, can the simple act of remembering — re-membering, making things whole — be a symbol of mortal defiance, as welcome as a life preserver in a roiling sea.

Watching my memory misbehave, I can't help wondering why the mind, that errant genius, forgets what it forgets and remembers what it remembers? Why do some parts of the past vanish while others seem to grow clearer with time? Why, as we age, do we find ourselves losing our memory while at the same time reveling in our memories, and why do both memory and memories seem so much more important to us now than ever before?

Losing It

Of the two mind games — forgetting and remembering — memory loss attracts more of our attention because its vagaries are the cause of so much frustration and embarrassment. The French say they have "a hole in the memory" when they forget something; an Israeli comedian refers to the condition as early Alzheimer's. The litany of middle-aged mind slippage seems to be as well grooved as tire treads: "Dammit, the word's on the tip of my tongue." "What's his name again?" "Have you seen my glasses?" "Where could I have put that parking stub?" "I can't remember if I turned off the oven." "These unmailed letters have been in my purse for a week!" "What am I doing standing in the bedroom with an eggplant in my hand?"

Supreme Court Justice Oliver Wendell Holmes was asked for his ticket on a train and couldn't find it. The conductor, recognizing him, said reassuringly, "Never mind, sir; I'm sure you have it somewhere."

"Mr. Conductor," replied Holmes, "the question is not where is my ticket, but where am I going?"

The great philosopher William James told of the time he lost his bearings while getting ready for a dinner party — he undressed, washed up, and then climbed into bed.

Stories of other people's absentmindedness always make me chuckle, but when such things happen to me, I feel a pang of nausea: Is this it? I wonder. The cold claw of dementia? The first sign that I'm losing my mind?

Journalist Marcia Seligson's survey of current memory research helped me rethink the issue. She became interested in midlife memory after she demanded that the supermarket give her a free replacement for the shampoo she'd bought that morning which she insisted had never been packed in her grocery bag — and two weeks later found the original in the refrigerator. Armed with her own apprehensions, she interviewed a number of specialists in the neurosciences and learned among other things: No one can predict who will be affected by memory loss or when. No one knows why we remember some things and not others (although scientists are sure that certain short-term memory skills, like phone number retrieval, do not change with age.) Memory can be affected by poor health, insufficient sleep, diabetes, hypoglycemia, depression, thyroid disorders, or prescription drugs. Brain cells don't die as we get older, though they may shrink. People start reporting memory declines at about age thirty, not just after fifty.

Many experts believe, according to Seligson, that the midlife memory is not much worse off than its younger incarnation; however, we tend to expect more of ourselves as we get older, or else we reinterpret our actions according to preconceived scripts about middle age that later become self-fulfilling. For instance, you may have been a tad absentminded all your life, but suddenly, at fifty, you see each misplaced object as a sign of doddering capacity and blame your forgetfulness on your advancing years. What changed was your perception of your behavior, not the behavior itself.

At a 1995 panel on "Aging and the Brain," sponsored by the Charles Dana Foundation, its chairman, David Mahoney, spoke of the incalculable toll that Alzheimer's disease takes on its 4 million American victims and on the families who must stand by in helpless anguish watching the decline of their loved ones. But, emphasized the panelists, severe cognitive impairment and memory loss are by no means inevitable accompaniments of aging.

Marilyn Albert, associate professor of psychiatry and neurology at the Harvard Medical School, said, "We used to think memory problems were a normal part of getting older, but now we realize that severe memory changes are not normal." People suffering normal memory loss have trouble learning something new — like directions to an unfamiliar destination or how to operate a digital alarm clock — but once the lesson is mastered, Albert said, they are able to retain the information as well as anyone younger. In contrast, victims of Alzheimer's disease find both learning and retention difficult or impossible. Albert also pointed out that while one-third to one-half of all healthy people have some minor memory problems as they get older, there is enough individual variability to account for someone like her grandmother, who was sharp as a tack when she died at ninety-nine, or George Burns, who, at this writing, is still rolling them in the aisles — or, one might add, the celebrated Delany sisters, centenarian subjects of the book and play *Having Our Say.*

"It's a matter of use it or lose it," declared Dr. Albert, echoing the rallying cry of this book. "People whose minds are very active can prevent declines in mental ability."

Corroborating that view, another panelist, Barry Gordon, associate professor of neurology and cognitive science at Johns Hopkins University, said all the evidence suggests that "the more you exercise your mind, the better," and that staying actively engaged in life can stimulate the brain cells and prevent memory loss.

Seligson draws a similar conclusion from her wide-ranging survey of brain research: "What we term memory loss appears to be, at least until we reach our late sixties or seventies, an issue of attention-paying."

Attention-paying is my thing. This whole book is, in a sense, a paean to the raised consciousness, a brief for paying attention to life, and yet all the awareness in the world cannot seem to change the fact that some categories of newly acquired information stick to the memory like bees to flypaper while others slip away moments after crossing my path. Sometimes, sound rather than sight holds the key to memory, and in other instances, it's the opposite. Certain past events can be excavated in one piece, original details intact, while other memories, if they reach daylight at all, surface in shards or faded beyond recognition. I, for one, can remember an interesting statistic the day after someone tells it to me, but not a joke. Your first day on your first job is very likely clear in your mind, but you probably can't remember what you did last Tuesday. I found that I could recall my high school years more vividly when I listened to the 1950s hit "Sh-Boom" than when I visited the school itself. The ways of memory are strange and mystifying — and wonderful.

Accessing Memories

I've tried every trick in the book to increase my focus and improve my retentiveness. As soon as I hear a person's name, I try to use it several times in our conversation, even if I sound like a finishing-school idiot. When I hear a funny story or a restaurant recommendation, I repeat it to myself immediately, then try to link it to some helpful association to aid me in recalling it in the future. Silly as it sounds, I associate a certain Richard with his riches, a certain black-eyed Susan with the flower of the same name. I rerun a good punch line in my mind, assuming that if I can retain that one sentence, the whole joke will fall into place. I visualize where the new restaurant is located in case its name escapes me. I use mnemonic devices for a round of neighborhood errands: SCARF tells me to go to the Shoemakers, Cleaners, and to Rent a movie and buy Flowers.

I suddenly recall that when I was eighteen and supposedly at memory's peak, I also used mnemonics to lock in the sequence of British monarchs. To a person in her fifties, this is reassuring.

Besides trying to download information into my cranial computer, I also have acquired a unique method of accessing stuff on demand. In San Miguel d'Allende years ago, I met a man (I forget his name) who told me about the elevator image he'd devised to retrieve information that eludes his immediate recollection. Say he's forgotten a woman's name: he imagines himself getting into an elevator and lowering himself to the first level, where he has told his mind to store visual memory triggers. ("First floor: lingerie, ladies shoes, lackadaisical memories . . .") At this level, he tries to "see" the person's name printed on her stationery, on her office door, on a message slip, or wherever he may have encountered it in written form. If this yields nothing, he takes the elevator down to the next level, where he keeps his auditory memories. Here, he tries to "hear" the sound of her name as she introduces herself, or as he might ask for her on the telephone. By this time, he says, he usually has recalled the first letter of the name, but he keeps hunting. He descends to level three, where he has told his mind to store more free-form associations. Here, mindful of the paradox, he consciously assigns the search to his unconscious and lets it proceed without his help. Soon, images pop up without warning, music enters the scene, he sees a guitar, a folksinger, dark hair — and he's got it! "Her name was Joan," he says, explaining that this particular woman had always reminded him of Joan Baez.

Flaky as it sounds, I get into my elevator whenever I'm stuck for a word or name and it works far better than you'd think. Moreover, I've since discovered that, though the elevator imagery is modern, its underlying methodology is hundreds of years old. In *The Memory Palace of Matteo Ricci,* Yale scholar Jonathan Spence describes how a sixteenth-century Jesuit taught the Chinese intelligentsia the art of memory. Ricci's technique called for visualizing a structure — a temple, palace, or other large building — and designating rooms therein as mental storage spaces for each category of knowledge. Later, a particular item of knowledge could be located by association with its precise physical location. The memory palace is too elaborate for my needs; the elevator usually gets me where I want to go, but not always.

The other night, my husband, Bert, and I and two friends had just entered a restaurant when we ran into a couple we've known for years, who gave us an effusive greeting and then glanced expectantly at our companions. Clearly, we were supposed to introduce the two couples but I drew a blank on the first name of one man and Bert's desperate expression told me he wasn't going to be any help. We blundered through with a last-names introduction ("Joneses, meet the Smiths"), but I was lousy company for the rest of the evening because I kept riding up and down in my elevator waiting for a revelation.

The guy's name came to me at 2 A.M. To a person in her fifties, this is *not* reassuring.

Ellen Langer, the Harvard psychology professor who studies mindlessness and mindfulness, woke up one summer morning and couldn't remember what day it was. She was in her late thirties. Had she been older, she says, she'd have attributed the memory lapse to aging. Instead, she realized that "in July, with no classes to teach and no appointments to keep, every day was pretty much the same as every other. There was no reason to remember whether it was Tuesday or Wednesday, so I didn't."

This insight led her to develop mindfulness-training exercises that eventually reversed memory loss in a group of elderly nursing home residents. She gave the group increasingly difficult cognitive tasks that required them to remember things like the names of staff members, activity schedules, dates, and the like, and she rewarded their correct answers with chips redeemable at the gift shop. But the real gift, she said, was to give them a "reason to remember" — an investment in the details of everyday life — something we can give ourselves at any age.

The exercise of active noticing had remarkable ramifications at the nursing home: it not only perked up the residents' spirits, it had a statistically measurable effect on their survival rates. Three years later, only 7 percent of the experimental group had died compared with up to 33 percent of the rest of the nursing home population. Why hasn't more been made of these astounding findings? Is it because no prescription drugs or medical treatments are involved in this method of possible life extension and therefore no one can profit from it? If we can prolong our lives by systematically ratcheting up our level of consciousness as we age, shouldn't we be doing mindfulness exercises along with our sit-ups?

I ask Langer for some simple suggestions. "Find a novelty in all that you do," she replies. "Get out of the other side of the bed for a change. Put on your clothes in a different order. Notice the buttons on your shirt. Take something you want to remember and notice five things about it. The more you notice, the better. Don't expect to notice everything, but at every moment expect to be noticing *something*."

But won't that make a person crazy? I ask.

"Thinking has gotten a bad rap, because to most people it means worrying," she says. "Noticing is *good* thinking; it keeps you alive." Langer doesn't call her system a memory exercise, she calls it mindful learning. "Most memory problems are a product of the mind-set you bring to them, and many problems attributed to poor memory are simply encoding problems [i.e., how we take life in and organize it in our minds]. Memory is about personal relevance. We remember what matters to us; that's why most women remember the calorie counts of foods they love. If you engage something mindfully, you're more likely to remember it."

As annoying as it is when memory fails us, that failure may also serve a purpose. By what it chooses to forget, a nation or a people determines which of its collective experiences shall be recorded as history and which shall be deep-sixed for posterity. Official American remembering goes by the name of Presidents' Day, Martin Luther King, Jr.'s Birthday, Thanksgiving, Memorial Day, the Fourth of July, while that which doesn't fit the nation's sense of itself — slavery, race riots, labor exploitation, Vietnam — is revised or repressed.

On a small canvas, each individual similarly determines, consciously or not, what personal history is worth recording and transmitting and what is better left in the deep folds of time. In a real sense, we choose our own past, creating it as we go along by deciding which experiences will be kept alive, surfaces polished, joints oiled, muscles exercised by frequent use. We decide whether a memory will be turned into simple narrative or made mythic, whether it will be reified in ritual, like the annual recitation of "how grandma came to America," or whether it will be left to sink or swim in the ocean of life experience. Part of building a past is deciding what to leave out. In 1960, a year out of college, I took a job as an advertising copywriter and was an abysmal failure at it. I'd been writing incessantly since childhood, but I turned out to be incapable of waxing eloquent in fifty words or less. I couldn't produce clever headlines or think in terms of "concept" and "positioning." I couldn't distill the essence of the product. Words like "campaign strategy" or "consumer habits" made my mind congeal. In short, I was a flop and by mutual consent, the ad agency and I parted company after six months. When I think about my thirty-five-year worklife, I usually leave that experience out. Although it taught me there is life after failure, I generally prefer to forget that humbling interlude, finding no purpose in revisiting the feelings of inadequacy that caused me so much anguish at the age of twenty-one. The pain wasn't about failing at ad copy, it was about facing my limitations, a difficult task at any age. Learning to forget pain, or letting oneself stop remembering, can be essential to self-image, psychological well-being, even to survival.

"Just as every species develops techniques for protecting and adapting, human beings do, too," says psychiatrist Robert M. Naiman. "And just as we have physical means for maintaining physiological homeostasis, similarly, humans have developed between twelve and fifteen mental defense mechanisms for protecting ourselves against overwhelming feelings of distress. One of those mechanisms is repression, or inhibition of recall, whereby things that are incompatible with well-being — for example, a heinous rape experience — are unconsciously pushed down into unawareness."

When remembering *everything* would hurt too much, selective amnesia is a balm. Mercifully, many of us have Teflon minds when it comes to moments of agony, public humiliation, the pain of childbirth, the cutting personal slight, and Velcro minds when it comes to the good stuff.

Aging with Our Heroes

A long memory bears fruits that are both sweet and melancholy. It might be easier for us to forget the flight of time were the icons of our era not galloping along on a parallel track. Much as we might want public figures to be models for productive aging, it can be slightly disconcerting to realize that the rebel writers Margaret Atwood and Germaine Greer are fifty-six; Joyce Carol Oates, America's most prolific "young" novelist, is fifty-seven; the ex–prom queen Alix Kates Shulman is sixty-two. Eleanor Holmes Norton, who started as a firebrand civil rights lawyer is now a fifty-eight-year-old congresswoman; the regally ageless Barbara Jordan died at fifty-nine; the history-making Geraldine Ferraro is sixty. I mention these women because we knew them *when* — when they were young and we were young and everything was just beginning.

This is especially true of film stars, whose past is trapped in images they can never escape. In Hollywood, where forty is over the hill for most actresses, it's hard to believe that Diane Keaton, the ditsy Annie Hall, is forty-nine and talking about menopause; Goldie Hawn, the original "Laugh-In" girl, is fifty; the winsome Blythe Danner is fifty-two; sexpot Raquel Welch is my age; Ellen Burstyn is playing old-lady parts; Barbara Eden ("I Dream of Jeannie"), Julie Andrews, and Sophia Loren are sixty; Sally Field, who was Tom Hanks's girlfriend a few movies ago, plays his mother in *Forrest Gump;* and the joke of the moment asks: "What is 10, 9, 8, 7, 6, 5?" Answer: "Bo Derek aging."

The movies are far poorer for the loss of stars like Marilyn Monroe, James Dean, Natalie Wood, and Judy Garland, yet one could say they did their contemporaries a favor by dying in their prime. Left behind is an image of youth intact, vitality caught forever in a cinematic time warp we can enter at will. Rent *Some Like It Hot* and you'll see Marilyn exactly as you always imagine her and as she will always remain, whereas the day after you watch her costars Tony Curtis and Jack Lemmon cavorting in the movie, you might catch them on a talk show or in the tabloids looking jowly and thick, *their* age reminding you of *yours.* Because we have no competing real-life Marilyn with face-lift scars and middle-aged spread, living with her sixth husband in Bel Aire, or getting detoxed at the Betty Ford Center — because Marilyn never changes — nothing stops you from reconnecting with the person you were back then when she looked like that. (A friend of mine, a passionate Monroe fan, says he actually *feels* younger after he's seen one of her movies. I'd like to believe he'd have loved Marilyn with wrinkles, but I wouldn't bet on it.)

This year, had she lived, Marilyn would be sixty-nine years old. Martin Luther King, Jr., and Anne Frank would be sixty-six. James Dean would be sixty-four, as would Sylvia Plath. Elvis would be sixty-one. Natalie Wood, who died at forty-three, would be fifty-seven. Bob Marley would be just fifty.

Meanwhile, Margaret O'Brien is fifty-five. There's no reason why little Margaret, child star of the 1940s, shouldn't be fifty-five; I've always known we were contemporaries (which is why I pledged my allegiance to her and not the "much older" Shirley Temple), so why am I feeling bruised by the news of her age? While I've been barreling through the decades, did I imagine she would remain the perennial "Tenth Avenue Angel" with her tiny triangle smile and her shiny pink cheeks?

That Margaret O'Brien is still around is great for her but an existential burden for me. Knowing this beloved child star is fifty-five tells me more than any mirror about how far I've traveled, for in some ironic sense, her age is more real to me, and harder to accept, than my own. If Margaret is fifty-five, then I am fifty-five for sure.

When I said this to a sixty-two-year-old friend, she shot back, "If Jackie Kennedy could die at sixty-two, then I could die tomorrow," which only goes to prove that the living and the dead can be equally relevant as long as their past and ours have crossed paths in time.

The Past Is Prologue

What is the past, or should I ask, when was it? Is thirty years ago ancient history or just yesterday? Is thirty years ago closer now than it was thirty years ago? People may never reach consensus on the abstract impressionism of time, but at least we can agree that the past ain't what it used to be. Once behind us, it used to be considered dead and gone; now, yesterday can seem hipper than tomorrow. Indeed, in 1994, people in their twenties and thirties were looking back with envy and admiration to the music and mystique of the original Woodstock twenty-five years before. But in 1969, when I was thirty, none of my friends were looking back twenty-five years to the music of 1944 with anything but amazement at how dated it all sounded. Now, of course, 1944 sounds good again: Frank Sinatra is Chairman of the Board, Tony Bennett is in the top forty, and Billie Holiday is a classic. Some memories get better with time; it depends on *how* we remember them.

At my birthday lunch, Annie, a stockbroker, said: "When I went into the stock market in nineteen fifty-nine, the great crash of twenty-nine was remote and irrelevant. Nothing that happened thirty years before was important to me. But from the vantage point of the nineties, everything that happened in the sixties seems relevant to me and my children. We're still listening to sixties music, we're still arguing about the Kennedy assassination and the Vietnam War." To help her outwit the flummoxing effects of hindsight, Annie has been keeping a journal, "so that thirty years from now I'll know who I was, and so will my children."

The personal diary is the raw material of memory, not doctored by hindsight with its revisionist tendencies, but captured on the spot in the words of the great and the humble who chose to write down "what happened today" and how they felt about it. We often discover deeper truths about the past in attic trunks and old shoe boxes than in the history books, and a deeper truth about ourselves in our own old diaries.

Years after she'd misplaced them (under the stairs in a room that was her ex-husband's old study), Wendy Orange, at fifty, came upon a stack of her old journals, twenty-five years' worth of them, a record of her life from age twenty-one to forty-five:

> She, they — my younger selves — had painstakingly written all through those years: all those moods, memories, details and descriptions, surveying all those cities and towns and the rooms that held her and her lovers and her friends and her attempts at work, her euphorias and her failures. . . . She had recorded all this for me, for the woman reaching fifty to reflect and remember, for I was her audience, her mother and her daughter all in one.

For weeks, Orange read the journals, couldn't stop reading, page after page, hours at a time, reading her life as if she had never lived it, and seeing herself clearly for the first time. "What I was left with, what those weeks achieved was a depth of empathy that I'd always reserved for the others and withheld from myself." In the full sweep of time, in twenty-five years spread out on the floor in her own handwriting, she saw "not the narcissism but the striving towards the good, not the mess but . . . the wish to clean up the mess, not the failed relations but the tenacity toward relation, and the atmosphere that all this left around me was this simple, singular blessing: the sense that I have earned my life and therefore finally have a right to live it."

Without active remembering, the past too easily slithers away from us, reverts to its wild, unruly state and escapes into the darkness, where we may lose it forever. To hold on, some of us make memories into stories, our fisherman's tales, spinning oft-told anecdotes into a narrative web that traps the past in our own ears. And some capture each day in a journal, hoping that writing a life won't substitute for living it.

"I suppose reminiscing is a sign of age," wrote Gwendolyn Bennett, one of the Harlem Renaissance poets, who decided on New Year's Day 1936 to start a journal. But before she got around to writing her first entry, it was April 7, which gave her cause to reconsider the whole business. Her procrastination had not only stolen time, she realized, it had stolen the immediacy of "the sting of pain and the exultation of joys that are at best ephemeral." Now she wondered if she could reconstruct her experiences or whether it was even worth trying: "Immediately, I ask myself, why use the pages up to April 7? Why not just let time remain suspended, unrecorded, unheeded? But such a consideration leads me to the question of why keep a diary at all. And here I really pause to wonder. . . ."

There are always excuses to justify one's reluctance to rake up the past and replant it on a page: there is the untrustworthiness of memory, the subjectivity of perception, the time commitment required to keep up to date on the vapid, boring, unworthy substance of everyday life. Nevertheless, for all practical purposes, time "unheeded" is time erased, and a life lost to memory is a life half lived. Willa Cather said of memories: "One cannot get another set; one has only those." Writers know this as well as anyone; when the memories run out, some novelists run dry, while a writer with a great stash of memories needs no other subject. "We write to taste life twice," observed Anaïs Nin, "in the moment, and in retrospection." But that double-dipping is available to anyone. You needn't be a writer to taste life twice, ten, two hundred times over. You only need a past and the will to remember it.

Ellen Langer goes even further, endowing nostalgia with the power to influence and rejuvenate the body, though she adds this proviso: "If you mindlessly return to the past, it has no effect. When most people step back in time, they do it as someone in the present looking at the past, as an observer watching from a distance. But if you are mindful, you try to conjure up the *feelings* you had in that past situation, as if you were a method actor *being* younger, not an observer watching your younger self. You get into your younger mind-set and act out of that perspective and feel like that person."

Mindful nostalgia works rather like a placebo, says Langer. If you believe a sugar pill is an aspirin, the sugar pill may cure your headache; and if you believe you are what you once were, you may become more like that younger, more vital self. The mind does the work, the body produces the result. If the process sounds familiar, it is because we've heard athletes describe how they use visualization to improve their performance; that is, they train their minds to visualize an image of themselves executing a perfect dive or tennis serve as part of their preparation for competition, and they do better as a result.

"I'm not a singer," Langer admits, by way of further illustration. "But when I'm in the shower being Barbra Streisand, I sing a hundred percent better than when I'm being me." The same sort of phenomenon can happen when nostalgia carries us back to the past; when we are being our thirty-year-old self, we feel younger and better than we do when we are being ourselves as we are now.

Moreover, entering the past in a mindful, method-acting way tends to be comforting because it is stress-free. "The present is like an unsolved puzzle, so it makes us anxious," says Langer, "but we've already solved the puzzles of the past, they're familiar, we know how everything turns out. So when we encounter an incident nostalgically — when we take out old pictures or try on old clothes — there is no accompanying anxiety, we have control over everything." She laughs. "It's surprising we don't do it more often."

I've always done it, but I never knew why I liked it. The control factor explains a lot. The possibility that we can prevent memory loss through more conscious engagement in the present, and can enhance our lives through mindful uses of the past, struck me as good news indeed for the "over-the-hill" gang.

In Praise of Nostalgia

"O! call back yesterday, bid time return!" In that poignant plea, Shakespeare could be defining the purpose of nostalgia as I see it. Though cynics and sophisticates have given it a bad press, nostalgia offers something that isn't easy to come by — a *usable yesterday.* Nostalgia can be many things — a warm bath in hindsight, experience capital, a way to refuel, a hedge against self-delusion, an ongoing conversation with one's former self.

Nostalgia is a big thing in our family, largely because it means so much to me. My husband says I'm so sentimental that I reminisce about the present. He exaggerates, but it is true that my memories sweeten my life. Home movies make me happy. So do old letters and photographs, and artifacts from my 1940s childhood, my teen years in the 1950s, the early married years, and the birth pangs of the women's movement. I save things. I'm a methodical collector of objects and memories. It has dawned on me that, having suffered the early death of a parent, I may be trying to preclude other losses by securing whatever can be nailed down — by saving "things," which, unlike time, can be framed and mounted and kept.

A thousand years from now an archaeologist could stumble upon the earth mound containing my apartment and in one swift dig know everything about me and the time in which I lived. I haven't been entirely successful at slowing time present, but I have captured whole segments of time past by writing my life on the page or saving remnants of it in a scrapbook where memories can "set" like aspic and stay firm. I keep a scrapbook for each year in which I mount the usual family snapshots along with dozens of quirky items that evoke time past with the power of a Proustian madeleine. The scrapbook of 1963, for example, conjures up the summer when Bert and I first met. It contains the flotsam and jetsam of our courtship: the balloon we bought at the Central Park Zoo on our second date (shriveled, of course, but still green); the fringed satin pillowcase he sent from his Army Reserve training camp; a strand of wool from the sweater I knitted for him while he was away (he still has it); a flyer he brought back from a civil rights march in Danville, Virginia, where he'd gone to do volunteer legal work; matchbook covers; *Playbills*; meaningful cocktail napkins; the newspaper announcements of our October engagement and December wedding.

From the perspective of more than thirty years of marriage, it's a kick to turn the pages back to where it all began, much as one rereads a favorite novel from the beginning despite knowing how it all turns out. And it's pure joy to watch our grown-up children pore over the scrapbooks of their early years, letting a tiny bundle of baby hair or a nursery school painting unlock a flood of memories.

I still have many of my kids' baby clothes and best-loved toys. I tell them I'm saving these things for *their* children but the truth is, memories cling to them like old paint and I can't throw memories away. In my kitchen drawer lies the silverplated flatware that I grew up with in my parents' house, its Queen Anne pattern so evocative that my mother and her kitchen materialize around a spoon or butter knife whenever I let them.

What I remember of my years with my mother, I keep fresh with an occasional assist from the few objects that belonged to her that I've managed to save since 1955. There are too few, because at fifteen I didn't have the foresight to ask my father for more "heirlooms" to take with me into my adult life. But I do have her red leather wallet with the odds and ends that were in it the day she died, and the chignon she had made from her own hair, chestnut brown and silky, caught like a sleeping kitten in a dark nylon hairnet. Some objects speak through their bouquet, and their eloquent redolence can break one's heart. On a shelf in my study sits my mother's white porcelain dresser set, a covered dish for face powder and two small perfume flasks, each topped by a corked stopper with a filigree crown. Years after she was gone, I could still put my nose to the lip of a flask or rub a few grains of pink powder on my skin and with the release of her scent bring memories of her more vividly to mind. One day, a day I never quite noticed, the perfume evaporated and the flasks lost their last traces of fragrance and the powder started smelling like nothing but dust. I miss them.

Forgive the tautology, but nostalgia takes us nowhere if we can't remember anything, so when memory grows sluggish, a faded snapshot or a pressed rose can give it a nudge, a bowl of pistachio ice cream can bring a summer back, a song that once mattered can connect us instantly with a place, a person, a time. Hearing "White Cliffs of Dover" doesn't just remind me of the 1940s, it returns me to 167th Street in Jamaica, to the tidy semi-detached brick house I shared with my parents and my big sister, Betty, until she left to get married in 1946, two weeks after I turned seven; back to the child I was during the Second World War, when Betty dated tall young men in uniforms, and Mommy and Daddy were air-raid wardens, and meat was rationed, and America was everybody's hero. "Love Walked In" evokes my first boyfriend, Billy, captain of the Jamaica High School basketball team as, to this day, does the smell of any school gym. Pete Seeger's voice sends me back to Brandeis University in the 1950s, when my friends and I thought we were the original Bohemians. The Modern Jazz Quartet playing anything at all reminds me of my single life in Greenwich Village. Mahler's First Symphony evokes the enchantment of outdoor concerts on the lawns of Tanglewood. And "The Eensie Weensie Spider" brings my children into focus singing in their dear, gurgly voices while their tiny fingers traced the spider's journey up the waterspout. Bittersweet memories, with an accent on the sweet.

Because it is so full of paradoxes and prone to distortion, nostalgia is best defined by what it is not: It is not homesickness, although it can derive from similar feelings of yearning. It is not a substitute for fulfillment, but rather an experience recalled for itself, and it is not pathological unless we overidealize the past or repress truthful memories. Rather than "a longing for something far away or long ago" (as one dictionary defines it), nostalgia is an acknowledgement of what that long ago something once meant to us, an exercise in appreciation, and an energizing, nourishing reconnection with who we were then.

Yet, some people fight it. "I'm always looking for antidotes to my inborn nostalgia," writes Daphne Merkin about being plagued by a string of losses of objects and people — an earring, a scarf, a friend — and annoyed that she misses them. Though moved by her account, I take a different view, having realized long ago that my losses are as much a part of me as anything I possess. All of us are the sum of our losses and our gains, but nostalgia lessens the losses by reminding us that nothing is all gone as long as it is remembered.

"I despise nostalgia," says Ken Burns, the documentary producer whose recent series on baseball was nostalgia squared. Yet he, too, protests: "Nostalgia is lazy. You have to separate nostalgia from history." History, shmistory. Baseball is the quickest nostalgia trip on record. Watching clips of Jackie Robinson's first game in the majors and Bobbie Thompson's home run in the 1951 playoffs puts me back in Ebbets Field with a hot dog in my hand. Why heap scorn upon sentimentality, the most human of emotions? Why can't we just feel what we feel, and feel good about it?

Edmund Wilson, struggling against nostalgia's seductions, wrote in his journal in the 1960s, "I find that I am a man of the '20's. I still expect something exciting: drinks, animated conversation, gaiety: an uninhibited exchange of ideas, Scott Fitzgerald's idea that somewhere things were 'glimmering.' I am managing to discipline myself now so that I shan't be silly in this way."

But surely there is nothing silly about cleaving to the mood and manners of another decade if we find strength or comfort there, or if drawing upon those memories helps to keep us whole.

Holly Brubach has a lovely way of explaining why she hangs on to her high-school cheerleading shirt, denim overalls from college days, the black leather jacket she wore when she first came to the city, a droopy cardigan that made her feel more literary, an old Chanel suit purchased to give herself authority: "I know that I'll never wear any of these clothes again," she writes; "their relationship to the person I've become is purely historical. Still, I can't bring myself to get rid of them, and in the end I left them in my closet, out of respect for the people I used to be. They meant well. Each one gave way to the next and disappeared, leaving only her clothes behind."

Gabriel, the main character in James Joyce's *The Dead,* realizes that "we're all in the act of becoming the past." Clearly, human beings have a great capacity for self-delusion in the face of this truth. The attempt to banish the past from the present is, to coin a phrase, a waste of time, since today becomes yesterday tomorrow. Each day moves into the past as soon as we've lived it. The future is only a prayer.

Many intellectuals assume that all nostalgia is mired in the swamps of middlebrow mushiness, or that being impervious to the past is a badge of sophistication. They put down personal nostalgia in the same breath as they disdain the latest theme park, suggesting that drawing pleasure from one's private memories is as morally corrupt as the mass marketing of a distorted American past. I have nothing good to say about people who create nostalgia for what we never had, or who give us a sanitized history — the nineteen fifties without McCarthyism, for instance; the nineteen sixties without My Lai; or the nineteen seventies without Watergate. I'm no fan of Woodstock '94, a giant promotion with product tie-ins, commemorative coins, pay-per-view broadcasts, and even an "official condom." (At Woodstock 1969, believe it or not, there was not so much as a T-shirt for sale.) But the fact that our collective memories may have been merchandized doesn't mean my memories and yours are misbegotten.

Still other nostalgia-bashers read political and cultural reaction into every backward glance, assuming that all manner of retrospection is doomed to be retrograde. Rita Mae Brown calls nostalgia "a sophisticated form of obstructionism." What nonsense! We can enjoy home movies without being a political Neanderthal just as we can appreciate I. M. Pei's glass pyramid without wanting to tear down the Louvre. Reasonable people can value the past, live fully in the present, and still be directed toward the future.

Underlying many of the nostalgia put-downs is the implication that we reminisce when memories are all we have. In fact, what most of us do is use the past as a cache of clues to the times that made us what we are. The texture of those times is recaptured in what I call *era* nostalgia, a frothier category of remembering, not as deep or as nourishing as personal nostalgia, but equally evocative.

Every generation stakes out its own nostalgia turf — the fads, clothing, music, and cultural stimuli that will forever have the power to tug at its heartstrings. The appeal of the sentimental journey is universal; only its landmarks are unique. If I tell you I grew up on Doris Day movies, read Robert Louis Stevenson in grammar school and Bertrand Russell in high school, brushed my teeth with Ipana, wore ankle bracelets and crinolines, listened to radio shows called "Our Gal Sunday" and "Mr. Kean, Tracer of Lost Persons," ate an ice cream known as Charlotte Russe, chewed Black Jack gum, and belonged to the Ruth Roman Fan Club, you'd know exactly where I come from on the twentieth-century time line, but you still wouldn't know what makes me tick. Era nostalgia doesn't reveal the inner person; it does, however, open the door to shared memories and instant bonding with others of the same vintage.

My friend Peggy Henretig writes from Yakima, Washington: "Recently, I stumbled across my original curler bag complete with curler cap, brush rollers and picks. What a find! I can also still locate my mousketeer ears, hula hoop, tie-dyed tank tops, go-go boots and charm bracelet. Ahh, the memories. Eventually I'm sure that Reeboks, Walkmans, and croissants will be as nostalgic."

In a recent column, Russell Baker catalogued some of the collective losses of the American people — the Princess telephone, the *Saturday Evening Post,* crowds of men wearing suits, neckties, and snap-brim fedoras and watching the Brooklyn Dodgers, Guy Lombardo on New Year's Eve, the Royal manual typewriter, Burma-Shave roadside verse, Edward R. Murrow, and most recently, the newsman Charles Kuralt, whose retirement sparked his nostalgia column in the first place. "As with so much of vanishing America," Baker writes, "we took it for granted that Charles Kuralt would always be with us, so failed to cherish him sufficiently, just as we failed to cherish mehitabel, and brushless shaving cream in a jar, and the movie stars who smoked, and the barber pole whose beauty had to be revealed to us by Edward Hopper, all of which now belong to America the Gone."

I share in these losses. I remember when I believed that everything I knew and loved would last forever, as though the world that existed when I was a child had always been there and would always be there, sealed in amber, its pleasures fixed forever in the universe. Needless to say, one can enjoy thinking about such artifacts and their era without wanting the era back. Era nostalgia must not be confused with ultraconservative yearnings for "the good old days." As a woman, I long for yesteryear about as much as I long for life under the ayatollahs. I remember the fifties and sixties well enough to know they had all the appeal of a long prison sentence when it came to women's aspirations. I want to *visit* memory lane, not live there.

That Edmund Wilson expressed a strong connection to the twenties is no surprise; people usually feel most nostalgic about the decade that corresponds with their own youth. In a 1995 commencement address at Brandeis University, Daniel Schorr reminisced about his youth, a simpler time when, "Pot was something you cooked in, and coke was something you drank and grass was something you mowed . . . [and] hardware was a hammer and software wasn't in the dictionary."

I happen to feel an almost visceral connection to the cars of my youth, a passionate nostalgia for certain models that carry very personal meanings — automobile as autobiography, you might say. A road sighting of a 1948 Dodge with Fluid Drive gives me palpitations because I *know* the car, I know the dials on the dashboard and the smell of the upholstery and where I was in life the last time I rode in one. It's the car in which I learned to drive. I've noticed, too, that my heart still skips a beat over the two-toned Chevy Bel Air hardtop, ditto the 1957 Corvette convertible, because I remember the boyfriends who drove them, usually too fast, whisking me away to Coney Island or Rockaway Beach, or a secluded make-out spot at the far end of a church parking lot. I loved other cars, too: the Cadillac Eldorado with its showy tailfins; the MG with spoked wheels, sloped fender, and running board; the Studebaker that resembled the cockpit of Lindbergh's plane; and those aerodynamic wonders the Nash and the "step down" Hudson, which we called "blimps on wheels." They rarely turn up on the highways anymore and I don't think I've seen a Henry J in forty years, but I remember them all because they remind me of my childhood, when getting there really *was* half the fun.

For ten or fifteen years after the Second World War, automobiles were as distinctive as people. You could tell a Pontiac from a Chrysler a half mile away, and you knew what sort of man would own each make. (I never knew a woman who owned her own car until I bought myself a French Simca in 1958.) My father was partial to the four-door Dodge. My uncle Ben was a Caddie man, though in 1954, he deviated for what I considered good reason — to buy the dashing Mercury Sun Valley with the green glass roof. My uncle Ralph always drove Pontiacs. My uncle Herman had a big old Plymouth that dated from the prewar years when "you could get your car in any color as long as it was black." No one in my family ever owned a Ford, because everyone knew Henry Ford was an anti-Semite.

to black-eyed peas have replaced language and ritual as the salient feature of group identity.

The irony in all this should be obvious: nostalgia is valued when it's an inspiration for style, identity politics, and pop culture, but not when it delivers satisfaction to the soul. In that case, it's cornball. Unhip. Passé.

If you ask me, discomfort with nostalgia is yet another symptom of people's fear of time and aging. To ridicule personal nostalgia is to ridicule the older generation, for who else has something to be nostalgic about but those with a sizable past? Younger people who are dismissive of the reminiscences of their elders may be acting out of denial — as though it is too painful to imagine that their hip and with-it lives might someday become nothing but words in their own dry mouths. Or they may be responding out of jealousy for what they never had and possibly never will. In other cultures, remembering makes one a valuable witness, a keeper of history, a teller of tales, but here in America, remembering marks one as an opponent of modernity and progress.

"Pay attention to what they tell you to forget," counseled the poet Muriel Rukeyser. Personal nostalgia is the taproot to one's past. Memory makes us into time travelers. The membrane between then and now is permeable because we are meant to move freely between the two.

We love old things because things can evoke people, and since people leave and change and die, there is great comfort in that which stays the same — or in the memory of it. For Nancy Mairs, "houses can literally embody the not-quite-discarded past." In *Remembering the Bone House,* she reimagines the many homes she has occupied throughout her life, returning to each location that was "important to my growth as a woman," resurrecting its constellation of inhabitants and their swirling crises, its cellars and attics, the wallpaper in every room, the hiding places, the color of the curtains and the cats. Remembering, she unlocks the tomb of the past, setting free echoes and images that tell her, and us, how she got from there to here.

Nancy Mairs writes about the House on the Hill, a house she hasn't seen for decades, a house full of light, glistening china, cobalt glasses and a table for twenty, the people she loved, guests, abundance, a house that may not even exist anymore:

> No, I'll never get the house back, not if by "getting it back" I mean holding a deed, owning a key, crossing the purplish shade of the porch to enter the side hall, slamming the screen door behind me.

I must content myself with another kind of possession altogether. My task is to house this house, which has vanished from the waking world, as it once housed me, to grant it the deed to my dreams. In the biochemical bath of my own body, through multiplex processes even neurophysiologists don't yet understand, I preserve and perfect the yellow house on the coast of Maine. As long as I do so, I get to dwell in it immemorially.

The Many Uses of Memory

Though I worry about my increasing forgetfulness and have made some effort to thwart the slippage, I'm far more interested in the phenomenon of remembering and the rewards it yields as we age. Why is remembering so pleasureful? It may be that what the mind saves compensates in some way for what the body loses, for the vividness of our long-ago memories is one of the consolations of growing old. Perhaps that incredible, after-the-storm vividness reconnects us with a sense of wonder of the sort that rejuvenates the mind and inspires creativity. But I'm inclined to think something else is at work here, something even more constructive and self-serving (in the best sense of the word): remembering is a way of affirming one's worth, the psychological equivalent of giving oneself a pat on the back, for in our reveries we usually arrange to recall our best selves, to revisit the people we've loved and those who have loved us, to review the best places we've been and the best things we've accomplished. If our memories amount to something, then we can believe our lives do, too.

Remembering waters my roots. It is one of my ways of being in the world. I don't indulge in mindful nostalgia all that often, but when I do — when I pore over the scrapbooks, or put on an old LP record from my high school years, or reminisce with my college roommate — it helps me carve a discernable shape out of the wild privet of the past. T. S. Eliot knew the joy that comes from reliving an event in the mind in order to understand it better:

> We had the experience but missed the meaning,
> And approach to the meaning restores the experience
> In a different form, beyond any meaning
> We can assign to happiness.

Some say chewing on old times is evidence of an undernourished present, but as I see it, the danger of living in the past is vastly overestimated and the greater peril, by far, is negating the Before of our lives. Memories are a touch of eternity in the present. I live *with* my memories, not *within* them. Looking back — not incessantly but now and then — helps me move forward on more solid footing. Just as immigrants incorporate elements of their native culture into their new lives rather than cut themselves off from their origins, we who are new arrivals in the land of aging must find ways to integrate our former selves into the person we are becoming.

I admit to being on speaking terms with my past — with no guarantee of factual accuracy — and to using my memories as a source of inspiration and strength, but I've never consciously manipulated those memories to make myself feel younger. In a remarkable experiment, Langer and her research colleagues did just that, effectively reversing the biological age of a group of elderly men (seventy-five and older) by systematically taking them back to a time when they saw themselves as young, and asking them to dress, talk, and behave as they did when they were in their mid-fifties. The experiment, which took place in 1979, required them to spend a week at a country retreat that had been furnished with magazines, books, music, and videos of movies dating from 1959. On their chests, the men wore I.D. photos taken twenty years before. All conversation was limited to events of that period. People like Eisenhower and Nixon were discussed in the present tense, and the participants were asked to interact with each other as if they still had jobs and active lives. Unbelievable as it sounds, after one week, impartial observers judged the men to look and behave more like fifty-five-year-olds than seventy-five-year-olds. By objective physiological measures they actually *de*-aged: fingers straightened, stiff joints loosened, posture became more erect, hand grips grew stronger, and I.Q. scores improved. Reentering their younger identities had such a dramatic impact on the way they saw themselves that their bones and muscles actually changed to keep up. If mindful remembering can be this potent — if it can reactivate the psychology and physiology of our younger selves — why wait until old age to try it?

Although her grant money ran out before she could reinforce the rejuvenation process in the men's everyday lives or do follow-up studies on the long-term effects of the experiment, Langer contends that what happened to these men in one week is ample proof of the power of the past to energize the present, and the potential for the mind to make the body younger.

Frozen Moments

Memories live as long as we remember them, and in that sense, so do people. It has always been important to me to be able to reconnect in some small way with what I no longer have, starting with my mother and the childhood that came to an end with her death. Many years before I discovered James Joyce's fascination with the "epiphanic moment" — that instant of illumination that suddenly forces us to reassess our lives — I had discovered the "frozen moment," a slice of time that demanded special attention, an experience so powerful that I knew I had to record it while it was happening, and remember it with conscious precision so I would have it always. My first frozen moment dates back to April 20, 1955.

It is morning. My mother has been gone for seven hours. We are in the car on the way to the airport to pick up my uncle, her brother, who is flying in for the funeral. I am sitting in the front seat, silent tears streaming down my cheeks. My father is dry-eyed and resolute at the wheel, his dispassionate profile floating at the periphery of my vision. I am staring out the window at the people in the passing cars. It seems miraculous to me, but I realize that their lives are undisturbed by my mother's death. I see that these people are going about their business, riding to work or school, laughing, smoking, listening to their car radios. They have no idea that my world has split apart; they don't care that my heart is filled with broken glass. If they notice me at all, they see a teenager with red eyes; nothing unusual — maybe I had a fight with my boyfriend, or my Dad has just tightened my curfew. No one glancing into our car can possibly imagine my grief. In a few hours, people at the funeral will hug me and say how sorry they are, but no one will ever know how it feels for this child to lose this mother. I am alone. My mother is dead. And life has dared to go on without her.

With adolescent clarity, I realize that though I am the star of my own movie, I am just an extra in everyone else's. There on the Van Wyck Expressway, at the age of fifteen, I understand that, in agony, in despair, in terror, each of us is finally, ultimately, alone. I decide to freeze this moment. I tell myself that I must never forget this.

And I never have.

Despite this early sadness, I don't see the past as a wellspring of pain. I remember happy experiences with just as much detail, a habit that protects me from Colette's hindsight regret. "What a wonderful life I've had! I only wish I'd realized it sooner."

I realize my happiness not only while it's happening, or after it has happened, but also in the form of anticipation. To put it plainly, I can remember in the present how it felt in the past to anticipate the future. If that still sounds convoluted, let me quote the Queen in *Alice Through the Looking-Glass:* "It's a poor sort of memory that only works backwards." Or, as my daughter Abigail wrote of her sixth grade graduation, "I look forward to looking back on this years from now." Talk about playing tricks on time! Remembering what the future looked like from the vantage point of a moment frozen in time is a special delight if one uses that memory to enrich the present and bounce happy memories back and forth across the years. It is also a wonderful way to treasure time, stop it in its tracks, and take it with us wherever we go.

It is 1965; I am twenty-six, my husband is thirty-one, We are at the original Broadway production of Fiddler on the Roof, *watching the wedding scene, in which Goldie and Tevye gaze at their daughter, the bride, as they sing "Sunrise, Sunset." The lyrics catapult me into the future: "Is this the little girl I carried? Is this the little boy at play? I don't remember growing older, when did they?" The scene on the stage blurs and behind my eyelids, on the screen of my imagination, I see our twin girls, then four months old, as young women. I see their father and me walking them down the aisle at their weddings and gazing at their sweet faces bathed in happiness — and I freeze the moment. Someday, I think to myself, before we know it, this will be us. We'll be wondering where twenty-five years went and what happened to our children's childhoods. Someday I will look back at this night and remember this moment when their lives were just beginning, and I'll hear these lyrics and I'll know how it all turns out.*

I defrosted that moment twice last year when Bert and I stood under the wedding canopy, first in January, then in December, watching each of our daughters marry. I remembered how I'd imagined this moment so long ago, twenty-eight years to be exact, and I thought about how the big things never change, for just as Goldie had done, I looked at my daughters in their bridal gowns and said to myself, "I don't remember growing older, when did they?"

My past is full of retrievable pleasures, frozen gems like this one that are as crystal clear today as the day they happened. I cannot imagine growing old without them.

PART III

Mortal Flesh and Mortal Fears

6

So, How Do I Look?

> No spring, nor summer beauty hath such grace,
> As I have seen in one autumnal face.
>
> —*John Donne*

The humorist Delia Ephron once said, "Preparing for the worst is an activity I have taken up since I turned thirty-five and the worst actually began to happen." In my case, the worst started happening in my late forties, and I was entirely unprepared. Needless to say, I'm catching on fast, since it's hard not to notice when one is falling apart.

In the interest of full disclosure, and with the goal of demystifying the middle-aged body, I am standing now in front of a full-length mirror ready to document my deterioration item by item from the top down. I don't love what I see; the discrepancy between my inner spirit (still thirty-six) and this outer body is hard to reconcile, but short of publishing a picture of myself naked, which would humiliate my children, the exercise of cataloguing my own physical collapse is the best way I know to redefine the "flaws" of aging as the norm of aging.

On me, *this* is what fifty-five looks like:

My hair, though not yet touched by gray, has lost its sheen and is even less full than it was twenty years ago when I was inspired to wear that wig for about a week and a half.

My face? Remember the opening scene from *Mommie Dearest,* when the aging, narcissistic Joan Crawford (Faye Dunaway) wakes up, takes off her lubricated sleep mask and chin and neck straps and plunges her face into a bowl of steaming hot water and then into a sinkful of ice cubes? Well, I *have* what she was trying to prevent.

Under my eyes are puffy fat pads surrounded by dark circles, each unfortunate feature doing its best to call attention to the other. My wrinkles materialized almost overnight when I was forty-nine. Now the lines in my face remind me of my palms. When I raise my eyebrows, my forehead pleats, and when the eyebrows come down, the pleats stay. Above the bridge of my nose, two creases stand up like rabbit ears, broadcasting to the world, even when I'm smiling, exactly how I look when I'm frowning — something I catch myself doing all too often lately while concentrating on a task or trying to read the small print.

Experts say that women live eight years longer than men but look old ten years sooner because we lack men's thicker skin and the hair follicles that hold their skin in place. That must explain why the cheerful parentheses at the corners of my smile have started looking downtrodden and my top lip is beginning to produce those spidery vertical creases that soak up lipstick.

Just this year, my jaw, the Maginot Line of facial structure, surrendered to the force of gravity. On each side of my chin the muscles have pulled loose from the bone. Once I had a right-angle profile; now there's a hypoteneuse between my chin and neck.

Which brings me, regrettably, to my neck, with its double choker of lines; and my chest, creased like crepe paper; and my shoulders and arms, which are holding their own for now except for the elbows, which are rough enough to shred a carrot. I don't yet have loose skin on the underside of my upper arm — you know, the part that keeps waving after you've stopped — but I can see it coming.

My "perky" bosom is a thing of the past. The breasts long ago flunked Bette Midler's test: "Put a quarter under each tit; if the coins drop, you're young enough to go braless." My twenty-three-inch waist is ancient history thanks to childbearing and a fondness for brownies. My belly, round even when I'm slim, is flabby, bisected top to bottom with an uneven cesarean scar and limned with pregnancy stretch marks courtesy of my full-term twins.

My pubic area has already been recorded in these pages. (I'm loath to revisit it.) Leeward of it sits a tush that seems to sink a quarter-inch every year, like Venice. My hips aren't as wide as some I've seen, but they're dimpled, which isn't as charming as it sounds. As for my legs — can these possibly be *my* legs? — their once-smooth surface is now splattered with purple capillaries and my knees remind me of the Saggy, Baggy Elephant.

Body Blues

What I've described here is not a maimed or disfigured human being but a *normal* female body in its fifty-fifth year of life. If this inventory conjures up a grotesque image, it's because most of us are not used to confronting the ordinary aesthetic of aging. Modesty demanded that our mothers hide their bodies from view and we have little experience observing other women unclad. While casual nudity is the rule in the men's locker room, shower, and army barracks, women have fewer opportunities for comparative viewing of female bodies of every shape, size, and age. Even in the ladies' locker or the communal dressing rooms at Loehmann's, older women drape their towels and maneuver their underwear so deftly as to keep the body under wraps.

(I happen to be one of them. I've spent the last thirty years hiding my belly from view. Though I don't think there is anything shameful about the way my babies were delivered — surgically, in a great rush after thirteen hours of hard labor — I've been so ashamed of my scarred and pouchy abdomen that I long ago abandoned hope of wearing a bikini and never undress openly anywhere but at home.)

The cultural sphere is as unedifying as the locker room. Rarely, in the lively arts, do we glimpse the older female body, or read adorations of it in poetry or prose (with few exceptions, like *Love in the Time of Cholera*), or see it eroticized in the soft-porn images of advertising. Lauren Hutton is modeling again at fifty, but not without her clothes. The nudes cavorting in classical paintings do not generally include nymphs pushing sixty. Nancy Sinatra posed nude for *Playboy* when she was fifty-four, but her breasts were suspiciously up-tilted and all signs of age, wrinkles, veins, and stretch marks had been airbrushed or excised, thereby making her a fifty-four-year-old impersonator of a twenty-four-year-old Playmate. And I can't recall any steamy sex scenes in the movies featuring over-fifty actresses in the buff, be it Dunaway, Streisand, or even the obsessively fit and lifted Jane Fonda.

How can I help but judge myself harshly as I stand here monitoring every crinkle, sag, and scar? Had I grown up observing the many-splendored incarnations of the aging female body, I might have been more sanguine about its normal permutations and transformations, but failing that, I can only compare my present body with its former self, which is why, when I look into the glass, I see only my flaws. This is not atypical. In *The Summer Before Dark,* Doris Lessing writes of her aging protagonist: "For the whole of her life, or since she was sixteen . . . she had looked into mirrors and seen what other people would judge her by, and now the image had rolled itself up and thrown itself into a corner, leaving behind the face of a sick monkey."

Sick monkey may be a bit strong, but I don't know one woman who harbors an altogether positive body image. My best-looking friends were complaining long before advancing age gave them something to complain about. Even in the early days of feminism, when we were public proselytes of body pride and benign self-acceptance, everyone I knew was griping about some anatomical defect or other. I will always remember the evening when my consciousness-raising group, which met weekly for three years with a different subject for each session, took up the question, "What do we love most and hate most about our bodies?"

The list of positives was short and sweet. One woman loved her hazel eyes, another was pleased she was tall, a third appreciated her curly hair, still another admitted she loved having a small waist though she knew we all hated her for it. I think I spoke well of my feet.

Then we took aim at our negative features — my scarred stomach, that woman's "obscene thighs," this one's small breasts, the next one's "hippo hips" or hairy arms or terrible teeth. Eventually, it was E.'s turn. E. is an elegant Daryl Hannah lookalike; what could she possibly complain about? She's perfect, I thought enviously. She'll have to pass. But E. was fidgeting and squirming like everyone else, trying to work up the courage to speak.

"What I hate most about my body," she said slowly while the rest of us sat at the edge of our seats, "are my nostrils."

It was hard to keep from laughing out loud.

Her *nostrils?!*

"I'm sure you've all noticed how disgustingly huge they are," she continued, covering her nose as if it housed a couple of unsightly sewage pipes. "I don't like people to look into my nostrils; that's why I usually keep my head tilted down." She lowered her chin to her chest, demonstrating the familiar pose that I'd always thought of as her coquette number. In one blazing epiphany I understood that, when it comes to our looks, none of us gets away unscathed, not beautiful young women like E. and certainly not older women, regardless of who they are. A smart, talented, fifty-seven-year-old California woman recently regaled me with the horrors of "UBF" — underbra fat, which I'd never heard of until that very day, though for her it was clearly a well-nursed grievance, one of those indignations she assumed *everyone* understood. "I carry my weight on my back," she explained, "just below the band of the bra. Can't wear anything fitted, or the roll of flesh juts out. Thank God for bustiers." Being one of the world's top-ranking intellectuals didn't spare Simone de Beauvoir, either: "I loathe my appearance now: the eyebrows slipping down toward the eyes, the bags underneath, the excessive fullness of the cheeks and that air of sadness around the mouth that wrinkles always bring."

Deep down, even as I stand here cataloguing my midlife collapse, I know that it's normal for a fifty-five-year-old woman to look more or less as I do and that none of it really matters in the grand scheme of things. "Wrinkles? I'd like to last long enough to *have* wrinkles," says a woman who is HIV-positive. "Bad hair day? Hey, I'm worried about my T-cell count." I realize how lucky I am to be healthy and how well my body has served me under stress. You're not maimed, you're not sick, you're reasonably able-bodied — so shut up, I tell myself, and my inner critic pipes down for a while; but before long, when I'm toweling off or trying on bathing suits in front of a mirror, the voice of self-loathing returns, ranting, "O! that this too too solid flesh would melt. . . ." Bitching about the physical corollaries of aging doesn't change a thing; it just casts a pall of discontent over our lives, and then, eventually, after years of grousing over this or that trivial imperfection, we realize that we should have been appreciating the glories of our younger bodies, flaws and all, because now we are dealing with serious decay.

In a society that reduces every woman to her appearance — a society where, according to Rutgers University psychologist Jeannette Haviland, being attractive turns up at the top of the average female's concerns from age ten on, a society where psychologists at the Oregon Research Institute in Portland found girls as young as twelve to be in a serious state of depression because of their negative body image, it's a brave woman who bucks the system and insists she couldn't care less when age takes the bloom off her rose. The rest of us suffer from what Rita Freedman, psychologist and author of *Bodylove: Learning to Like Our Looks — and Ourselves* calls body-loathing — the "preoccupation and dissatisfaction with appearance . . . anxiety about body parts . . . guilt and shame over flaws that are real or imagined." We care too much and try too hard to resuscitate the rose any way we can.

I, for one, have experimented with mudpacks and moisturizers, herbal wraps and hot tubs, foundations and concealers. I haven't succumbed to collagen cream, Retin-A, face massagers, shark-liver oil, Flash-Lifting, Bag Balm (a salve used to keep cow udders from chapping), or any of the other "revolutionary" antidotes to aging, but I probably would if someone I trusted were to tell me they worked. I also know how tempting it can be to solve all of one's beauty kvetches with a quick fix — a shortcut through the office of a plastic surgeon. Just last spring, I entertained the idea myself.

Cosmetic Surgery and the Politics of Transformation

It started with a small cyst on my back and two bumps, each the size of a lemon pit, on my thigh. For no apparent reason, my skin occasionally produces these outcroppings — my friend Gale calls them the "barnacles of age" — and, given the gaping hole in the ozone layer and the idiosyncrasies of skin cancer, I've learned to take them seriously. Off I went to the dermatologist, who performed minor surgery on the lemon pits and, to my relief, pronounced the bumps benign. At the end of the checkup, the doctor glanced at my face, then at my chart, then again at my face. "You look pretty good for your age," he declared. "But you'd look a hundred percent better without those fat pouches under your eyes."

Like many skin doctors, this guy was also a plastic surgeon and quite the salesman. He sent me home with a stack of brochures describing a half-dozen cosmetic procedures — liposuction for fatty deposits, subcision surgery for wrinkles, exfoliation and dermabrasion for dark circles, sclerotherapy for varicose veins — and a strong pitch for the merits of "cleaning things up a bit." Assuring me that my "problems" would be a simple job for a scalpel or a heavy-duty Hoover, he made it sound just as easy and natural to undo a half-century of wear and tear as it had been to excise the suspicious little barnacles that had brought me to his door.

At first I dismissed the idea out of hand. After all, I was a feminist. But then again . . .

A friend of mine recently had her neck done, and she's thrilled with the results; rightly so, I might add — her turkey folds are gone and she looks fabulous. It took her three years to save up for the $7,000 operation, but she says it was worth every penny because she feels "born again and cute as a kid." Hers was a trouble-free recovery, but I know another woman, Ann Scheiner, who suffered the torments of hell after she had a face-lift. In an article in *Ms.*, she told how her corneas were bruised and her eyelids were stretched so tight that her eyes wouldn't close and her eyeballs dried out, causing her excruciating pain. Though everything turned out fine, when she tallyed the score, the negatives won out.

> On the plus side: a smoother cheek and neckline. I have fewer lines. I know more truths about myself. On the minus side: serious eye problems. Fear of blindness. Hideous swelling and swollen eyes. Numb face and neck which may last for months. A nasty fight with my husband. Loss of identity. Long-lasting scabbing. Loss of weeks of work. Lack of exercise for six weeks. The results last only four to eight years. After that, it's sags and bags again. Cost: $5,300 [in 1986] plus eye-doctor bills.

Several other friends of mine have suffered no ill-effects from their cosmetic procedures, but their faces look strange to me — taut, drawn, expressionless, not-quite-familiar, in the way that Carole Burnett has become almost unrecognizable. I know a woman whose face-lift left the rest of her looking older in comparison — her young head topping off a body with varicose veins and liver spots. In two cases I can think of, nose jobs left women looking almost the same as before. But despite these contradictory outcomes, the possibility of radical transformation inspired me to spend a couple of days reading the brochures and fantasizing about how I might look all "cleaned up." Never mind the cost for the moment (from $400 for collagen injections to about $10,000 for surgery); the first question was, Could I? Would I?

Just thinking about it made me feel like a feminist heretic. But, ironically, the process of exploring the surgery option helped me sort through many ambivalent feelings that I'd managed to repress when I was in the thick of the women's movement and forced me to confront the meaning of appearance and its role in female identity in a more probing way than ever before. Though not every question had an answer, in the end, I knew what I had to do.

I could claim none of the pragmatic excuses that people often cite to justify plastic surgery. I didn't need a youthful appearance to compete in the job market, since writers can hide behind their words. I wasn't disfigured by an accident (other than the accident of age), and as a long-married wife, I didn't have to compete with thirty-five-year-olds in the man market. My husband said he thought I looked just fine as is, which seems to be the typical reaction of men who haven't opted to trade in their older wives for younger versions. Long-married husbands are guilty of many sins, but disdaining their wives' laugh lines isn't usually one of them. Witness Karl Marx, of all people, who wrote to his wife, "There are actually many females in the world, and some among them are beautiful. But where could I find again a face whose every feature, even every wrinkle, is a reminder of the greatest and sweetest memories of my life?"

What are wrinkles after all but time's signature, etched proof that one has lived? "After a certain number of years," writes Cynthia Ozick, "our faces become our biographies." When the rings in a tree trunk reveal a redwood to be thick with age, we are taken with the thought of how much the tree must have seen and survived. Shouldn't we be at least as respectful of the time lines in our own faces? And shouldn't birthing scars count as much in the annals of heroism as any soldier's battle scars?

If my fatty pouches have had no injurious impact on my love life or professional status, and if I wasn't planning to pass myself off as a forty-year-old, why was I even *thinking* about surgery? The answer that kept coming back at me was, Why not? When my husband and I got tired of the cramped layout of our house, we took down a wall between two rooms and everything was transformed. We didn't agonize over the politics of home improvement, we made a purely aesthetic judgment. Why shouldn't I do the same when it came to *self*-improvement? Women all over the world were doing it, including professors of women's studies, and old warhorses of feminism. (In 1990, nearly 50,000 face-lifts were performed in the United States, 91 percent of them done on women, 58 percent on those fifty-one or older. The total number of tummy rehabs was 20,213, 93 percent done on women.) What would be so terrible about giving myself a nip and tuck as a midlife present? It might even be an adventure.

When all was said and done, my dilemma was shaping up as a straightforward face-off between me and my face or, one could say, between personal aesthetics and the politics of transformation.

A Tale of Two Artists

Orlan, a forty-seven-year-old French multimedia artist, uses plastic surgery as a sculptor's chisel. Over the last few years, she has undergone seven operations on her face, each of them transmitted via satellite from her hospital room to a gallery audience as part of her work in progress — having her skin and bones reconfigured into a perfect amalgam of the faces of Venus, Diana, and Mona Lisa.

Orlan's "art" strikes me as certifiably pathological, but it does put my flirtation with plastic surgery in bas relief. I ask myself what female archetypes are guiding my fantasy of perfection? Where would I draw the line? Is making young bodies and beautiful faces God's turf or ours? If I believe human beings were put on earth for a purpose and that purpose is to improve and repair the world, how does self-repair contribute to that goal?

The second artist, Joan Semmel, is a painter who depicts women in the process of aging. Perhaps her most provocative series is "Over-Lays," in which she reworks — paints over — pictures of women that she originally painted in the 1970s, altering their faces and bodies in much the same way that nature alters any woman over the course of twenty years. "It is difficult to believe that an artist would, in effect, destroy her earlier work to present a more mature perspective," commented one admiring critic, "but no artist has created a more convincing way to convey the changes brought by time." Semel's work reproaches me: shouldn't I let time's artistry paint over my youthful image?

Two women artists, two attitudes toward women's aging. Orlan's face — sliced, stitched, smoothed, and reconstituted — strikes me as the sculpture of self-loathing. Semmel's canvases — youth revisited and revised, lined with age, and layered with reality — are the paintings of self-acceptance. Despite the pain and risk in Orlan's choice, Semmel's is the braver art. Yet I can't stop thinking about liposuction.

What keeps popping into my mind is the big difference a small operation can make. A few years ago, a friend had surgery to "fix" her large, prominent nose, and while meaningful life changes are not supposed to happen from the outside in, it is clear to all who know her that this woman's new profile has affected her soul and psyche. She no longer covers her nose with her hand when people look at her. She smiles more often. She's more relaxed; even a bit flamboyant. Where once she wore only browns, blacks, and grays, now red is her favorite color.

"It's not that I needed to be gorgeous," she tells me, "but I needed *not* to feel ugly. Now I don't have to think about my face anymore. I can just be me."

Still another friend, who looked perfectly presentable before, gave herself an eye-lift for her fiftieth birthday. For the life of me, I can't tell the difference, but she says, "Now, when I look at my face, it matches the way I feel inside."

What's a feminist to say to that? If someone believes that a natural "God-given" physical feature distracts from her true self and makes her feel uneasy, is it more sisterly to lecture her about the superficiality of beauty or to support her decision to look better so that she can feel better? Likewise, if a woman — or a man, for that matter (men account for 28 percent of facial plastic surgery), feels diminished or disoriented by the natural manifestations of the aging process, why shouldn't she be able to change them to make herself feel better? (For argument's sake, I'm assuming she can afford the surgery.)

Fundamental to these questions is the tension between artificiality and authenticity, and the issue of whether the former can legitimately serve the latter. If, during her search for a self that is at peace with all its parts, a woman feels the need for a closer fit between her exterior and interior, between surface and substance as it were, who's to say artificial means should not be used to achieve a deeper authenticity, a more integrated wholeness? What's so terrible about a relatively safe surgical procedure that doesn't harm anyone else and leaves her feeling more in tune with herself? And why should such a private decision be subject to coercive philosophical debate? Because, you might reply, each person who elects cosmetic surgery is helping to sustain the oppressive youth=beauty standard by bowing to it and validating the idea that aging is something that has to be "fixed" or "cured." True enough; however, isn't it also unfair to expect any one individual to ignore her private pain (or social and economic needs) in order to prove a point?

Face It: Looks Count

Arthur Marwick, a British professor and an expert on beauty, claims that physical attractiveness is more important to individual success today than at any time since the Renaissance. A host of studies by American psychologists and plastic surgeons have determined beyond a reasonable doubt that positive changes in a person's physical appearance can, as one put it, "directly enhance her or his social value" and lead to "more satisfying and comfortable lives." Nola Rocco, author of *A Facelift Is a Bargain,* argues that the average face-lift costs $10,000 and takes ten years off a woman's life, which amortizes the cost of instant youth to $1,000 per year, or less than

$3 a day. And the surgery pays for itself within two years, says Rocco, because youthful looks lead to job advancement and social contacts that yield increased financial rewards.

If youthfulness is so economically potent, how far should a woman go to gain its advantages? Should she draw the line at makeup? Hair coloring? Diet? Surgery? Or should she just keep complaining about the coercive power of youth and beauty?

One reason why these questions drive middle-aged women to distraction is that we prefer to believe others admire us for ourselves, and we define our "selves" as more than our surface appearance — although I'm not sure why how we look is any less *us* than, say, how we sing, which also is genetically determined. People are criticized for "using" their looks but never for "using" their God-given voices or other inborn talent. Furthermore, if self-improvement is a reasonable rationale for voice lessons that might help a person sing better, why shouldn't self-improvement be a reasonable motivation for cosmetic surgery that might make a person look better?

Then again, whose idea of "better" are we talking about here? Obviously, what is making me question my looks at this moment in time is the incessantly touted youth-and-beauty ideal. But am I not already surrendering to that ideal every time I put on blush or pluck my eyebrows? When do cosmetic improvements pass out of the realm of acceptable enhancement and into the realm of vanity, self-absorption, or self-mutilation?

Another reason why the whole discussion makes us dizzy is that we're not sure attractiveness is a legitimate value in the first place. By drastically altering her looks, the older woman affirms the supremacy of youth and perpetuates the value of appearances, thus handing a victory to the advertising folks who made her uncomfortable about her looks to begin with. But wait a minute: if the will to improve on nature is strictly the result of commercial manipulation, how do we explain the elaborate face painting and body adornment found in some tribal societies 6,000 miles from Madison Avenue? Those folks didn't need 30-second spots to sell them on elongating their necks or wearing rings in their noses. Since every culture responds to *some* well-defined beauty ideal, and the existence of an ideal is an anthropological fact of life, why single out the Western beauty standard for special criticism? Is it any more reprehensible that Western-trained eyes respond to our standards of beauty than that Western-trained ears prefer harmony to dissonance?

We're told that beauty is in the eye of the beholder, as if it were some quirky individualized perception, yet survey after survey shows a remarkable consensus among people of all ages and races about what makes a face attractive. In women, the preferred features are symmetrical and youthful, large wide-set eyes, high cheekbones, narrow jaw, full lips; for men, it's the all-American look, a strong, well-defined jawline, and traditionally even "masculine" features. While our mothers may have taught us that beauty is only skin deep, psychologsts Ellen Berscheid, Karen Dion, and Elaine Walster have identified an "attractiveness stereotype" — a common belief that "what is beautiful is good." In addition to benefiting from the bias toward attractiveness, good-looking people enjoy a "halo effect" — a much-enhanced image that inspires many positive associations. Specifically, better-looking individuals are assumed to be "more sensitive, kind, interesting, strong, poised, modest, sociable, outgoing, exciting and sexually warm and responsive persons [who] will capture better jobs, have more successful marriages and experience happier and more fulfilling lives." Since human beings tend to rise to others' expectations, it's no surprise that beautiful people often *become* more sensitive, kind, interesting, strong, poised and so on. (Syllogism: if what is beautiful is good, and most people equate beauty with youth, we can surmise that what is young is good, and conversely, what is old, isn't.)

In the social science literature, one finds innumerable examples of the halo effect working its magic and bringing its rewards to good-looking people throughout the life cycle. For instance, studies show that baby nurses attribute higher intelligence to cuter babies; mothers hold, kiss, and cuddle attractive babies more often but offer unattractive babies more stimuli as if to develop other strengths to compensate for the infants' lesser looks; teachers are more likely to attribute high IQs to good-looking children than to plain-looking kids and tend to discount a cute child's misconduct while the same behavior from a homely child is thought indicative of poor character.

By the same token, looks prejudice can have far-reaching impact in both social and economic terms. Child development researchers have found, for instance, that by age three or four, kids show a clear preference for more attractive playmates and call their unattractive peers — and old people, in general — scary, aggressive, and unfriendly. Other studies discovered that managers faced with a pair of job applicants with comparable qualifications tend to hire the more attractive of the two. In the courtroom, jurors are less likely to find attractive offenders guilty, and when good-looking culprits *are* found guilty, jurors are more likely to impose shorter sentences on them than on plainer defendants. More attractive mental patients receive more visitors and are discharged sooner than unattractive patients who may be equally disruptive or disturbed. And prison convicts who underwent plastic surgery to correct their physical deformities had a far lower recidivism rate than deformed convicts who did not improve their appearance.

This calls for a few rounds on the chicken-and-egg front: Which comes first, being attractive (or young) and therefore likable, or acting in likable ways that make one *seem* attractive? Do we merely *perceive* unattractive (or older) people as unpleasant or have they actually *become* less nice as a result of years of disdain or discrimination? The answers to these questions and others raised by the research on attractiveness have obvious relevance to women over fifty, because if the aging face is scorned as ugly, then every older woman is subject to the same prejudices that are directed to people who are judged to be unattractive from the git-go.

Since most of the attractiveness surveys use photographs to measure a subject's response to a given face, and since a two-dimensional image can't capture such three-dimensional "looks enhancers" as personality, energy, warmth, or style, the research results may not be borne out with complete accuracy in real life. Nevertheless, even with their limitations, the findings are troubling, for they make clear that, as much as race, class, and gender, the face a woman is born with, and the face that ages with her, elicits a particular set of reactions from almost everyone who crosses her path and thus affects how she is treated in all aspects of her life.

It is obvious that plain-looking women suffer in a beauty-biased culture, but so do the golden girls when age finally dims their halos. Several studies indicate that the more a woman relies on her looks when she is young, the harder it is for her to get older. Put another way, exceptionally good-looking women are less happy in their middle age than those who had been average-looking. While that result may seem to contradict the weighty evidence of looks favoritism, it makes sense in a culture where faded beauty is discarded as quickly as yesterday's newspaper. It can be a rude shock for a beautiful woman to find herself unseen in midlife or judged on other merits after years of having been adored simply for *being*.

Our mothers were right when they instinctively enriched the development of their less attractive daughters. If a little girl knows she can't win attention by being adorable, she tends to build on the strengths she finds in books, sports, art, and doing the best she can. As she ages, she has those other resources at her disposal, and rather than abide the withdrawal symptoms of the femme fatale, she has other means of attraction. On the other hand, the punishments of beauty may include being taken less seriously, being given less academic training, and being expected to survive and flourish on her looks.

This may offer some belated satisfaction to us average types, but whether or not the game of looks evens out in the end, we can all agree that it's not worth the suffering it costs us: for both sexes, feelings of inadequacy and rejection; for all women, objectification and internalized shame; for minority women, the pressure to meet a beauty standard defined by the white majority; for beautiful women, the built-in obsolescence of aging; for moderately attractive women, the gnawing sense of never being pretty enough; for plain women, the feeling of being unlovable and unloved; and for aging women, the fear of losing whatever advantages their looks may have given them in a world that doesn't offer very many other advantages to women.

Knowing all this, we continue to be confounded by the youth=beauty imperative and oblivious to its many contradictions: We complain because looks count so much to others, yet we can't seem to admit to ourselves that looks count to us, too. We claim to find a variety of faces appealing, including older faces, yet the vast majority of us have been found to respond most positively to faces that are young and conventionally pretty. We know from experience that looks become less important the more people know or love each other, yet most of us still make an effort to look good for our friends and loved ones. Bert and I often marvel at how pleased we are when one of our kids says, "Gee, Dad, you look terrific," or "Mom, I love your hair." If looks don't matter — if inner beauty is what counts — why do they notice and why do we care? We teach children that looks don't matter, yet we live in a country in which millions more dollars are spent on beauty and fashion than on education or social services. We purport to hate vanity, especially in women, yet advertisers use women's beauty to sell everything from shaving cream to automobiles.

In the process of battling the beauty ideal, many thinkers have denied the undeniable, which is that we respond to one another's outward appearance before we have the opportunity to explore each other's inner beauty. What attractiveness boils down to is the capacity to *attract*, to draw others to us, and for a person to want that capacity is normal, nonsexist, and human. So, too, is the pleasure we derive from putting ourselves together artfully, from bringing our particular aesthetic vision to life on our own bodies and, yes, from looking at ourselves in the mirror and pronouncing the image fair. In her search for a more authentic self, her essential self, a middle-aged woman may discover that authentic doesn't necessarily mean unembellished. For some people, decorating the surfaces of life — the human body, a garden, architecture, the wall over one's desk — may be an expression of the artist in Everywoman, a deeper impulse to beautify the world. And without that impulse, the earth would be a gray and gloomy place.

Though dilemmas related to physical attractiveness continue to plague women of every age, race, and class, surprisingly few feminist thinkers write about or study beauty, weight, clothing, and personal style, except as instruments of oppression, or retrograde bourgeois concerns that are beneath concern if not contempt. During my seventeen years at *Ms.* magazine, whenever we ran an article on looks, a large portion of our reader mail contained letters from purists who thought the subject too trivial to engage the interest of serious minds. Such sanctimonious attitudes make many women, including feminists, feel guilty when they attend to their appearance, whether to take pleasure in it or because they are worried about how they look. Such was the ideologically induced guilt that plagued me after my visit to the dermatologist while I was grappling with the implications of cosmetic surgery.

Then something curious happened. Though I'd taken a detour through my brain, the answer to my dilemma came to me straight from my body. Weeks after the procedure, my barnacles still hurt like the dickens. They were not healing properly; twice a day, I had to bathe them, change the dressings, and take antibiotics to deal with an incipient infection. I had no patience for it. If the aftermath of such minor surgery demanded so much fuss and bother, how would I ever tolerate recuperating from having my face stapled? The wounds took months to heal and, if you ask me, the scars look worse than the original blemishes. I chose to read this development as a sign. My skin was telling me that it did not want to be messed with. I would keep my first-edition face. I would make the best of my maternal belly. There would be no dramatic transformation in my future.

Even if the barnacles hadn't spoken, my obsession with time would have decided the issue. Though most surgeons say patients are back to normal in three to ten weeks, an actress friend of mine, a veteran of three operations, told me that it takes six months after each face-lift before she is fully able to resume her everyday life. And she has to repeat the surgery every six or eight years to keep pace with gravity. Plus she's beginning to feel like an old house with freshly painted window frames that make the rest of the exterior look shabby. "So I'll probably have to do something about these flabby upper arms," she says, "and have a tummy tuck, and maybe some liposuction on my thighs. Oh, where will it all end?"

Recovering from liposuction, currently the most popular cosmetic procedure in America, can also take six months when one factors in the pain, numbness, bruising, depigmentation, weeks of limited activity trussed up in a girdle, not to mention possible infection and clotting.

In the end, it wasn't politics but fear that turned me away from the quick fix — fear of pain, misery, and medical mishaps. I would not risk all that to be rid of a couple of fat pouches. But even with a guarantee of safe recovery, trading time for looks struck me as a bad bargain. Time fanatics like me do not have six months to kill waiting to heal behind closed doors. I could see that an actress has her career to protect, and other women might be motivated by economic or emotional needs, for which I don't condemn them. Each of us must make this decision for herself for her own reasons, and I decided I had no compelling reason to sacrifice the time of my life for the possibility of looking a few years younger. The physical improvement would be a short-lived illusion, but the lost months would be real and they would be gone forever.

Diversionary Tactics

For women past fifty, these are the choices: We can consider each new sign of age a cause for shame, or a badge of life experience. We can say that we are degenerating — or transmogrifying. We can devote our remaining years to what Zelda Fitzgerald called "the art of being: being young, being lovely, being an object" or we can use that time — time our treasure, time our life, time that is all we have — to turn our attention to other things. But that is precisely what the capitalist system cannot permit to happen, because women who turn their attention to other things cease to be a "market" for all the products whose bottom line depends on the youth=beauty equation. As has been well documented by Susan Faludi in *Backlash* and Naomi Wolf in *The Beauty Myth,* formidable forces have conspired to prevent women from turning their attention to other things, which is what started happening in the late 1960s with the rise of the women's movement.

As soon as millions of women began focusing on their larger aspirations, demanding economic and political power and eroding the male monopoly of public life, the color of their eye shadow became less important to them. That's when the defenders of the status quo shifted into overdrive to promote the idea that a woman *is* her body, and whatever else she might be is secondary, and what matters most is not just how pretty she looks but how young. Both Faludi and Wolf have shown how the cosmetic business and the media systematically upped the ante on youth, targeting this message to older women, since we were the ones gearing up to storm the barricades. With our credentials, our relative freedom from family responsibilities, our new sense of entitlement, and our sudden disregard for makeup, bras, and beauty, the older woman became a serious threat to corporate interests. As Carolyn Heilbrun put it, "Nobody ever made money saying: 'If you just want to gain weight, do it. If you just want to let your hair go gray and wear it in a bun, do it.'" So the older woman's attention had to be redirected to her looks; she had to be persuaded that her first priority was to attend to her inadequacies and try to recondition her pathetically aging face and body.

Of course, besides creating consumers of beauty products, the pursuit of youth creates consumers of time. If we can be kept busy competing with women for men's approval, we will have less time left to compete with men for power. If we can be sidetracked into searching for the right anti-age cream, the right diet, and the right hair color, we will have less time to devote to the struggle for our rights. If we can be convinced that it's possible for us to compete with younger women on the youth=beauty scale, we doom ourselves to certain failure, fighting a losing battle. Like Sisyphus, who was condemned to keep pushing a heavy rock up a hill in Hades only to have it roll down again as it neared the top, we keep falling short of the beauty goal, leading to a steady loss of confidence and a consequent need for even more products to fight the youth game; our jealousy, anxiety, and body-loathing erode whatever midlife energy might otherwise be channeled into worldly pursuits. We become so preoccupied with how we look that we lose sight of how we want to spend our lives, or where we might contribute to society, or what's wrong with this picture. As one woman put it, "If I could stop thinking about my weight, my hair, and my face, I'd have time to make the revolution."

In *Backlash*, Faludi charts the rise of an ever more stringent beauty ideal that has glorified the girlish, if not the absolutely infantile, in an attempt to intimidate the average woman out of her growing aspirations. Faludi documents how, just as the largest portion of the population was entering middle age, American commerce and culture promoted the teenager as the feminine ideal. Just as women were entering the workplace in droves and breaking into management and other nontraditional fields, and just when most families needed two incomes to make ends meet and more and more single mothers were struggling to support their families alone, the reigning look in fashion became the street urchin and the disheveled, erotically degraded Guess girl, neither of whom seemed capable of balancing a checkbook, not to mention holding a day job. And just when the average "real" woman weighed 143 pounds and wore a size 10 or 12, the weight of the average fashion model fell to 23 percent below her ordinary sisters', the beauty magazines hyped the emaciated waif, and the Miss America contestants and *Playboy* centerfolds became increasingly thinner. The hedonistic message of our culture is, do it if it makes you feel good, but society's unrealistic ideal means you'll never feel good no matter what you do.

Four studies reported in the journal *Sex Roles* by psychologists Brett Silverstein of City College of New York and Lauren Perdue, Barbara Peterson, and Eileen Kelly of the State University of New York at Stony Brook proved that the female bodyweight ideal as seen on television and in movies and magazines "is slimmer now than it has been in the past." With the obvious exception of Roseanne, the typical media star has gotten steadily slimmer over the last few decades, far thinner than what was considered attractive at any previous time in the twentieth century, and far thinner than any weight standard that might reasonably be expected of the average woman, especially if she is over forty. According to Vivian Meehan, president of the National Association of Anorexia Nervosa and Associated Disorders, "The current female ideal is only apropos for 5 percent of the population."

It can't be mere coincidence that all this has come to pass since the rebirth of feminism. Making the impossible obligatory turns out to be a highly effective form of social control. As long as the profit motive requires that women believe aging is unattractive, there is nothing so threatening as a woman who feels good about herself and ready to take on the world. So that's when they zap us: Watch out woman, you're losing your youthful glow! Beware of sagging skin! Sinking sex appeal! Younger women on the prowl for your man! Middle-age spread! The propaganda put forth incessantly by the beauty industry has made the aging female appear unsavory and in dire need of repair. "They call these age spots," pouts a woman in a skin cream ad. "I call them *ugly!* But what's a woman to do?" Such messages have intensified the demonization of age, warning women of the penalties for wrinkles and gray hair, traits that might otherwise be seen as honorable markings of wisdom and power.

Reviewing *The Beauty Myth* in *The Nation,* Gayle Greene, a professor at Scripps College, writes:

> As Wolf emphasizes, the devaluing of older women also eradicates female power. Whereas older men move into positions of prominence — and power is eroticized for men but not for women — older women have to be made to disappear. Making our aging appear unseemly, unsightly, unacceptable assures that we will. Moreover it performs the crucial work of cutting the links between generations of women and assuring that power is not passed on. This is why the caricature of the Ugly Feminist appears with every backlash — to scare young women away from identifying with older women and prevent the transmission of authority. The Beauty Myth not only sets women in competition with one another on a daily basis but sets younger women against older, which is part of the reason the struggle for women's rights has to begin anew with each generation.

The intimidation works because women know the punishment for nonconformity. If we fight the youth=beauty imperative and let age have its way with us, it's a good bet that we will lose out on something — respect, attention, love, money.

"Women are not forgiven for aging," said Jane Fonda, now fifty-eight. "Robert Redford's lines of distinction are my old-age wrinkles."

Kathleen Turner, who is just past forty, said she paid an emotional and professional price when she put on fifteen pounds to play a character part. While actors like Robert De Niro and Tom Hanks have been admired for accommodating to the physical demands of their movie roles, Turner was punished for it. "The assumption was not that I was acting, but that I was losing my attractiveness because I was getting older," she told an interviewer. "I was quite shocked, and I became overly sensitized to the incredible pressure of 'How do you look today?' . . . All I could hear in the last couple of years was people commenting on my looks. 'You look great today,' or 'You look better,' which is even worse — I hate that. Or 'You look tired.' . . . The body of work that one has built . . . is not considered as important a factor as appearance."

Hollywood may be a bit heavy-handed in policing the female beauty standard, but women in all walks of life are punished just as systematically when they dare to slack off or rebel against the youth imperative. The nonconformist is called "hag," "witch," "old bag" or lately, "feminazi." She is stigmatized as a lesbian. (She must hate men, why else would she refuse to look pretty?) High achievers have more on their minds than headbands; they worry about bigger things than the length of their hair, skirts, or nails. Yet women like Hillary Clinton, Attorney General Janet Reno, Secretary of Health and Human Services Donna Shalala, former congresswoman Bella Abzug, Ambassador Madeleine Albright, the U.S. representative to the U.N., or Carol Bellamy, the director of UNICEF, are routinely subjected to media judgments about their looks. Journalists have had unkind things to say about their clothes, hairstyles, and general attractiveness, and columnists and talk show blatherers who rarely comment on the physical appearance of men in comparable positions have floated innuendos about the women's sexuality. The message is clear: You can be as successful as you want, girls, but guys won't like it if you don't give them something good to look at. So you may as well play the game.

That's how the system works. That's why the manufacturers of diet products rake in $33 billion a year; the cosmetics industry, $20 billion; the plastic surgeons, $300 million and climbing. That's why American women bring a terrible ambivalence to the issue of age and appearance. In a 1994 Clinique survey, 74 percent of the respondents said they "accept aging as a natural part of life and are not concerned with looking young," and nearly 96 percent answered the question "Does beauty equal youth?" with a resounding "No." Yet in the same survey, seven in ten said they are willing to do whatever they can to stay young-looking!

That's why "How do I look?" has become the dominant question in so many women's lives. Susan Faludi documented the phenomenon in the 1990s, but Mary Wollstonecraft had the whole thing figured out back in the 1790s, when she wrote: "Taught from infancy that beauty is woman's scepter, the mind shapes itself to the body, and roaming around its gilt cage only seeks to adorn its prison."

As sometimes happens with me and feminist theory, I agree completely with the analysis but not necessarily with where it leads. I may want to fight the commercialization of youth, but that doesn't mean I choose to age au naturel. I may deplore the way advertising manipulates my "needs" to get me to buy more beauty products, but I'm not sure I want to go through the day looking exactly as I do when I wake up. Brainwashed or not, it's too late to undo the damage. And now my problem is that, while I wish it weren't true, the fact is, I care about how I look, therefore I invest time in my appearance, therefore I worry that the older I get, the more time it will take to keep myself presentable. To lose so many precious hours every week attending to one's lost looks strikes me as a bad bargain, especially for women over fifty, who have shrinking futures.

Youth, Truth, or Something In-Between

"I'd give a year for an inch off each thigh," said a friend. I've heard that sort of hyperbole often enough to wonder, *would* anyone actually forfeit time to be rid of a bodily imperfection? The question is not rhetorical. Like everything else, beauty isn't just about looks, it's about time. According to the Clinique survey, the average woman spends slightly more than fifteen minutes getting ready in the morning and slightly more than ten minutes on her nighttime routine for a total of nearly a half hour a day, every day. But 22 percent of American women spend an hour or more each day on their beauty routine, which, assuming eight hours of sleep, translates to at least one-sixteenth of their waking hours. Put another way, every sixteen days, these women have lost a day of their lives just by fixing their faces.

I'm not sure how much time my looks are worth, or how many hours (months? years?) of the rest of my life I am willing to devote to the energy-depleting, high-maintenance effort to get the old carcass up to snuff. Is it worth the time it takes to follow the fashion magazines, the time it takes to prowl the cosmetics counters checking out the most up-to-date anti-age products, the time it takes to visit the hairdresser, or shop for flattering clothes (never mind what these things cost, for the moment, which is absurd in itself). Is it worth the time spent applying makeup and taking it off, over and over again, day after day, year after year? Is it worth the time it takes to earn the money to wage this incessant war against age? Right now, in the shank of life, the best of the last good years, how many quarts of this lifeblood, time, am I — is any woman — willing to sacrifice on the altar of youth? And suppose I decide to claim that time for other uses — suppose I "let myself go" as they say — am I prepared for the consequences?

Doris Lessing said she welcomed the consequences: "All one's life as a young woman one is on show, a focus of attention, people notice you. You set yourself up to be noticed and admired. And then, not expecting it, you become middle-aged and anonymous. No one notices you. You achieve a wonderful freedom. It is a positive thing. You can move about, unnoticed and invisible."

Carolyn Heilbrun has expressed similar views with an even more assertive conclusion. She believes that as women accumulate power and accomplishments, we won't need youth and beauty; we'll keep the attention of the world the way older men do, and the way Margaret Mead did when she stood five feet tall, weighed 180 pounds, and wore her gray hair in a bun. Heilbrun writes, "As older women we will have to be what we do; we will watch ourselves grow invisible to youth worshipers and to the male gaze. Despair is inevitable, but must be wrestled with. . . . We will be mysteriously unseen. We will not be noticed immediately upon entering a store, a party, a meeting. We will move invisibly for a time, to relearn seeing and to forget being seen. As we grow slowly visible, we will be heard more and seen less. Our voices will ramify, our bodies will become the house for our new spirit."

Not me, thank you. I may protest women's bodies being objectified, but I don't want my body to exist solely as a container for my spirit. I don't want to be defined as present or absent in the world according to the judgment of youth worshippers or the whimsy of the male gaze. Still, I'm confused: I admire accomplished women in gray buns — women like Heilbrun herself, and Mead, Golda Meir, Hannah Arendt, and Maggie Kuhn, the late founder of the Gray Panthers and a fierce opponent of age discrimination — women who care about ideas, justice, and other people, and don't give a fig how they look. I admire what they do and what they stand for; the trouble is, I don't necessarily want to look like them. Of course, female human beings should be taken seriously, heard more and seen (gazed at, slobbered over) less, but in return we shouldn't have to be corporeal nonentities. "You can be a sex object or you can be invisible" strikes me as a Hobson's choice. There's got to be another way for the older woman to be physically present in the world.

To consciously promote the beauty of the seasoned sex symbol and make older women appear okay in their own eyes and the eyes of the young would take a billion-dollar advertising campaign, assuming any company had the motive to do it. They probably couldn't make bifocals erotic, but there might be a bright future for slogans like "Laugh lines are lovable," "Gray is glamorous," or "I want to be around someone who's been around."

Right now, I can think of very few manufacturers whose ads use attractive older women (or men, for that matter) to sell their products, but the campaigns that do exist are heartwarming and memorable.

Revlon features the headline "This is our prime time. Let's make the most of it," illustrated by the gap-toothed supermodel Lauren Hutton, who is now past fifty and enjoying renewed success. When the news media interviewed Hutton about her career comeback, she described what it had been like to hit bottom in her mid-forties: "I'd stopped looking at *Vogue*. It was painful to always see very young girls, because you compare yourself to them. Now I understand how always seeing tall, skinny white girls is bad for everybody. We should have a choice of what's considered beautiful in femininity." For her sake and ours let's hope Hutton is allowed to keep working as she ages. Maybe she'll be as lucky as Carmen Dell'Orefice, a favorite model of such designers as Donna Karan, Isaac Mizrahi, and Jean-Paul Gaultier, who is busy doing magazine fashion layouts and runway shows in Paris, Milan, and New York — at the age of sixty-four.

Nike classes up one of its full-page ads with a beaming, confident-looking woman, identified as fifty years old, who calls her time of life "the age of elegance." Another Nike ad features two great-looking outdoorswomen in their seventies, canoeing guides in Minnesota, who "don't have time to grow old." Neutrogena shows pretty women who have discernible time lines and crow's feet and who openly discuss aging. In one ad, the actress Nanette Fabray reveals herself to be "over sixty." In another, instrumentalist Eugenia Zukerman says, "I want to keep playing the flute until my teeth fall out. . . ."

Banana Republic has run ethereal full-page pictures of young people lounging around with a much older couple who are immensely striking though white-haired and deeply wrinkled. The headline simply says, "American Beauty."

"Beauty isn't about looking young, but looking good," trumpets Clinique, whose current campaign accentuates health, not youth. One of their most appealing models is sixty-four; it says so right above her picture. The company's chief executive told the *New York Times* that Clinique has banished the word "young" from all its advertising, and its sales people have been given sensitivity training to help them interact with customers of every age.

Of course, what fuels these campaigns is not a sudden attack of feminist guilt, but a fiercely competitive profit motive. America is aging fast, and business is beginning to realize that appealing to older women via our inferiority complex has its limitations. However cynical the conscience of capitalists, we thank them for small favors. In the process of enhancing their sales, they also happen to be enhancing our self-esteem by showing us examples of vibrant females well beyond the age of consent.

In *The Beauty Myth,* Naomi Wolf describes the cognitive choices that are required in order for the image of the older woman to become positive, respected, and lovable:

> You could see the signs of female aging as diseased. Or you could see that if a woman is healthy she lives to grow old; as she thrives, she reacts and speaks and shows emotion, and grows into her face. Lines trace her thoughts and radiate from the corners of her eyes after decades of laughter. . . . You could call the lines a network of 'serious lesions,' or you could see that in a precise calligraphy, thought has etched marks of concentration between her brows, and drawn across her forehead the horizontal creases of surprise, delight, compassion and good talk. . . . The darkening under her eyes, the weight of her lids, their minute cross-hatching, reveal that what she has been part of has left in her its complexity and richness. She is darker, stronger, looser, tougher, sexier. The maturing of a woman who has continued to grow is a beautiful thing to behold.

This portrait was enough to send me back to the mirror for a rematch.

Finding One's Own Look

Stated broadly, the question I have to answer for myself is, will I let myself go to seed or will I spend my life pruning and irrigating? In my middle age, I seem to prefer the middle ground. At this point, I am happiest when I steer clear of extremes — both the doctrinaire ideal that disdains makeup and fashion and the mainstream ideal of painted perfectionism. I hope never to become a caricature of femininity but, much as I respect Heilbrun and Lessing, I also refuse to voluntarily disappear.

Where does this leave me, a feminist in her fifties who cares about her looks and wishes she didn't; a woman torn between her aesthetic imperatives and her refusal to waste the time it would take to satisfy them? The simple answer is, I've opted to work at my appearance to whatever extent helps me feel good enough to free myself to work at what really matters to me. In other words, I spend as much time on my looks as it takes to get myself to the point where I can forget about them.

This policy translates into some admittedly quirky habits. Even when I'm alone in the house, I wear perfume and lipstick; without them I feel incomplete, like a painting without a frame or a stool missing a leg. I choose to color my hair, use blush, and wear mascara when I go out, all because I can't stand myself in drab. I could bore you with more of this, but the point is not what I do or don't do, it's that each woman should do only what is right for her and what makes her feel comfortable, confident, and relaxed about her looks.

Coming to terms with my face and body has been part cop-out and part compromise. As much as I might wish for an ideal world in which only the *person* matters, I've stopped kidding myself or trying to deny that appearance plays a major role in our lives when nearly every woman I've ever known and all the research I've ever read tell me otherwise. After a quarter-century of feminist proselytizing, I don't hold out much hope for a grassroots revolution on the beauty issue. Sure, substance should win over surface, but I've come to accept that surface counts for something and must be reckoned with because how we look is one of the many ways we express who we are.

These days, I'm into the truth, and the truth is, I'm not crazy about my looks, but I can live with them — in a different way, with a different emphasis. What jolted me out of my low-grade Body Image Blues was the death of friends felled by cancer in the prime of their lives. Sitting through my third funeral within six months, I wept for the forty-eight-year-old woman who was no more; I watched her children trying to absorb their loss, and I suddenly flashed on the absurdity, the colossal arrogance of vanity. How *dare* anyone complain about this wrinkle or that bulge when we have the incredible gift of life, I thought — as if I were the first person ever to stumble over a truism in the dark. Why should it take three deaths to make someone see the enervating foolishness of women's youth quest?

Because the desire to be beautiful runs that deep in the psyche; because it is rooted in the tender soil of our parents' praise and irrigated by male tributes and buried beneath all the rich topsoil of cultural propaganda.

After the third funeral, I tuned into life on a new dimension. I saw my body not as face, skin, hair, figure, but as the vehicle through which I could experience everything my friend would never know again. For days, I felt so grateful to be alive that I nearly burst into tears at the sight of my husband and children. Ordinary pleasures seemed so precious that I vowed to set my priorities straight before some fatal illness did it for me. Since then I have been trying to focus on the things that really matter. And I can assure you that being able to wear a bikini isn't one of them.

I still think about my appearance, but it doesn't rule my life. I try to make my own rules. Most of the time, I concentrate on how I feel and what I'm doing rather than on how I look. Better yet, I concentrate on other people, and real problems, and how I might make a difference. I'm much kinder to myself than I used to be — or than advertisers would have me be. I try not to judge myself by impossible beauty standards nor to compare myself to younger, prettier women. I try to decode social pressures before they can make me feel inadequate. Though I am the beholder whose opinion matters most, I try to see my body through the eyes of my husband, who says he's quite pleased with it. I try to focus on my good features (my feet are still nice), and I don't feel guilty when I give my bad features a helping hand. I believe a woman need not look entirely natural to be entirely real, and shouldn't have to be drab to be taken seriously as a thinking person. I do what feels right to me. I don't look in the mirror more often than necessary. And though it makes me feel well taken care of to take care of myself, I try not to spend a lot of time fixing my face. At my age, I have more important things to do.

When it comes to hair and clothes, my new motto is NO MORE PAIN. No matter how gorgeous it is, if it makes me uncomfortable, forget it; I've done my time suffering for feminine fashion. "Beauty hurts," said my mother, as if that explained everything. She wasn't being insensitive, she was just initiating me into womanhood. When I was little, beauty usually hurt from the neck up as I endured "one hundred strokes" with a bristle brush to make my hair shine, and braids plaited tight enough to raise the eyebrows. Once, my mother gave me a foul-smelling home permanent, a "cold wave" that turned my fine hair into frizz. Even more disastrous was our beauty parlor outing in 1951 when I was strung up to hot curlers on a machine that resembled a Gorgon's head dangling from an electric chair. Tresses singed beyond salvation, I ended up with a poodle cut.

In adolescence, "beauty hurts" translated to: pluck eyebrows, shave legs, curl eyelashes without chopping them off, tolerate crinolines scratchy as burlap, and high-heeled shoes that pitch the body forward and pinch the toes. In my teens, I also learned to master the art of dressing attractively but not provocatively, a subtle distinction that explains why, scrawny as I was, I had to wear a full latex girdle to flatten my buttocks. The merest suggestion of two definable cheeks was sure to give a boy the wrong idea.

The 1960s and 1970s took me a long way from corsets, crinolines, and the fashion dictates of my mother's world. Today I wear what my daughters wear, the casual, unstructured, age-irrelevant, morally neutral, invent-your-own-look clothing of the nineties. Since Abigail, Robin, and I have been the same size since the early eighties, we often trade clothes, something my mother and I could never have done even when I was fully grown, not because she was thirty-nine years older than I and wore a size 14, but because women's apparel was not something a teenager would be caught dead in. Now, stores like the Gap have bridged the generation gap and all of us, regardless of age, are traipsing around in jeans and T-shirts, but when I was a child, fashion didn't blur the age difference, it *defined* it.

Despite my embrace of the more relaxed fashions of the last couple of decades, it is only in recent years that dressing for comfort has become an article of faith for me. It began when a night on the town left me with two screaming blisters on my feet, and I decided to toss all my three-inch heels into the Goodwill bin and start wearing only flats and boots. Since then I've noticed that people associate shoes with age in odd ways. "High heels make you look taller and thinner, and your legs look longer — coltish and adolescent," observes Francesca M. Thompson, M.D., an orthopedic surgeon who specializes in foot and ankle problems, bunions, hammertoes, and the like, which, in large part, are attributable to women's shoes. Who wants a colt's legs if your hooves have the bunions and hammertoes of a workhorse?

After an interminable eighteen-hour day in a brassiere whose infrastructure branded my chest with U-shape rings, I cast away my underwired bras. (Since then, new studies have shown some linkage between wearing wired bras and the incidence of cancer — a provocative if not causative connection.) Itchy fabrics were the next to go. After that came heavy jewelry — the chains that weighed like a noose, the hair ornaments that gave me a headache, the lobe-numbing earclips, the bracelets that dug into my arms. Retired next were the mammoth shoulder bags that were responsible for my Leaning Tower of Pisa posture. Now I carry nothing; I wear backpacks and fanny purses that strap to the body and leave the hands free. Lastly, tight waistbands were banished from my closet, never to bind again. Ah, liberation! My clothes fit like pajamas, I feel healthier, and I never have to leave a party because my feet are killing me.

Having spent years in fashion hell, I have no trouble recognizing a sister in agony. She's the woman who keeps scratching her head because her hat is too snug; she's the one limping along with Band-Aids on the backs of her heels; the one grimacing each time her arms move in her too-small armholes; the woman in the tight dress who can hardly speak because she's holding her breath so her tummy won't stick out. Since turning fifty, I've said good-bye to all that and good riddance, regardless of the trade-offs. I may have sacrificed some sex appeal as the culture defines it — high heels do flatter the legs and push-up bras work wonders — but that's not my problem anymore. I've decided if I have to get older, at least I'm going to do it in comfort.

Meanwhile, as I try to strike a balance between the need to accept my body and the urge to transform it, I can only hope that as the years progress and the balancing act changes in response to further signs of age, I will never allow myself to devote more time to my looks than they're worth.

That formula ought to hold me to five minutes a day. Maybe less.

7

Know Thy Body, Know Thyself: In Sickness and in Health

> The body is an instrument, the mind
> its function, the witness and
> reward of its operation.
>
> — *George Santayana*

When I was forty-two, my eyes aged overnight. I'd worn glasses to correct my nearsightedness since I was fourteen, and for years, I put them on the minute I woke up and didn't take them off until bedtime. But then, one night at a concert, I suddenly realized I couldn't decipher the program, couldn't make out a single word — a rather terrifying moment, I might add — and then I discovered that I could read it just fine if I took my glasses *off*.

"What's happening to me?" I asked the ophthalmologist.

"What's happening is, you have forty-two-year-old eyes," he replied, and gave me a prescription for bifocals.

Let's face it: the body is where mortality makes its intentions perfectly clear to anyone who is paying attention. What's ahead for us is written, gradually but unmistakably, not only on our faces but in our flesh and blood, bone and muscle, health and stamina, whose every tiny fluctuation threatens to awaken the sleeping giant, our fear of death.

When I was younger, if I had a couple of bad headaches, it never would have occurred to me to think I had a brain tumor; pain was something you got rid of, not a portent of terminal disease. In my twenties and thirties, a beauty mark didn't conjure up cancer. If I tripped and fell, I didn't foresee the onset of perceptual degeneration or crippling osteoporosis. These days, though, now that the worst-case scenarios are becoming plausible, every twinge, every injury, every bodily change, however slight, seems to contain the possibility of ultimate doom. In short, I'm becoming a hypochondriac, my sleeping giant is turning into an insomniac, and we're quite a pair.

Regardless of all those extended-longevity predictions, after age fifty, mortality tremors shake up the psyche on a more regular basis, largely because the body keeps reminding us that we are losing control. (Control again — and still.) In the middle of my middle age, I couldn't help but notice my faculties fading, strength diminishing, and contours expanding in all directions, but rather than surrender to the encroaching anarchy, rather than let age have its way with my body, I decided to fight back. Eventually, of course, I will have to accept whatever infirmities and physical deterioration may be programmed into my karma or hardwired into my genes. However, for the last six or seven years, since I've been in a resistance mode, I've found that the struggle for control of the body can yield some measurable results that, at this stage, are not to be sneezed at. The poet Adrienne Rich writes, "In order to live a fully human life we require not only *control* of our bodies (though control is a prerequisite); we must touch the unity and resonance of our physicality, our bond with the natural order, the corporeal grounds of our intelligence."

As I see it, one's relationship to one's physicality has much in common with one's relationship to time. If heightened awareness can extend and prolong the time of one's life, perhaps this same degree of mindfulness applied to the workings of the body can ultimately prolong health, energy, and life itself. With this as my guiding premise, here is where I wage my battles:

The Senses

Since I started wearing bifocals, I've been able to both see and read, though I do neither to my complete satisfaction. The plain fact is, I can no longer count on my eyes. If the light source is dim, I have to squint, and in low light I cannot read at all. Pushing a strand of thread through the eye of a needle can be a ten-minute task; it may as well be a camel. I'm constantly readjusting the contrast and brightness knobs on my computer screen. Once upon a time, I used to look at something and see it; now I have to think about whether the conditions are right for seeing to take place, and it seems to get worse every year. Still, I've noticed that I would rather struggle, squint, and screw 100-watt bulbs in every socket than avail myself of the large-print books and newspapers on sale in my local bookstore. How old do I have to be before I can admit that I have a problem?

My husband, who has the farsighted vision of a hawk, cannot decipher anything up close that is smaller than a billboard unless he's wearing his reading glasses. Because he's the epitome of the absentminded professor, he owns eight or ten pairs, several of which are bereft of one earpiece as a result of having been stepped on or sat upon wherever he misplaced them, a daily occurrence that inspires my usual: "Honey, if you added up the time you spend looking for your glasses, you'd have. . . ."

I've also picked on him for his hearing loss, poor man, because I was convinced he was hearing but not *listening*. It's been well established that hearing slowly deteriorates after forty, most commonly with a loss of high frequencies at low volume levels, reduced dynamic range, and a poorer understanding of speech in the presence of background noise. But it's also been well established that men tune out things that don't interest them, so when Bert didn't hear someone, namely me, who was sitting right next to him, of course I accused him of not paying attention. Then one of the hearing-aid manufacturers offered an audio test that could be taken on the telephone. When I called, an automated voice said if your hearing was normal, you would soon discern three descending tones, a few seconds apart. I heard all three tones, but when Bert took the test he heard only one.

Despite my stellar performance, I will admit that over the last few months, I've found myself saying "What?" and "Come again?" in noisy, crowded rooms when the speaker is close by. Not long ago, I would have heard the whole sentence the first time. It happens to all of us. At a party the other night, above the din of background music and lots of chat, some friends asked the subject of my new book. As always, I answered, "It's about time and aging."

"Time and Asia?" asked one of the men, obviously baffled.

"No, age and Asia," joked his wife. "His hearing's going," she explained, then repeated closer to his ear what I had actually said.

"Ah, euthanasia," said the man, topping her and laughing off his infirmity.

The thought that I might ever lose my hearing makes me feel afraid. I imagine great, thick curtains dropping all around me, barricades of silence, baffling me from the world. Even now, with just the rarest hearing lapses, I hate straining to tune out background noise, hate asking people to repeat themselves, hate the impatient look I see on their faces when they have to stop and reiterate, hate the thought that someday I may be "out of it" simply because my ears have shut up shop. People tell me it takes years before audio loss gets bad enough for the average person to need hearing aids, but I'm fighting back now, hoping to postpone that eventuality as long as I can by sharpening my powers of concentration. Already, I've found that I can hear better when I focus my mind more intently on the person speaking. I've even started lip reading.

And I've become more sympathetic to Bert; I no longer accuse him of tuning out, but I do expect him to *try* harder, which pretty much summarizes my approach to everything physical these days. Try harder, I tell myself. Don't disengage. Don't let things slide. Don't surrender to loss. Don't give in to weakness. Don't let death come one symptom closer.

This campaign to save my body from itself actually began nearly two decades ago when I decided to undo twenty-four years of nicotine addiction and quit smoking by the time I was forty. Though it seemed inconceivable that I could end a meal without a cigarette, talk on the phone, sit down at the typewriter, or finish making love without lighting up, I managed to kick the habit (after two failed efforts) with the help of Smokenders, and found myself a confirmed nonsmoker before my thirty-ninth birthday. In my mid-forties, drawing strength from this success, I felt ready to take on the big one, my brain's conspiracy against my biochemistry, the most debilitating weakness of all: my blood phobia.

The Body-Mind Connection

I cannot remember a time when I wasn't afraid of blood. The sight of someone with a cut, the glimpse of a vial of blood, the picture of a stabbing victim, visiting someone in the hospital and seeing the intravenous contraption, would set off a spiraling feeling of weakness ending in a dead faint. Even the *thought* of bleeding or veins put me into an anxious state, intruding on my consciousness like a bee buzzing around my hair and with the same potential to turn menacing.

Thankfully, blood isn't something a writer encounters in the normal course of a day, and for the most part I was able to live my life without worrying about the phobia, other than to avoid situations that might bring it on. My children got their first aid from their father, a friend, or each other. "Mommy faints from blood," they'd say matter-of-factly, as though announcing that I like tulips. If a movie was gory, or we had to drive past an accident on the road, I averted my eyes. We accommodated to my phobia the way one learns to put up with an eccentric neighbor: never provoke.

The first time I passed out, I was five years old. My cousin Danny and I were at the movies watching a pirate torture scene in which the victim's blood was being pumped out of his body, and the next thing I knew I was on the floor under my seat, with a flashlight shining in my face and the movie matron shouting, "Wake up!" (Remember movie matrons, and smoking sections, and cartoons before the double feature?) For nearly four decades afterward I continued to faint at the sight of blood — theatrical or real, my own and other people's — more times than I can count or remember.

I had what is called a "specific phobia," an intense, irrational terror that triggered an *involuntary* physical reaction (medical term: vasovagal syncope) to almost anything associated with the vascular system — including the word "vascular." I couldn't tolerate the sight of the red stuff on a gauze pad, not to mention a person, couldn't stand blood tests, couldn't even take my own pulse or look at protruding veins without feeling woozy. I fainted from shaving cuts and nose bleeds (but not from menstrual blood or animal blood, which my unconscious seemed to put in a different category). As an adult, these incidents happened only two or three times a year — usually after an accidental razor or knife cut, self-inflicted in my own bathroom or kitchen, where I was able to lower myself to the floor before I blacked out. Although my fainting episodes lasted less than a minute, I found them disconcerting, as did whoever happened to be with me at the time.

Sometimes, I could stop myself from losing consciousness by lowering my head between my knees as soon as I felt the first wave of weakness. But whenever I had to have blood drawn, in fact the moment the tourniquet appeared on the doctor's side table, I was a goner. Nurses teased me. Doctors put me on a slant board, head down, feet up, but even upside down and in violation of the laws of gravity, I still blacked out.

The whole syndrome was annoying and embarrassing but not life-threatening until I was forty-one, when, in the midst of a routine blood test, instead of fainting in my usual perfunctory fashion, I went into shock.

I knew something untoward had happened, because when I came to, the doctor's face was ashen; he told me he'd had to administer a shot of adrenaline to bring me back. He warned me that the possibility of a shock reaction, dangerous in itself, would compound any health problems I might develop in the future. He said that if I was going to survive the diagnostic blood tests and intravenous treatments of my later years, I'd better get myself cured — admitting, incidentally, that he had no idea how to do it.

Colette once wrote, "Look for a long time at what pleases you, and longer still at what pains you." I looked long and hard at my phobia, ruminating on what the fear of blood might represent, trying to talk myself out of it, reason my way out of it, interpret it into oblivion. Surely I wasn't afraid of literally bleeding to death from a shaving cut. What was I really afraid of? Ebbing away? Leaking what little strength I had? Emptying out? Losing fuel? Hemorrhaging? Letting what's inside out? Seeing red? Losing control? The fainting began with the trauma of the pirate movie, but could it have been sustained as I got older by an unconscious need to exhibit feminine vulnerabilities to neutralize my controlling nature, or to compensate for other strengths that I knew society deemed inappropriate in a woman? Was the phobia an expression of these unresolved conflicts? Or could my fear of blood have absorbed all my other fears, concentrating them in this one tight little pocket of madness so I wouldn't have to face them one by one — the fear of helplessness, of grief and loss, of random disaster, of aging, of dying. How clever of the unconscious to devise this manageable, concrete pathology to contain all the unmanageable, amorphous terrors that beset humankind. Other people, the ones without phobias, have no focal point for their apprehensions. But when you're scared of something in particular, you have a *reason* to be afraid. Which may explain why phobias are so hard to let go.

Whatever its roots, my fear of blood had now been eclipsed by a more realistic fear of death. If I went into shock again, I might be miles away from a shot of adrenaline. In other words, I could die.

I decided to find help.

My search took seven years of intermittent consultations with an internist, a neurologist, a psychiatrist, and assorted practitioners of biofeedback, hypnosis, and biolinguistic programming. Nothing worked. Finally, in 1987, when I bought my first computer, it occurred to me to use the modem to access Medline, the medical database, and do a search for exactly what I needed — a doctor who'd had repeated success treating vasovagal reactions to phobias. That's how I found Katherine Shear, then director of the Anxiety Disorders Clinic at New York Hospital. During our first visit, she asked me to describe the phobia's history and to list the stimuli that triggered a faint, ranking each from the worst to the least disturbing (Worst: having blood drawn. Least: thinking about veins.) Next, she wanted to witness the phobic reaction while I rated the progress of my anxiety numerically — discomfort rated a 1, weakness and hyperventilation a 3 or 4, stomach-churning misery a 6, scary lightheadedness an 8, up to a 9 for fading vision, and 10 for an unstoppable faint.

Believe it or not, to activate the fainting process so she could observe it, I had only to press my fingers against the veins in the crook of my arm. Immediately, I slumped in my seat, felt weak, nauseous, the whole bit. As the symptoms overtook my body, I rated them in a steadily weakening whisper: at number 9, just before darkness closed in, I let go of my arm, put my head between my legs, and breathed in the ammonia pellet that the doctor stuck under my nose. Our goal was not to have me pass out, but to deconstruct my escalating physiological response to the phobia and unlearn each reaction one by one.

In the ensuing sessions and in my homework assignments, I learned to very gradually increase my exposure to each negative stimulus, forcing myself to think about, see, touch, and endure everything I'd ever associated with blood. I took on one problem per week — veins, my own pulse, tourniquets, needles, syringes, intravenous equipment, bloodstains, vials of blood — until I was actually able to sit in a lab watching dozens of people have their blood drawn. Over and over, I exposed myself to these formerly intolerable sights, working to control my breathing and reduce my anxiety from a 9 to a 1 for each succeeding stimulus, until finally, one triumphant day ten weeks from my first visit, I had my own blood drawn — sitting up with my eyes open. Talk about asserting control over one's body! Eureka! After forty years, mindfulness over matter. Unbelievable!

Since that day, I have endured all manner of exposure to blood and bleeding and haven't fainted once. Can you blame me for drawing grandiose conclusions from this victory over myself? If a person could unlearn a physical reaction so deeply embedded in the unconscious that it had been coded into the involuntary nervous system — if four decades of dysfunctional behavior could be changed by mind-work in a matter of ten weeks — then, it seems to me, anyone can conquer anything.

An estimated 11 million Americans are "deathly" afraid of dogs, cats, snakes, insects, crowds, driving, bridges, tunnels, heights, elevators, thunderstorms, and similar everyday situations. In addition to these well-known phobias, people endure other terrors, just as overwhelming, that don't necessarily make it into official clinical categories. At various points in his life, the great essayist E. B. White suffered from his fear of darkness, school bathrooms, collapsing on the street, fear that the brakes would fail while he was riding in a trolley on a hillside, fear of the future, of dying, of writing, which never ceased to be an anxiety-ridden enterprise for him, and of public speaking. Describing a terrifying lecture appearance at Dartmouth College, he wrote to his wife, "The old emptiness and dizziness and vapors seized hold of me. . . . Nobody who has never suffered my peculiar kind of disability can understand the sheer hell of such moments."

In childhood, Joan Didion was afraid of ski lifts, snakes, and certain comic books. "As an adult, she remained anxious but with less certainty about what was scaring her," says Ralph Keyes, author of *The Courage to Write,* in which he catalogs writers' terrors and their means of overcoming them. James Joyce was frightened by dogs, rats, and thunder. Emily Dickinson was probably agoraphobic. Barbara Grizzuti Harrison is afraid of stairs. (In *Italian Days*, she quotes experts who claim going up and down steps approximates "'feelings of aspiring to heaven and then returning to earth.' If this is true," she writes, "a fear of steps may represent a fear of achieving that transition, that is, a fear of death. . . .")

Since I identify most closely with writers, it reassures me to know that no matter how honored, established, or productive they are, their anxieties match my own — if not in phobic form, then in the form of familiar fears of failure, criticism, humiliation, ridicule, the blank page. "Far from being fearless, authors tend to be anxious people who are duking it out with their anxieties on the page," says Keyes. "They don't write *despite* their fear but *because* of it. . . . Over time, writers learn how to manipulate fear, bargain with it, harness its power." (Those who admit converting their worst fears into fiction include not just White and Didion but Rosellen Brown, Catherine Drinker Bowen, David Grossman, Ernest Hemingway, Jessamyn West, Raymond Chandler, and probably most writers you've ever read.) Recognizing how his apprehensions had fed his work, White himself once said, "I am not inclined to apologize for my anxieties because I have lived with them long enough to respect them."

Indeed, most human fears deserve respect — for their fervor, tenacity,

aging. Having said this, I mean no general condemnation of large people; I admire women who occupy their fullness with the untroubled grace of a Lucille Clifton, author of the wonderfully lusty poem "Homage to My Hips," or a Jane O'Reilly, the writer, who gained more than 100 pounds during menopause and recently told an interviewer, "I am fat, aging, and yes, libidoless and to my surprise, it doesn't matter to me. . . . I have whole categories of things not on my mind anymore, and I'm pleased."

I was not at all pleased, and my body was on my mind constantly. Never before had it been a burden to me; now it was literally weighing me down. I felt estranged from my skeletal structure, surrounded and overwhelmed by flesh, as though I were the tiny figure trapped at the core of those multiple nesting dolls. When I'd gained weight during my pregnancies, there were babies to show for it, and after each delivery my body bounced back. Now, all I had to show for it was flab, and no delivery date to put an end to the discomfort. Leaden and lethargic, I wasn't me anymore; I was turning into someone else. It was an out-of-body experience.

That disoriented feeling reminds me of something the singer Barbara Cook once told me. When I interviewed her, in 1977, the former 113-pound ingenue in such Broadway musicals as *Candide, She Loves Me,* and *The Music Man* had become a woman of indeterminate size, maybe 200 pounds, maybe more, having yo-yo'd up the scale in full view of her public. "I understand people's fascination with weight," she said, "but the truth is that my fat surprises me. I bump up against it unexpectedly. Passing a mirror or store window, I'll see my image and say, 'Jesus, who the hell is *that?*' Or a friend will offer her sweater when I'm chilly and I'll be amazed when it doesn't fit me." It was as if she'd become a stranger to herself.

Feminist theorists speculate that women who hate their own fat are really afraid of female power, of taking up too much space in a world that belongs to men. They say, somewhat paradoxically, that fat frightens us because it embodies superabundant femininity — the enveloping maternal figure — and, at the same time, is a transgression of femininity, a violation of the delicate female ideal. I won't say they're wrong, but these theories failed to explain my state of mind. To me, the extra pounds were the embodiment of aging, harbinger of all the other time-related physical transformations I'd been dreading, and undeniable proof that the years were changing me for the worse. My strange new form symbolized deterioration and loss of control of the sort one associates — I associate — with dying.

I felt a powerlessness I'd never known before, the powerlessness people experience when they are in the clutches of some terrible disease, unable to control their bodily functions and fighting for their life against a force they can neither understand nor subdue.

Some say that the truly mature person is one who rejects the whole concept of control and learns to "let go." Maybe this fits the male model of maturation, but women are another story. Women already know what it means to let go of power and control; that's just another definition of traditional femininity. Some of us have managed to change the rules and gain some power over our time, work lives, money, sexuality, and reproductive decisions, but the thrill of self-mastery is still new to us. So when age suddenly zaps us with another kind of out-of-controlness — say, when our metabolism goes off half-cocked — it touches deeper chords. I was not surprised to read in the 1994 Clinique study that when American women think about aging, their two biggest worries are the fear of being "less in control" of their lives and the fear of losing their figures.

I have never craved power over others but only over myself. When I don't feel like the captain of my own ship, I go under. It would have been nice if I'd been able to accept my new body weight and go with the flow of the aging process, but I simply couldn't do it. My body fat was an unbearable daily reminder of decay and death. Furthermore, I couldn't imagine I would ever *stop* gaining weight because I hadn't a clue about which foods were fattening and which weren't. Until now, I'd never had to learn the difference.

When I was little, people were always feeding me. Not only did my bag of bones cast aspersions on my mother's cooking, but with children starving in Europe, it was considered rude and ungrateful for an American kid, especially a Jewish-American kid, to be skinny. Fattening me up became a family project. My relatives distracted me with songs and games to get me to finish what was on my plate. To this day, when I raise a forkful of food to my mouth, I can almost hear, "Open wide / Don't you hide / Let it glide / deep inside." And whenever I cook spinach or peas, I'm tempted to bury them in a buttery pillow of mashed potatoes, which is how healthy things were smuggled into my diet in those days.

My mother, who kept a kosher kitchen, produced her purposely fattening meals from two food groups. For dairy menus, she drew liberally on anything with the word cream in it: ice cream, sour cream, whipped cream, cream cheese, creamy salad dressing, cream of tomato soup. For meat meals, she put her faith in chicken fat. I was schtupped with chopped liver sandwiches on thick hunks of rye bread slathered with *schmaltze* (chicken fat the consistency of yellow peanut butter). Friday nights, I had yellow chicken soup, slick with fat and embellished with matzoh balls that were, pardon the expression, larded with *schmaltze*. I snacked on mounds of *griebens*, small wads of solid chicken fat rendered in a hot pan until they contracted into crispy cracklings — Jewish popcorn — which I loved better than anything, except brownies.

Now and then, my mother resorted to all-American "health" foods (I think she was covering her bets), by which she meant ice cream sodas and malted milk, cod liver oil, cream cheese and sweet butter sandwiches on Wonder Bread, and a daily rasher of what I came to call "medicinal meat." Somehow, my mother had decided that the difference between me and my sturdy gentile friends was bacon — yes, *bacon,* which she served to me on a paper plate under the alias "lamb chops on paper." (She cooked three strips at a time in a special pan that she kept in a brown paper bag well hidden under the kitchen sink, where it could not contaminate her koshered cabinets.) But no matter what I ate, I gained nothing. More to the point, these early gastronomic habits turned me into an adult who approached food with mindless self-indulgence. Even when I was well into my forties, I thought nothing of polishing off a brownie every afternoon, eating bagels with butter and cream cheese on both sides, and taking my coffee with heavy cream. For years, I didn't own a scale and never thought about or even knew my weight until such time as I had reason to visit a doctor's office. But now, here I was among the 100 million Americans who are overweight, half of whom are dieting at any given moment, and none of whom had an ounce of compassion for a woman who didn't have a weight problem until she was almost fifty.

I've since learned that it is normal for most people, even the relatively young, to increase their weight and body-fat percentage as they age. In a multiracial study of eighteen- to thirty-year-olds, researchers found that over seven years, the men gained between 13 and 17 pounds, the women who'd had no pregnancies gained an average of 6 to 14 pounds, and the women who'd had babies in those years ended up between 10 and 19 pounds heavier. It gets worse for women over forty who lose muscle mass through lack of exercise. For every pound of muscle lost, one's resting metabolic rate drops by nearly 50 calories a day. Metabolic slow-down explains why a female who could consume 2,000 calories a day as a teenager and not gain an ounce needs only 1,200 calories to keep her weight level by the time she's my age.

The problem was, I didn't know a calorie from a ketone. Having spent nearly half a century paying attention to nothing but how food tastes, I had no idea where to begin. Every weight loss program I read or heard about sounded hopelessly complicated or utterly unappetizing, and there seemed to be a serious downside to each. Low-carbohydrate diets left people with low energy. Low-calorie diets could take off as much muscle mass as fat, resulting in a reduced metabolic rate that would make fat-burning even less likely. The Scarsdale diet was insipid, repetitive, and gave people gas. A friend of mine almost died on a macrobiotic diet. Weight Watchers seemed to work, but measuring every portion required more discipline than a beginner could muster, and I'd heard that people tended to put back the weight after going off the regimen. Juice fasts scared me because I get faint on Yom Kippur. While searching for the perfect program, I read a statistic that stopped me in my tracks: only one dieter in 250 loses weight and keeps it off. I was desperate, but I was also convinced that if I were to go on a diet and fail, I'd become clinically depressed. So I did nothing — and kept on gaining.

Turning It Around

God knows what would have happened if Bert and I hadn't been invited to a friend's house for lunch one August afternoon two summers ago. Gerry, whom I've known for twenty-five years, had never looked better. She'd lost 9 pounds in eight weeks. The lunch was delicious.

"Is all this wonderful food on your diet?" I asked.

"It's not a *diet,*" she insisted. "It's a *way of life* and it's easy. All you have to do is cut down on fats."

I wasn't exactly sure what a "fat" was, but I got a little booklet that listed the number of fat grams in everything edible, and the next day I swore off cheese, butter, and red meat, which turn out to be the main culprits. Bert and I started eating lots of grains, vegetables, chicken, baked potatoes with garlicky yogurt, and pasta with tomato-based sauces. We checked the fat content listed on food packages and bought only those foods containing fewer than three grams per serving. We discovered fat-free frozen yogurt and low-fat mozzarella, dipped our bread in olive oil, and gave up butter.

By Thanksgiving, I'd lost 16 pounds. Bert, who is six feet tall, dropped more than 20. His reduction was the most fortuitous by-product of our new regimen, since he'd put on 30 pounds in the thirty years since we'd been married, and a Harvard study has shown that men who are heavy have a 40 percent higher death rate and a two-and-a-half-times-higher heart attack rate than men of normal weight. For Valentine's Day, I bought him a fancy upright scale, which I rank among my most loving presents. And watching him enjoy the return of his former physique has been half the fun. Together we've become our own weight-watching support group. We applaud one another's progress, monitor each other's splurges, and get as excited as kids in an ice-cream shop when we find a new low-fat product that tastes like food. I'm not saying I wouldn't be thrilled to go back to my mindless eating habits and that daily brownie, but the truth is, I don't feel seriously deprived. I have yens and urges, sometimes an irresistible craving for pecan pie, or a nonnegotiable need for a cheese enchilada, but I've found I can indulge in those treats occasionally and still stay the course. I don't beat myself up if I have dessert in a restaurant, eggs and bacon for breakfast when we're on vacation, or two steaks a year. If the needle on the scale creeps up more than a pound or two, I cut out a few more grams until I'm back where I want to be. This may sound fanatical to some people, but I've discovered that for me, keeping my body a familiar housing for my spirit is, psychologically speaking, a survival issue.

At this writing, the extra weight has stayed off, give or take the two-pound leeway for splurges, and except for my omnipresent rounded belly, I look more or less as I did in my thirties and forties, which suits me fine. I don't want to be a skinny kid again, I just want to feel at home in my skin.

If this account sounds self-congratulatory, I don't mean it that way at all; I mean it as testimony to the fact that, just when you think you must give up and let age have its way with you, regaining control is possible — not easy, but possible. I mean to suggest that while other midlife body changes cannot be stopped — the sag and drag, the aches and pains — this particular project of physical transformation offers the prospect of reversal. For older people, losing weight is not just an issue of vanity; it rewards us with visible evidence that *we still can change for the better because of something we decide to do,* and thus, to some degree at least, we are still in charge of our destiny. All this I gained from losing. Oh, and one more thing: I gained compassion for people with a weight problem — something I could never understand until I had it myself, something too easy to ridicule as vain or weak or trivial unless it is one's own flesh that refuses to yield.

The Conversion of a Couch Potato

The only thing harder than altering my eating habits was changing my sedentary ways, yet everyone kept telling me that, with or without low-fat foods, if I wanted to control my weight, I would have to get out of my chair.

Movement is not my forte. Growing up, I was the proverbial 99-pound weakling who couldn't throw a ball or even run for a bus without putting myself into the early stages of cardiac arrest. My mother, who had an Old World superstition for every occasion, believed that athletic activity could "jumble" the female reproductive system. She was convinced that contact sports — in which she included dodgeball, if I remember correctly — could bruise a girl's breasts and jeopardize her ability to nurse future babies or, worse yet, give her breast cancer.

My mother's apocalyptic view of physical activity was exacerbated by the inferior sports programs offered to girls in the public schools of my day. As a result, I took modern dance to satisfy my Phys. Ed. requirement, and except for three years as a college cheerleader (which involved more synchronized shouting and strutting than actual exertion), all my life I have been athletically challenged, a huffer and puffer, and a physical coward. I used to joke that my favorite activities were exercising discretion, jumping to conclusions, and running amok. Therefore, it was a major move on life's chessboard when, at about the time I gave up butter, I took up walking. Not strolling, but serious, arm-pumping, hard-breathing walking, in Central Park or on a treadmill, with the aim of burning calories and building strength.

"Walking is the best medicine," said Hippocrates, and in the beginning I took my walks like castor oil, grudgingly, and ruefully aware of my limitations, which manifested themselves in instant exhaustion. I started doing one mile a day at the rate of 2.5 m.p.h., which is about as fast as you travel when you're window shopping. After a year of trudging on the treadmill three or four times a week, I gradually built up my speed and distance to three miles a day at 4 m.p.h., which is actually quite strenuous and speedy. Little by little, my confidence level rose above zero as I noted the absence of my usual death rattle, though the minute I set the treadmill on

Incline, the wheeze returned and my pulse leapt into my ears. These days, in keeping with my self-imposed "try harder" regimen, I try to set the treadmill on Incline at least once a week to give my heart as much of a workout as my legs. Going uphill without pain is my new goal, which I suppose is appropriate for one who is trying so hard to keep from going downhill.

Like the weight loss, this account should be taken not as a boast but as a case history with a larger point. For a confirmed wimp like myself to be fast-walking twelve miles a week at age fifty-five is not chopped liver (which, incidentally, is no longer on the menu at our house). It proves that physical weakness is neither irreversible nor inexorable. It says that each passing year need not be a measure of things lost (looks, strength, health), but can be symptomatic of things gained (strength, health, endurance). I haven't exactly climbed Everest, but given my pitiful athletic past and formidable collection of frailties, my experience suggests that there may still be time for any aging couch potato to turn things around — to feel better, look better, grow stronger, and thus become more optimistic about a future in which we might achieve similar turn-arounds as age takes its toll in other ways.

"The true value of exercise is pyschological," says John Foreyt, professor of medicine and psychiatry at Baylor College of Medicine in Houston, adding expert testimony to the mix. "It increases your sense of well-being, of control, what we call self-efficacy. People feel more in charge of their lives."

And isn't that precisely what we are searching for at this age? Furthermore, by starting a regular exercise regimen right now, we may be sparing ourselves a miserable dotage. Ralph Paffenbarger, Jr., a professor emeritus at Stanford University, who has done several long-term studies on the effects of physical activity on Harvard graduates over the last thirty-five years, says, "Starting to exercise is comparable from a health-benefit standpoint to quitting smoking," and it's never too late to profit from those benefits. Research shows that exercise can help the heart, strengthen immunity, control weight, promote mental health, and lower the risk of developing osteoporosis, arthritis, diabetes, and some cancers, including breast cancer. What's more, says David Nieman, professor of health and exercise science at Appalachian State University, studies published in 1990 and 1993 strongly suggest that regular walking may even keep the common cold at bay in women of all ages.

To older women, Joan Ullyot, sports medicine physician and veteran of over seventy marathons, says, "The more you use your body, the better it will perform." Ullyot's own record proves her point. At age forty-eight, she ran the 26-mile race in 2 hours and 47 minutes, four minutes *faster* than her previous best time, which she'd achieved when she was thirty-six.

Those of us who haven't been running marathons since puberty have reason to worry, as do the nearly three-quarters of American women who, according to federal health officials, are not getting enough exercise. (The Centers for Disease Control and Prevention recommend 20 minutes of heavy-breathing aerobic activity three days a week, or five days a week of less-strenuous 30-minute sessions.) Of all the nasty outcomes predicted for the aging female body, perhaps none is more alarming than the prognosis of structural weakness: women run an increasing risk of osteoporosis and arthritis and after about age forty-five start losing both bone density and muscle mass, which can lead to fractures and enfeebling weakness. The bad news is, by age sixty-five, the average woman has doubled her fat content and dissipated half her muscle; by seventy-five, two-thirds of women (and 28 percent of men) cannot lift 10 pounds. The good news is, we can annul these losses and rebuild muscles *at any age.*

Jane Brody, the *New York Times* health columnist, cites a study published in the July 1994 *New England Journal of Medicine* describing a ten-week strength-training program that helped fifty frail men and women in their eighties and nineties increase their walking speed by 12 percent, their stair-climbing ability by 28 percent, and their weight-lifting capacity by 118 percent. "Impressive though these accomplishments are in stemming some of the costly and debilitating incapacities of old age," writes Brody, "they pale in comparison with what strength training can do for younger people who want to maintain or improve physical prowess even as their biological clocks keep ticking toward decline."

A recent study done at Tufts University on healthy women between ages fifty and seventy found that one year of strength training (lifting weights twice a week) yielded important gains in bone density, strength, gait, and balance, results that have dramatic implications for preventing falls and fractures when we are elderly.

Though walking may be the best medicine, it is clearly not enough. To avoid further physical decline and escape the ranks of the infirm, midlifers need a balanced workout — aerobics to increase oxygen intake and fortify the heart; strength-training exercises to build muscle tissue, lose body fat, and speed up the metabolic rate; hand weights to increase the bone mass in the arms; abdominal contractions and back extension exercises to develop the muscles in the spine and hips; sit-ups and bar-hanging exercises to work the upper body; and resistance and stretch exercises to counteract the rounding of the shoulders and back so typical of older women. I would gladly add these exercises to my life if I could figure out what to give up to make time for them. As it is, my day groans and cracks from the weight of its current schedule. How can I find time for fifty sit-ups, isometric contractions, and biceps curls? The answer is, I must.

Jane Brody, herself fifty-three, takes an aerobic walk and a half-mile swim every day, plays singles tennis four times a week, goes skating and cross-country skiing in winter, bikes often, and started rollerblading at fifty. (I'm tired just writing this.) Other women are tap dancing, scuba diving, and ice skating for the fun of it. April Martin, a forty-five-year-old psychologist whose girlhood sounds a lot like mine ("By seventh grade, my life contained no physical activity at all. . . . The worst part was that I never even noticed what was missing"), can be found every morning before work at the ice rink, where she puts herself through two hours of spins and jumps. Then there are the women who are *really* serious: Bonnie Frankel, fifty, took a course in recreational running five years ago and is now training for the 100 meter dash in the national Senior Olympics. Helen Darnall ordered a discus by mail, taught herself to throw it by reading the enclosed instructions, and, at fifty-nine, won gold medals in that event and sprinting, silver medals in track, and a bronze in javelin. And probably no one can top the Vermont woman I heard about who competed in the Senior Olympics shotput event when she was eighty-one.

Though I will never be a competitor in anything more active than gin rummy, I will keep walking and I *will* start that strength-building regimen one of these days, because the results of exercise are clearly so salutary and I've found no better rebuttal to what Edmund Wilson called "the dark defile of age."

Preventive Measures

Since time began to zoom along, since my body started changing and the sleeping giant started stirring, I've also tried harder to stay healthy. Not long ago, I had the temerity to take good health for granted — though not the ability to pay for such things as doctor and dentist visits, prescription medicine, insurance, and new eyeglasses when I need them. Maintaining one's health costs money, and the sorry truth is, many people can't afford the treatment they need. Under our current system, nearly 37 million Americans, many of them women, have no health insurance whatsoever, and those who do have insurance are less likely than men to have the premiums covered by an employer; rather, they are covered under their husband's policy, which leaves them vulnerable to loss of benefits after divorce or widowhood or in cases where an employer terminates coverage for dependents. At this writing, cuts in Medicare, the nation's primary form of health insurance for citizens over sixty-five, present a looming threat to that age group and to the future health security of those of us presently in middle age, especially to women, who comprise 57 percent of Medicare beneficiaries.

Getting decent health care when I'm sick will always be my first priority, but practicing *preventive* health care should run a close second because timely efforts may actually forestall the ailments of age. I don't intend to become self-obsessed, but I am trying to be a reasonably active partner in my own health care and to monitor my well-being the way I used to watch over that of my children. The last time most of us paid close attention to our changing bodies was in adolescence, when we lived in front of the mirror. At midlife, I think we need to develop a different kind of body awareness, to watch for telltale changes, the early-warning system for many serious diseases.

Regular medical checkups are an obvious part of any preventive health plan, but that doesn't mean a person can leave her well-being in the hands of experts. Too often, as my friends' experiences have taught me, people attribute symptoms like depression, muscle degeneration, and fatigue to the aging process when they should have been noted as possible indicators of serious problems such as brain or lymph tumors or multiple sclerosis. Systematic self-monitoring is just as important as lab tests or doctors' visits, and it doesn't cost a dime. Though I started relatively late (after some age degeneration had already set in), I've memorized my baseline physical condition so that I can recognize future lumps, skin discolorations, systemic changes, or other abnormalities as soon as they develop. This is not an enterprise I relish, but one I'm convinced is essential if I want my health to last as long as my spirit.

It's amazing what you notice when you zoom in on the details. I've become aware, for instance, that I wake up feeling stiff in at least one body part, usually the neck, back, or legs. My eyesight is at its worst when I first open my eyes but improves by the hour. My bra straps and sock bands now leave long-lasting indentations. (Poor circulation? Or maybe it's fluid retention.) My bite is different from what it used to be; not exactly buck-toothed but definitely encroaching on my lower lip. Outdoors in cold weather, my eyes start watering after about five minutes. Indoors, my bare feet freeze at night, even in the summer. If I'm not at home, where I can warm my icy toes against Bert's legs (you can imagine how he loves this), I have to wear socks to bed. My diurnal clock belongs to an owl; left alone on an island I would go to bed at 2 A.M. and awaken at 10, but lately I seem to need less rest and sleep less soundly, no doubt due to my having to get up at least once a night to pee — a necessity that materialized quite suddenly when I turned fifty and a source of annoyance ever since. Ditto for the recent changes in my elimination habits, which now require me to spend a half hour in the bathroom every morning before I leave the house, or else regret it for the rest of the day. (You get to do a lot of reading.)

Lydia Bronte, an expert on longevity, is a strong proponent of the know thyself philosophy: "A doctor sees your physical system once a year, during a checkup. You *live* in it *all the time.* In that sense no one else can possibly know as much about your body's functioning as you can. You can use that understanding to head off problems while they are still small, and stay active and vigorous throughout your life."

I'd go a step further. At this age, knowing the body may be a prerequisite to knowing the soul, since the soul is so often besieged by the body's transmutations and we tend to confuse the worth of the self with the failures of the flesh. It makes sense to fight back through self-discipline, exercise, diet, behavior therapy, hormones, preventive health care, and just plain grit, not because each triumph over physical degeneration is something to crow about in the car pool, but because each is a rebuke to death, a way to buy time, and a reminder that, no matter how old we are, we can still change our lives for the better.

I've also bought into the importance of dietary supplements. I've become one of those crazy people with 42 bottles of vitamins lined up next to the salt and pepper. Since it's only logical to load the artillery before the enemy appears on the horizon, I take enough pills to fill a howitzer — calcium, niacin, lysine, odorless garlic capsules (garlic is supposed to help boost immunity), glutathione, vitamin D, all the B's, plus vitamins C, E, and beta carotene. Those are the antioxidants that are said to block the action of "free radicals," the highly reactive oxidizing substances that cause cellular damage when they form in the body during normal metabolism or enter the body as environmental insults like smoke, pollution, and carcinogens. I think of free radicals as rust producers, and antioxidants as rust removers, an image that helps me justify swallowing a full glass of water just to get all my pills down twice a day. Though still in the experimental stages, studies suggest that antioxidants help prevent heart disease, cancer, and the worst ravages of age, so I figure, for what they're worth, why not put them to work?

Sick Calls

Some things, of course, are out of our hands.

Illness (especially cancer) terrifies me, not just because, as Mel Brooks once said, "You could die from it," but because serious illness is the quintessential loss of control. Yet, I am also fascinated by sickness, respectful of the extraordinary way that it reorders one's priorities and changes one's perspective on every aspect of human existence — love and work, friendship and beauty, time and aging, death and life. Although sick people are often shunned — for their exposed mortality, I suspect, even more than the potential for contagion — if you get close enough to someone who is gravely ill, or read a memoir by a writer who is dealing with a dreadful malady, you often discover that they know more than the rest of us about everything that matters.

When the critic Anatole Broyard was battling cancer, he wrote of feeling "concentrated as a diamond, or a microchip." Answers came to him fully formed: "I see everything with a summarizing eye. Nature is a terrific editor. . . . I see now why the romantics were so fond of illness — the sick man sees everything as metaphor. . . . I'm infatuated with my cancer. It stinks of revelation."

Others who have wrestled with disease describe having had insights of such clarity and force, and having developed such an exuberant love of life, that I've actually envied them, which makes me wonder: Do we have to face death — or three friends' funerals — before life can be fully apprehended? Is it necessary to experience agony before we can appreciate simple contentment? Must the body be decimated before we can recognize, in hindsight, the miracle of uneventful good health?

I hope not, on all counts. I don't want to have to put in time in the intensive care unit in order to appreciate that ordinary life, with all its petty annoyances and routine ups and downs (and infuriating depredations of age), is, in fact, a marvelous thing. Yet, like many people, I sometimes need a reminder of the alternative before I can discern the obvious. After one of those wrenching funerals, I fall in love with life. I feel fresh waves of gratitude for my health and that of my loved ones. People seem universally endearing, the world suddenly appears brighter, more wondrous, and I become as mawkish about ordinary pleasures as Emily was in *Our Town* when she returned to Grover's Corners from the grave. I understand why Wallace Stevens wrote, "Death is the mother of beauty."

"Death, even the hint of death, has a way of making nearly everything else trivial," writes Joseph Epstein of this changed angle of vision. "I was walking away from reading a petulant review of a recent book of mine, beginning to work up a temporary but genuine sulk about it, when I met an acquaintance who told me he had been discovered to have colon cancer. I'll take, I thought to myself, the bad review. Can it be that I am gaining a modicum of perspective, some distant hint of what is important and what is utterly beside the point in life?"

Similar moments of realignment and humility have persuaded me of how much can be learned from people who have been forced to cut to the chase before their time. Sick friends have taught me how to be more mindfully well, more focused on what matters, more grateful for what is. Friends with sick children — a youngster with cancer, a college kid permanently damaged by drug abuse, a grown son who is schizophrenic — have shown me the astounding power of hope, undeviating hope, and indefatigable love. From those who are close to death themselves, I've learned how to live with the fear of death, how to set it off to the side where it can be acknowledged but doesn't get in the way. And thanks to what Nancy Mairs calls "the literature of personal disaster," a subgenre of autobiography whose narrator "wants not to whine, not to boast, but to comfort," I am always being enlightened by the epiphanies of people I've never met.

In *Ordinary Time,* Mairs, a self-dubbed "connoisseur of catastrophe," writes about accepting her lot, a difficult life that has included multiple sclerosis, suicidal depression, incapacitating agoraphobia, a husband with cancer — and finding within it a kind of liberation: "Horribly constrained in a body that can no longer roll over in bed reliably, much less be trusted to arise and get to the toilet before the flood, I have never felt freer to cherish and celebrate my husband and children. . . ." In *Voice Lessons,* Mairs says she has discovered that "it is possible to be both sick and happy. This good news, once discovered, demands to be shared."

In Love with Daylight, subtitled "A Memory of Recovery," shares with the reader the lessons Wilfrid Sheed has learned from having had polio since childhood, then, as an adult, fighting depression, dependence on alcohol and sleeping pills, and finally, cancer of the tongue. Each affliction "caused me to lose something quite irreplaceable, something I would have sworn I couldn't live without." The polio took his mobility; after beating the addiction-depression, "the whole congenial drinking life" was closed to him; and the cancer "made some mean little inroads into the joy of eating, the last redoubt of the sensual man." With it all, Sheed remains a lively, dare I say cheerful, man, his prose devoid of self-pity, his life fueled by debonair wit and informed by the clarities of both suffering and age, which have given him the means "to face sickness and death with something like equanimity."

Reynolds Price, the novelist who has spent the last ten years paralyzed with spinal cancer, writes in his memoir *A Whole New Life* that the past decade has "brought more in and sent more out — more love and care, more knowledge and patience, more work in less time." Despite every manner of devastation and discomfort, Price wrote the same number of books (13) during the ten years since the start of his affliction that he did in the preceding fifty years, and he insists that except for the most harrowing months of his illness, "mine has been a happy life."

The poet Audre Lorde counted her blessings by default. In *The Cancer Journals,* she begins, "I'd give anything not to have cancer and my beautiful breast gone, fled with my love of it. . . . I guess I have to qualify that — there really are some things I wouldn't give." She meant her life, her partner, her children and friends, her poetry, her eyes, her arms . . . "and no, I would not give up love."

But, of course.

The Scare

At this point, I don't need a catastrophic illness to remind me to treasure life. Since the calamity of turning fifty, I've been doing my treasuring on a regular basis, what with my commitment to sacred moments, frozen moments, mindfulness, noticing, slowing time, and all the rest. Still, it took a

I think I might pass out just from the video. I do the shallow-breathing exercises I learned in natural childbirth classes, trying with each intake of air to calm the panic in my chest. Whatever happens in the next hour, I know I will never be the same.

The nurse escorts me into a room with machinery and computer screens along one wall. Off-center stands the operating table with the hole near one end of it. I lie down on my stomach. The nurse lowers my left breast into the opening, straps me to the table, and cranks it up several feet, almost to the ceiling. From this height, I can see nothing but the top panes of a window and the face of the nurse, who is holding my hand and talking to me in a gentle, accented voice. Her presence is the only human component in this high-tech encounter. She blots my eyes with a tissue. "You can cry," she says, "but you must not move." Doctors seem to be scurrying around under the table. I try to imagine how my breast looks to them sticking out of the hole all by itself; not erotic, I'm sure.

They take their x-rays, pinpointing the suspicious spot on their computer screens and discussing what they see in words I cannot understand. They warn me just before I am to feel the quick puncture of the anesthetic; moments later I have the dull, vague sense — more a knowing than a feeling — of the hollow-core needle pushing in, rooting around, and then pulling out. This happens three times. After each probe, I hear the door open as the pathologist takes the tissue sample with him out of the room, my fate in his hands.

The whole procedure lasts about forty-five minutes, during which time my immobilized head, neck, and arm go numb as a stone. The air-conditioning has dried my tears. I can hear my own breathing, as though I am a large bellows fanning a fire. Want to slow time? Strap yourself into a paralyzing position on a hard table in a cold room and wait there for someone to tell you if you have cancer. I don't care what kind of unbeliever you are; if you're human, you'll say enough vain prayers to cover a block of burning houses.

The door opens. I cannot see him from my position, but I can hear the pathologist's voice: "It's normal tissue," he says. "You have very dense breasts, and the new mammography equipment is so sensitive it sometimes picks up cystic tissue as shadows. But all three samples are normal."

I exhale more air than I knew I had in me. Thank you, God. Thank you, Doctor. Thank you for sparing me the C-word, the search for "the best oncologist," the hospitalization, lumpectomy, chemotherapy, the nightmares. I would remain in the realm of the healthy, for now, but I would never forget what it felt like to stand on the brink looking into that other world.

At a time like this, an Orthodox Jew would recite *gomel,* the blessing of thanksgiving appropriate to having survived a dangerous ordeal. I say the *sheheheyanu,* the blessing over time. For me it is, very simply, a sacred moment, so I decide to freeze it — the whole experience, both the terror and the reprieve, to keep it with me, clear and sharp and ready to thaw the next time a friend is sick and scared so that I can enter the experience with her and maybe help her through. I freeze the whole awful hour, the panic, the waiting, the vulnerability, the verdict; how it felt to float like a balloon off the operating table, to burst out of the building and see the sun and sky as if for the first time, to bound up Lexington Avenue and back into my dear, glorious, normal life.

Happiness is "having two breasts to put in my brassiere," wrote Judith Viorst. It's true.

Talking It Out

I've told this story often, to more people than need to know. For some reason, I feel I have to keep going over it, to get it off my chest, as it were. Maybe talking about the biopsy dissipates some of the terror I feel in hindsight, and I need to hear myself repeat the happy ending so I can believe it — that I am still alive and (presumably) well. Maybe I also need to reassure myself that it wasn't my fault, since women are expected to take partial responsibility for breast cancer detection by doing monthly self-examinations, and we tend to feel dumb and inept — i.e., out of control — if we've missed a suspicious symptom. I may be retelling the story to convince myself that I didn't fall down on my part of the bargain: I couldn't have known. The mammogram was wrong. The doctors were confused. Or maybe I just want to let other women know that suspicious mammograms can turn out to be nothing, biopsy doesn't automatically mean mastectomy, and having three needles shot into your breast isn't as bad as it sounds. I want us all to remember that, despite our frail mortality, sometimes there is no cancer, there is only fear of cancer, and you don't die of that.

My friends soak up every word; they bombard me with questions, just as I do with anyone who's been through a health crisis. At this age, other people's organ recitals are like music to my ears. I don't just toss out a wide net and ask, How are you? I trawl for details: How did you find the lump? When did you realize you were having a heart attack? What does a breakdown feel like? What do you take for it? Did the test hurt? How long after the operation could you resume sex? and — if we're really close — how *was* the sex?

I ask because I genuinely care about my friends and want them to be able to talk about what they've been through, but, in all honesty, I am also motivated by a streak of self-interest a mile wide. Questions are a form of do-it-yourself medical research, and our friends' answers set down the foundations of the layperson's database — symptoms to watch for, treatments to find out about, good doctors, bad hospitals, medication that works, predictable side effects, and coping skills that may come in handy when it's our turn.

After describing her joint pains and failing eyesight, Barbara Macdonald writes, "What I am always aware of, somewhere in the back of my mind . . . is that I am in the process of dying. . . . I am self-conscious in writing this. For after all, no one speaks of dying until they have only a few months or weeks or hours to live. This is society's definition of dying. It asks that I deceive myself and others about my daily awareness that my body is using itself up; it prevents me from calling this process by name for myself and others."

The notion that we shouldn't discuss our bodies rests on the stereotype of the complaining old shrew and the impression that such conversation is unique to this stage of life. "But the fact is," says Macdonald, author of *Look Me in the Eye: Old Women, Aging and Ageism,* "we spend our lives conveying to others how we feel in our bodies." Babies do it through crying or gurgling; adolescents talk about their growth, height, pimples, and puberty; lovers talk about how one another's bodies feel; childbearing women talk about their pregnancies and deliveries; and fiftysomethings talk about their menopausal symptoms. But when the talk is of the discomforts and diseases attendant on aging, it is perceived as complaining, not communicating, and some women feel censored. "I have to ask myself, 'Why am I being silenced? What is the message that I have to tell you that you are forbidden to hear?'"

The answer is, of course, that we are *all* in the process of dying.

A disability rights activist once told me we're all in the same boat; hers just happens to be a wheelchair and she's in it now. "You're temporarily able-bodied," she said. "But you'll catch up." She was talking about aging —

the great leveler. Sometime or other, *something's* going to get me, and I'll have to zero in on that condition ("the sick person has only one problem"), but right now I'm a generalist harvesting information from all quarters. This is why I had no trouble reassuring a friend who had colon cancer that I was glad to be her postsurgery sounding board despite the concerns she expressed in a letter:

> It suddenly occurred to me that our talks often involve my illness and my operation. One of the things I had hoped to avoid was the sickness syndrome: the CAT scans, the reports, the progress, the treatment, the anecdotes. And here I am — discussing it A LOT.
>
> The fact of the matter is that I have had cancer, and I don't want to bore people with it. If our talks are useful to you, that is fine with me. . . . But if you think you SHOULD talk to me about it, please relieve yourself of that burden. I don't want you to dread being with me. And I don't want to go into utterly uninteresting details that are really yawn-yawn time.
>
> Let us re-evaluate this situation. Please tell me how you think we should proceed. I don't mind being impossible, but being BORING and self-involved is just too terrible to contemplate.

When I assured her she wasn't boring me one bit, it was the absolute truth. It isn't every day that someone speaks candidly about colon cancer, which is, after all, one of the most common afflictions of middle age. Happily, my friend has decided to write a book about her experience to put an end to the shame factor surrounding this disease — and she has every intention of making her colostomy *funny.* "The three greatest pleasures in life are health, sex, and a great bowel movement," she tells me, "and for the time being, I've lost all three." She will regain the first two eventually, "but I'll never have to shit again." And then, with a nod toward my obsession, she adds: "Think of the time I'll save."

Another friend, who is fighting both brain and lung cancer, has taught me more than I ever could have taught myself about the power of self-healing. Though she is undergoing chemotherapy and radiation, and cooperating with her doctors in their all-out assault on the disease, she is simultaneously pursuing alternative paths, like meditation, yoga, holistic nutrition, acupuncture, deep relaxation, and creative visualization. She visualizes her body welcoming the chemo into her cancer cells and imagines the cells being devoured. She works at loving herself, finding things to laugh at, and steering clear of negative environments. She tunes in to a reality beyond the senses. While I'm awed by her discipline, what I admire most is her capacity to empty her mind and sit perfectly still. "You have no idea," she says, "how full emptiness can be." She's right; I don't, and I've often wished I could sweep away the clutter and find that kind of peace.

My friend will never know whether it's the self-healing exercises, the Indian shaman, or the megadoses of chemicals that did it, but the fact is, her most recent CAT scan revealed no trace whatever of her brain cancer. The lung tumor has shrunk to about an inch in diameter and, she says, "very soon I'll be getting that under control, too."

Even here, the word "control" forces itself onto the page. Maybe it's wishful thinking. Battered by illness, we take refuge in science, mysticism, or faith, hoping to wrest our fate from carcinogens or clogged arteries, or to beg a reprieve from God. If we love life, we have to do *something* — act, think, breathe deeply, visualize, eat differently, find some way to persuade ourselves that we still have a hand on the tiller and can turn things around.

I was raised on the axiom "Without your health, you have nothing." But that's not the whole story; there's more. Without our health, we learn about suffering and, trite as it sounds, suffering deepens our capacity for empathy. When we don't have our health (or think we're about to lose it), we appreciate whatever else we have all the more. In that sense, I suppose, illness can be redemptive. Without our health, or when it is gravely threatened, we face two stark choices: give up or fight back. The decision to fight for one's life — for control, if you will — marks the difference between a sick person and a sick dog. It is the telltale of the human spirit.

I look upon my "scare" as a preview of things to come. Ill health is inevitable, the only unknowns are when, what, how bad, and how well we are going to cope with it. I wish I could be sure that when my turn comes, I'll be strong enough to fight back with the courage of my friends and the writers I admire. Having glimpsed my own panic, though, I'm not too confident in this regard, and while the scare has left many insights in its wake, I can assure you I would rather stay healthy than be further enlightened. At the same time, the preview did teach me something rather fundamental: when your health goes, life doesn't end, it just asks more of you.

8

Sex, Lies, and Menopause

The mind of a postmenopausal woman
is virtually uncharted territory.

— *Barbara G. Walker*

Let's free-associate: What comes to mind when I say "postmenopausal woman?" What adjectives? What images? What memories? Be honest. Are you thinking "vibrant," "energetic," "dynamic," "vigorous," or are you thinking "dull," "desexed," "irritable," "old?" Are you visualizing a plum or a prune, a lovely, happy woman or a crone (a prefeminist crone)?

I am not saying all postmenopausal women are dried-up old prunes, but I am suggesting that when we reach this time of our lives — the average age at menopause in the United States is fifty-one — menopause is not an empty slate in our minds but rather a jumble of half-conscious preconceptions and misconceptions that color our experience as it unfolds.

Growing up in the fifties, my head was stuffed with dozens of aphorisms that were supposed to guide a girl through life. Along with such vital prescriptions as "Never wear white before Memorial Day or after Labor Day," I learned that "No man will buy the cow if he can get the milk for free" and "You can't get pregnant if you do it standing up." Most of these tidbits have gone the way of the rotary phone and the box step, but at least three menopause maxims endure to this day, tempered by modern science, embellished by feminist rhetoric, but still permeating the collective consciousness and misleading millions:

MENOPAUSE CHANGES A WOMAN'S LIFE

MENOPAUSE IS A NATURAL BIOLOGICAL PROCESS, SO YOU JUST HAVE TO LIVE WITH IT

NO ONE WANTS TO TALK ABOUT MENOPAUSE

Though they sound simple and straightforward, reasonable, innocuous, and descriptive of common experience, I'm convinced all three are lies, or rather half-truths — myths that function as mechanisms of social control.

Myth #1 — Menopause Changes a Woman's Life

The year I turned fifty (*anno horribilus*, to quote the queen), my menstrual periods petered out. For a while there, I did battle with one pesky menopausal symptom but, like the interview subjects described in Betty Friedan's *Fountain of Age,* I basically "didn't have menopause" — that is, I had nothing resembling the momentous, pivotal "change of life" I'd heard and read about since I was a teenager.

I'm not saying nothing happened; menopause happened — it's just that it wasn't traumatic, or even close. Hot flashes, yes. The end of my life as a woman, no. The hardest part of menopause for me was dealing with what Friedan calls "menopause hysteria" — the *expectation* that it was going to be a crisis that would change my life in profound ways. From the outset, however, the facts never added up to crisis material. With three grown children, my biological clock wasn't an issue, and I had only scant evidence that my sex drive was in decline. As for gut-level feminine identity, I was never one to wax rhapsodic about monthly bloodlettings that lasted seven or eight days; there were better ways to feel affirmed as a female. Then, too, while I can't quite agree with whoever said that "the end of the curse is a blessing," there were distinctly positive changes associated with menopause — no more cramps, tampons, tender breasts, contraceptives, marking the calendar, pregnancy scares, or inglorious seepage on the seat of one's white jeans. Marge Piercy's poem about menopause ends with "I will burn my last tampons as votive candles." She calls the poem "Something to Look Forward To."

Complaining of her hot flashes and wavering libido, Dena Taylor wonders whether women in the United States have "a privileged way of going through menopause. If I were in Central America, the mother of a disappeared child, would I be feeling any menopausal symptoms?" Overall, in my experience, menopause fell somewhere between a welcome development and a nonevent. Compared to other seismic happenings in human experience, it truly did not qualify as a *major* change. Want to see your life change? Lose a parent while still a child. Lose a limb. Have a baby. Get fired, get divorced, get AIDS. *Now* you're talking change.

I'm far from alone in my sanguine views. (Pun intended.) A Massachusetts study of 8,000 women found that fully 70 percent felt either relief or neutrality at the onset of their menopause, and when reinterviewed five years later, they felt even more *positive* about it. A Gallup poll discovered that more than seven out of ten menopausal women experienced no change at all in their interest in sex. Another large study found that 25 percent of American women are altogether *symptom-free*. If the majority of us find menopause to be either positive, tolerable, or no big deal, why, I wondered, is it still given the ominous designation "The Change?"

I'm not denying that some women go through the torments of hell. Friends of mine have suffered not just hot flashes but crying jags, headaches, incontinence, weight gain, and desert-dry vaginas. Other women report atrophy of vaginal and genital tissue, urinary tract problems, stress, pessimism, insomnia, and limp libidos. In a *Ms.* article entitled "Benched," Florence King writes, "I haven't felt a trace of horniness since completing the menopause." *Women of the 14th Moon*, a collection of women's essays on their menopause experiences, attests to the full range of reactions, psychological and emotional as well as physiological. Jean Mountaingrove says she had brief thoughts of suicide, suddenly feeling, "It's no use. My life is meaningless. I can't go on." Erica Lann Clark asks, "How can you be a woman and not be fertile?" Frances Ruhlen McConnel describes her hot flashes as "death closing in against my heart." Pat Miller, who endured six years of fevered flushes, calls her menopause "world class."

I do not for a moment question the truth of these accounts, nor the testimony of Gail Sheehy, author of a bestselling book on the subject, who suffered "unexplainable fatigue, feelings of sadness, free-floating depression, loss of sexual desire, mental confusion, hot flashes, changes in memory and brain clarity, unexplained nervousness, etc." What I do question, however, is the tendency to generalize a set of norms from them and to formulate negative predictions based on reports from that portion of the female population that happens to have suffered the worst side effects.

Since one out of four women is symptom-free, we are just as likely to know someone (or be someone) who sailed through the climacteric with no sign of it other than the cessation of menstruation. (Technically, "menopause" refers to a particular point in time — the last menstrual period — while the "climacteric" refers to all the years from the beginning of ovarian decline and reduced hormonal production to the postmenopausal phase when the symptoms are gone.) Why can't menopause be personified by that *woman*, for a change, the one with no symptoms? Or by a woman from the majority that falls between those with "no symptoms" and the "extreme sufferers" — the group that had some problems but found ways to make them tolerable with the help of doctors, therapists, herbs, creams, exercise, yoga, nutrition, or estrogen replacement. Women like Amber Coverdale Sumrall, who has hot flashes *and* a lover ten years younger than herself and says, "I am amazed by my newfound sexuality." Or like Clara Felix, who writes, "Free of the burden of menstruation, I think of my body as being under my control, rather than subject to omnipotent hormonal forces. . . . My physical health is fine. My emotional health is far better than it was through all the tumultuous years of my youth." Or like Meridel LeSeur, who proclaims, "After a woman passes menopause, she really comes into her time. . . . I have never felt so well or had so many images before me."

Why aren't these women as visible in the menopause literature as the women who are in extremis?

The climacteric is a highly individual biological process, marked by different manifestations of varying intensities, but because we rarely hear about the less notorious case histories, each new wave of older women goes into it as I did, expecting the worst. One can understand why a catastrophic interpretation of menopause might have taken root in generations past, when life was short and, as Friedan put it, the end of reproductive potential signaled "the end of life as a woman." However, that doesn't explain why my generation is perpetuating the myth that caused so many of us to approach this biological inevitability with such dread. Although disavowing the "you are your uterus" perspective, and denying that a woman's sex life is over at fifty, today's most prominent commentators persist in describing menopause in apocalyptic terms. The title of Germaine Greer's *The Change* could be the title of an Anne Rice or Stephen King novel. Gail Sheehy's title, *The Silent Passage,* is vaguely forbidding. *Newseek* put a picture of a dying tree on its cover to illustrate its lead story on menopause. Many writers approach the topic the way journalists cover a train crash, piling up the disaster stories while ignoring the survivors who were thrown clear of the wreck. While Sheehy admits that some women told her they had an unremarkable, trouble-free menopause, she dismisses them, saying they may be "one of the lucky few," or they may be "lying." In her view, menopause is still the "most profound change of our life."

Since I approached my fifties fiercely resistant to the whole idea of change, you can just imagine how *The* Change — the Big One with all the bad news — loomed in my mind. My mother finished menopause a year or so before she died, leaving me with no specific memories of it other than the impression that a lady keeps her "change of life" a secret, like her age. My sister, who is fourteen years my senior, never talked about her menopause, either. Now she tells me this was because it was not worth mentioning; at the time, I assumed it was because it must be worth hiding. Today, of course, the mystery and modesty are gone, but the atmosphere of melodrama endures — regardless of the facts.

I'd always heard about women's off-the-wall moodiness, for example, but I've since learned that depression actually decreases during menopause and is most common in women *under* thirty-five. "It is important to say at the outset that no peak of emotional illness is found in the menopausal years," writes physician Sadja Greenwood in her commonsensical guidebook *Menopause Naturally: Preparing for the Second Half of Life*. "Surveys of women in their mid-forties to mid-fifties show that hot flashes and night sweats are the only symptoms *directly* related to menopause."

The health columnist Jane Brody is just as unequivocal: "Menopause by itself does not cause depression. In fact, the studies show, there is no particular link betweeen menopause and depression." The link, it seems, is elsewhere: some researchers have found that depression in middle-aged women is related to their degree of acceptance of the traditional feminine role. Others posit that menopause blues may actually be midlife blues, or that women who are depressed usually have good reasons — fear of aging, divorce, widowhood, discrimination, economic hardship, loneliness — reasons unrelated to whether or not they're still ovulating. Writes Greenwood: "If a woman in her late forties gets angry or cries, her emotion is often blamed on 'the change of life,' just as in her thirties it was blamed on her periods or pregnancy. This kind of thinking can make women feel helpless, at the mercy of their hormones. It often prevents them from examining the factors in their relationships, families or jobs that may well cause anger or depression."

Then, too, I was intimidated by the horror stories around the issue of sex. I'd heard of vaginas so dry that a penis felt like a sanding machine during intercourse (an image that could depress anybody). Yet I knew women who had solved that problem with topical lubricants, testosterone cream, or hormone replacement. As for the postmenopausal woman's legendary lost libido, that, too, seemed greatly overdramatized. "Sexual responsiveness changes with aging in both women and men," says Greenwood. "The sex drive may seem less urgent and arousal may take longer. However, many women continue to be sexually active into old age, both with partners and by masturbating. . . . Some women report being less interested in sex after the age of fifty, feeling other aspects of their lives are more important. Others say sex is more enjoyable than ever." The good doctor also reminds us that there is more to sexual expression than intercourse: "One of the problems with sex in younger years for many women is the lack of prolonged caressing and foreplay, and the rapidity with which sexual encounters lead to intercourse. In later life there is an opportunity to correct this imbalance."

Whether or not women suffer from vaginal dryness — and men from erectile difficulties — Greenwood and other menopause experts counsel using this time of life to experiment with forms of gratification other than penetration: the loving touch, deep sensual massage, mutual stimulation with hands, mouth, or vibrator, and lots more affection, touching, hugs, hot tubs, and erotic conversation between partners — all of which might have a distinctly life-enhancing effect on sex at any age.

Some women are more sensitive than others to hormonal changes, and, having experienced premenstrual tension, PMS, or postpartum depression, they seem likelier candidates for menopause-related depression and changes in their sexual responsiveness. Cause and effect remain cloudy, however, since the female sex drive is influenced by androgen, not estrogen, and almost all of a woman's androgen is produced by the adrenal glands, which are unaffected by her reproductive status or decreasing estrogen levels. (The ovaries produce a very small percentage of the androgen supply.) Nonetheless, about 35 percent of American women report a gradual or sudden drop in sexual interest.

Some physicians have been administering testosterone supplements in addition to estrogen replacement therapy to rekindle the libido, and their patients have reported the return of their sex drive, fantasy lives, and ability to reach orgasm. One might reasonably be concerned about doctors giving women the male hormone that, in high doses, can produce facial hair, a deeper voice, acne and weight gain, as well as raising the "bad" cholesterol count and increasing the risk of cardiovascular ailments. At the same time, there is something to be said for the fact that the libido of a fifty-year-old woman is considered worthy of medical attention at all. Not long ago, only male sexual dysfunction was important enough to worry about. People believed older women were not sexual human beings so it made no difference if they felt desire or not as long as they remained available to their men for intercourse.

Whether testosterone therapy is safe for women may not be known for years. By the same token, science has yet to fully understand the role of biochemistry in creating or relieving negative mood states, and until that is established, most doctors seem inclined to look for the cause of menopausal anxiety or low-libido problems in the social or psychological realm. Indeed, anyone can understand why a fifty-year-old woman might feel unloved and unlovable in this youth-crazed culture, or why her juices might stop flowing if her spouse or lover (straight or gay) takes her for granted or leaves her for a younger woman, and new sex partners aren't knocking at her door. Finally, it should be said that if older women are turned off by sex, older men may have something to do with it. Make of it what you will, but, according to Clark Gillespie, M.D., author of *Hormones, Hot Flashes and Mood Swings: Living Through the Ups and Downs of Menopause*, "Lesbian women complain much less of menopausal symptoms than do their heterosexual counterparts."

I'm told some men are amazingly inept in the sack; either they don't know or don't care what makes a woman responsive. Or, they're having troubles of their own associated with the "male change of life." After fifty-five or so, the level of testosterone (which fuels the male sex drive) gradually begins to drop and, though men keep producing sperm well into their eighties or even nineties, it may become more difficult for the penis to become hard and stay erect. In *New Passages,* Gail Sheehy says many older men experience a "virility crisis" — called the viropause in England — brought on, not just by changes in their sex drive or performance, but by their having become aware of a decrease in their general stamina, overall muscle mass, physical strength, and capacity to command attention in the world, which, in turn, makes them irritable, lethargic, or depressed.

"And unless a man is in a good relationship with a knowing partner," mobility and power, but *decreased* when women's power and freedom grew." In the United States, where women are valued for youthful beauty and reproduction, for instance, older women exhibited many severe menopausal symptoms. Moreover, American women's discomfort runs tandem with the value placed on older women in each ethnic subgroup, writes Steinem, citing studies in which "African-American women reported the fewest negative symptoms and Jewish women reported the most; arguably because of the relative importance of the role that older women play in those communities."

In countries like Pakistan, where women are restricted during their childbearing years but emerge from isolation after menopause and are allowed more authority, social mobility, and conversation in the marketplace, women had very few symptoms. Likewise, Mayan women in Mexico and blue-collar and professional women in Britain and Hawaii looked forward to postmenopausal lives that were active and free compared with their own premenopausal pasts. Instead of worrying about spiritual emptiness or lost femininity, their only question was, what next?

Yewoubdar Beyenne, an Ethiopian, says that in her country, the climacteric is associated with no negative attributes, and she is surprised by the American obsession with the subject: "Coming from a non-Western background, I was not aware that menopause causes depression or any other emotional or physical illness. I only knew that menopause was a time when women in my culture felt free from menstrual taboos." Beyenne, a medical anthropologist who studied the impact of menopause in a variety of countries, has concluded that the climacteric is a "biocultural phenomenon."

Summing up, Clark Gillespie writes, "In all studies of menopausal symptoms, regardless of race, creed, color, or economic status, one fact stands out: Women who are well-integrated in their environment, who are surrounded by friends, and who possess a good social network and have meaningful activities will have less intense menopausal symptoms."

Some women dump on menopause when the actual culprit — the force that makes them feel melancholy and doubtful of their agency as females — is more likely to be sexism, ageism, the beauty imperative, and the unfortunate bottom-line equation of femininity with youthful sexuality and motherhood. In Western society, "femininity" has always been a word with too much power and no real meaning, except as it's been manipulated to maintain stereotypes, coerce women to behave in traditional ways, or make us think we're not measuring up. Though it has been more than five years since my last menstrual period, I simply cannot relate to words like "empty," "unfeminine," or "sexless." Although I've noticed a change in my libido — less of a driving desire to have sex — I also feel a surge of sexual freedom. Being able to have intercourse without worrying about an unwanted pregnancy can liberate a woman and let her concentrate on pleasure. For forty years, the fertility goddess was hyperactive on my behalf; after three abortions and three children, I had reason to say good riddance to her and to welcome menopause — though not the advanced years that come with it. And that, I believe, was the real source of my malaise. What troubled me was not "the change" but "the end."

The underlying trauma of the climacteric is that it gives us an advance inkling of death. We tend to conflate the accompaniments of aging, such as feelings of anxiety, fatigue, or inadequacy, with the physiological effects of menopause, because it is preferable to focus on big, bad hormonal chaos rather than on the trickling away of time. Menopause is a convenient repository for the nonspecific dread and inexpressible rage that come with the territory when you're fifty. Almost anything that happens at this age is blamed on menopause, an all-purpose transference mechanism that becomes a temporary distraction from the truth, but also an inescapable reminder of it. In short, I've come to understand that the change I feared most, the change we all fear, was the end of *deniability*. Men this age can keep kidding themselves, pretending they are still young and pushing mortality out of view. Even if the penis falls down on the job now and then, their bodies can still do what they've always done: make babies well into their sixties and seventies. We women, on the other hand, cannot hide from our age or mortality; menopause reminds us of what lies in store by forcing us to acknowledge that the body we've known and trusted has suddenly shut down in one area, foreshadowing all the stoppages to come. Menopause tells us — not in the abstract, but in the altered workings of our flesh and blood — that we are closer to the end.

Because of my fixation on time, and my need to reframe the aging experience wherever possible, I warmed to Lonnie Barbach's *The Pause: A Positive Approach to Menopause*. She begins by renaming this phase of women's lives to help us overcome the many negative expectations associated with it. She finds "The change of life" a problematic phrase, since it "can easily be misinterpreted as the change from life to death." She chose "The Pause" because it seemed to capture "the most positive aspects of the experience. It speaks of a break, a time to reflect. This transition from our childbearing years to the next stage of life, in which our own needs can play a more central part in the story that unfolds, promises excitement."

The concept of "the pause" appeals to me because it suggests that a woman's life is still moving forward in time; that menopause doesn't shut us down or turn us into a husk of our former self, but gives us time to get our second wind and rethink our future. "It's sort of like pushing the pause button on your VCR player," Barbach writes: "you take a break for a few minutes to answer the phone or scoop out some frozen yogurt. You can do a lot of things during this interlude, but ultimately you expect to continue from where you left off. . . . While The Pause may be a period of disequilibrium, of physical discomfort, it also heralds a new equilibrium, a period of renewed energy, and often a new sense of purpose."

Myth #2: Menopause is a natural biological process, so you just have to learn to live with it

I've told you I only had one symptom, hot flashes, but what I haven't told you is, they were lollapaloozas. People who've never had one ask, "How hot could a hot flash be?" Think scorched earth, I tell them. Think pizza oven, think iron smelter. Menopause mavens report that during each hot flash, the skin temperature suddenly rises 7 or 8 degrees Fahrenheit, but at the height of my conflagrations, I felt as if Mount St. Helens was erupting inside my body sometimes twenty, sometimes fifty times every twenty-four hours, saturating my clothes with sweat and leaving my hair dripping wet, much to the puzzlement of colleagues who witnessed these sudden lava flows in the midst of a meeting. Even when it was Artic-cold in the room, it was Africa-hot in me. I couldn't wear sweaters, long sleeves, or shirts buttoned at the neck. The flashes happened so often that I had trouble concentrating on my work for more than a few minutes at a time. A good night's sleep was out of the question — for Bert as well as me — since every night, several times a night, my personal furnace blasted out enough BTU's to drench the bed linens and send me crawling to an open window or an air conditioner, in January.

About 80 percent of women experience some version of hot flashes, accompanied by dizziness, headaches, heart palpitations, and drenching sweat on the face, neck, and upper body. These usually last for two or three minutes — although in some women they can rage for as long as an hour. Untreated, up to 50 percent of women suffer for more than five years, and some for ten years or more.

Feminism had taught me that menopause is a natural biological process and not something to be "cured." It had also taught me that a woman must take control of her own body, so after about six months of this torture, I consulted my women's health manuals and tried some of the natural remedies recommended to deal with this heat wave that many people insist "you just have to live with." I cut out caffeine, alcohol, and hot showers. I tried ginseng, papayas, motherwort, vitamin E, self-hypnosis, and a Chinese doctor who read my aura and prescribed herbs to replenish my depletions. Since women have fewer symptoms in cultures where older women are revered, I tried self-reverence, focusing on my achievements and telling myself that, since I was never solely invested in my reproductive powers, ovulation should go out like a lamb. No dice. It went out like a pyromaniac.

My gynecologist, Lila Nachtigall, who happens to be an authority on hormone replacement therapy (HRT), monitored my condition for six months, then came to the rescue with a prescription for small daily doses of estrogen (supplemented each month by ten days' worth of progesterone). I refuse to feel guilty about this, although many antihormone absolutists think taking estrogen for menopause is like doing the New York City marathon by subway. They think it's cheating or chickening out or interfering with one's natural biological processes, and they insist that every woman should use positive thinking and homeopathic remedies regardless of her circumstances. (Hey, I want to ask them, if you're letting Mother Nature do her thing, how come you're not pregnant more often?)

Of course, they're right to attack doctors who "medicalize" women's bodies, and pharmaceutical companies that reap huge profits from women's discomfort. They're right to keep reminding us that Premarin, the top-selling brand of estrogen, is now the most-prescribed drug in the U.S., and the HRT consumer market already exceeds half a *billion* dollars — even though fewer than 18 percent of today's 40 million menopausal women are taking hormones, and the drug companies have only begun to tap the nearly 50 million baby boomers who will enter menopause over the next two decades. Still, it is also true that many of the proponents of HRT are committed feminists like Penny Wise Budoff, a gynecologist and author of *No More Hot Flashes,* who is motivated by what is best for women and who was an early and insistent promoter of replacement therapy that includes *both* estrogen and progesterone. Budoff has been administering HRT to her patients with no ill effects since 1964.

Although their hearts are in the right place, many of the anti-HRT forces, the die-hard supporters of natural remedies, sometimes overdo it. They remind me of home-birth missionaries who make a person feel she has betrayed all of womankind by choosing to deliver her baby in a hospital. If I'd been bullied into a home birth with my twins, who, you'll recall, were delivered by emergency cesarian section, all three of us might be dead; and if I'd been forced to endure menopause without HRT, I might have killed someone. Dehydration and sleep deprivation would have driven me to it. Louise Mancuso writes in *Women of the 14th Moon* that not only couldn't she bear to have the sun touch her skin, she also couldn't understand why the newspapers weren't filled with accounts of menopausal women going "berserk, strangling, bludgeoning, maiming whoever happened to be near them when their, yes, *runaway* hormones took the express elevator up their backs, chests, and necks, straight on through to the tops of their heads." Surely, it was an inferno like hers or mine that inspired the T-shirt that read:

"I'M OUT OF ESTROGEN. And I've got a gun."

More power to those for whom the natural remedies work. For me, however, HRT has been the right solution. Less than forty-eight hours after I swallowed my first estrogen pill, Mount St. Helens subsided, and, in the five years since I started on the regimen, I've felt exactly as I did before the flashes began. As Nachtigall explained it, HRT returned my hormonal system to the equilibrium in which it functioned for forty years. Maybe that's why I feel so "natural" about taking it.

Of course, one can't be a woman today and not know that estrogen replacement carries with it some risk of cancer of the breast, although Lila Nachtigall has been prescribing it since 1975 (though never to women in high-risk categories) and of all her patients who've gotten breast cancer, only one was on HRT. We also know that there is some risk of cancer of the endometrial lining of the uterus, although in 1983, the American College of Obstetrics and Gynecology issued a bulletin stating that the addition of progesterone during each cycle "has been shown to reduce the risk of endometrial hyperplasia to near zero, and this should be accompanied by a significant reduction in the risk of developing endometrial carcinomas." Nonetheless, anyone who remembers the DES debacle is surely sobered by the fact that the long-term effects of HRT are still unknown.

On the other hand, the positive trade-offs are compelling. There is strong evidence that women who take estrogen live significantly longer than those who don't. One study found HRT users enjoy a 46 percent reduction in rate of death from all causes. Estrogen protects against bone loss and against osteoporosis, which currently afflicts about one out of four women over age fifty. Osteoporosis is far more serious than most women realize. It doesn't just give you dowager's hump or rob five inches from your height, it causes fatal falls and fractures and ten times more deaths than endometrial cancer.

Estrogen also seems to guard against heart disease, reducing its morbidity by 50 percent. (While we're worrying about cancer, nearly three times as many women over fifty-five die of heart problems.) Two more just-released findings also fall on the plus side: women who take estrogen seem to be somewhat protected from colon cancer, and they are 40 percent less likely to get Alzheimer's disease. Furthermore, those who *do* get it suffer less memory deterioration than women who aren't on hormones.

Some would have us believe estrogen does everything for a woman except hang her pictures. I'm no fanatic, but after weighing the benefits against the risks, I came out pro-HRT. For *me.* I don't advocate it for anyone else, and I'm not claiming to have based my decision on more than an informed guess and a burning desire to rid myself of those hot flashes. If estrogen didn't exist, I'm not sure *I* would.

Going through "the Change" never changed anything but my thermostat — not my moods, not my vaginal walls, not my sex life — however, if another woman's symptoms are as discombobulating to her as the hot flashes were to me, I'd say it's cruel and unusual punishment to ask her to "just live with it" simply because her symptoms were precipitated by a natural process. Teething is natural, too, but we don't want babies to suffer and we don't feel guilty when we alleviate their discomfort.

As one doctor noted, while it may not seem natural to fiddle with body chemistry, neither is it natural from an evolutionary standpoint for a woman to live to be eighty. Although menopause is clearly programmed into female biology, until a generation or two ago most women didn't survive long enough to experience it. In 1900, remember, female life expectancy was forty-nine. Judging by all the elderly women walking around with brittle bones and curved backs, it's fair to ask whether the female body was intended to endure more than one-third of its life span in a state of estrogen deprivation. Given humanity's relatively brief experience with longevity, maybe this is one area where nature needs our help.

In any case, the HRT decision is ours to make, each of us according to younger women know what's coming, I can't help feeling nervous about where this openness is taking us, why the media is eating it up, and how this flood of menopause information could be used and abused — especially now that reactionary conservative forces are moving into the driver's seat all over America. Could all those well-publicized menopausal symptoms someday be used to argue that older women are too unstable to be trusted with responsibility? If the phrase "male menopause" connotes irrational or aberrant behavior in men, can there be any doubt that menopause in women could be used to discredit us?

This is not paranoia speaking, this is caution informed by a long memory. I can still remember when the mere fact that women menstruate was reason enough to question our abilities and accuse us of "raging hormonal imbalance." If being "on the rag" once disqualified us for worldly pursuits, is it so far-fetched to imagine that being "off the rag" might be used to make similar claims against middle-aged women, a group that some observers find offensively assertive and independent anyway? Now that we Second Wave feminists are past fifty, and the female baby boomers have begun entering the climacteric (3,500 new ones every day), what better way to keep those uppity women in line than to rally 'round menopause; what better way to put the difference back in vive la différence than to shift the spotlight off a woman's cool competence and onto her hot flashes?

If history repeats itself, it is possible that this heightened awareness of menopause could be used by pronatalist forces to draw attention to all those boomers with wombs-on-the-wane and to underscore the need for a new generation of (white) baby-makers. The religious right is already demanding that women return to the kitchen and nursery. Given America's relatively low birth rate, and given the fact that the largest contingent of women in history is about to leave its reproductive capacities behind, the propregnancy advocates could find statistical support for their campaign. Thus could the current open discourse on menopause be distorted into a "profamily" message that would reverberate in the lives of women who are still of childbearing age.

By going public with our bodies ourselves, by revealing our symptoms and giving credibility to the concept of the Big Change, we could unwittingly be providing our detractors with proof that biology is destiny. In educating ourselves and each other, we could inadvertently be handing the antiwoman forces the weapons to cut us down to size.

Of course, all this is speculative. But with the conservatives coming on strong, speculation may well be a form of prescience. I'm not suggesting we should censor ourselves or back away from the knowledge we need to get through menopause in fine fettle, but I am saying that vigilance is the price one pays for open access to that knowledge. Women of every age ought to be keeping tabs on right-wing rhetoric and political strategies in general, and older women ought to keep monitoring the menopause boom in particular to make sure it keeps working for us, not against us.

Once again, the issue boils down to control. Everything is fine so long as women are in control of menopause and its meanings, so long as each individual woman controls her own body, makes her own treatment decisions, and defines her own capabilities. But the situation bears watching. Just as younger women cannot exercise self-determination in a society that interferes with their reproductive freedom, older women cannot exercise self-determination in a society that equates our reproductive shut-down with the end of our usefulness.

Women cannot control when or how menopause happens to us, but we must be able to control how postmenopausal women are treated in our society and to strike back if and when this "biocultural" event is used as a club to keep us in our place. If Pakistan and Ethiopia can value postmenopausal women, America can, too.

PART IV

Rethinking What Matters

9

Love in the Time of Caricature

> Getting along with men isn't what's truly important. The vital knowledge is how to get along with a man, *one* man.
>
> — *Phyllis McGinley*

I warned you at the beginning that this book wasn't going to be a comprehensive survey of midlife, but a meditation filtered through one sensibility and one set of experiences. Renewing the disclaimer is important here because, as I begin these chapters on relationships, I am aware of my circumscribed perspective. I have one husband, three biological children, a family of origin, relatives-in-law, and a few dozen friends. I can't speak with authority about divorce, widowhood, stepparenting, adoption, being a grandmother, lesbian relationships, or what it's like to be single over fifty. Nevertheless, when it comes to universals like love and intimacy, one needn't have seen it all to figure out what matters. Individual experience, however idiosyncratic, can resonate with more richness and depth than all the generalizations in the big tent.

On that theory, I shall proceed to tell it as I see it — meaningful relationships at midlife — starting with marriage.

Marriage and Memory

At this writing, I've been married for thirty-one years — forever to some people, a trice to me. More than anywhere else, it is within marriage that I have discovered time's mischief: the years pass faster when you share them.

"Where did the time go?" long-wed spouses ask each other, because almost everything seems to have happened just yesterday. Since so many of the landmarks of married life are such high-concept events — wedding, honeymoon, kids, family, home, illnesses, accidents, graduations, deaths — we can run through our past like a bullet train whose passengers needn't stop at every station to know the terrain. Or we can say, "Remember when . . ." and, using a shorthand only we understand, conjure a single experience, reveling in the memory like army buddies reliving their glory days, or baseball fans feeding each other the stored imagery of seasons past, or comedians who make each other laugh by number. This, I think, is one of the unadvertised bonuses of long marriage: it gives your life a witness. In a long marriage, spouses are each other's historians of record.

I sometimes wonder what happens to shared memories when a couple get divorced. Do they cut each other out of the past like a teenager trimming an old boyfriend out of last year's prom picture? How do they detach recollections of a place from thoughts of the person they saw it with? Does their mind's eye recall a pleasant image but blur the face of their former spouse, as if he or she were one of those undercover agents unwilling to be shown on camera? As you get older, what do you do with the holes in your memory when memories mean so much?

"After the breakup, I had no desire to look back; I was trying desperately to look ahead," says Carol, one of the women who was at my fiftieth birthday lunch. "I worked so hard on separating from my former husband, not relying on him, not being disappointed when he didn't come through for the children, and in the process, I probably wiped out *all* my memories of him, the good with the bad. But when I'm reminiscing with the kids, I try to remember the happy times. I tell them stories of their father and me when we were young. I guess I haven't obliterated him altogether."

Harriet, another guest at the lunch, sees it altogether differently. Looking back on her eleven-year marriage, which broke up more than twenty years ago, she says, "We fought, we had issues that couldn't be resolved, but even though we couldn't make a go of it, I have extremely happy memories of our time together. My ex-husband was my first love, and I look back on our marriage as a great adventure. It was my youth.

"I have joyful memories of giving birth, and he and I doing the Lamaze method together. And I have no problem recalling our wonderful odyssey in 1970, when we spent four months in England and Ireland with our two-year-old daughter in tow. It was a perfect idyll and we were totally carefree.

Couples who are sensitive to other people's perceptions, and who don't want to arouse either ridicule or envy, learn to censor their love in public, which, in turn, perpetuates the culture's mixed messages: whereas love songs and romance novels promote dreams of devoted, long-term unions, the absence of living, breathing examples of such unions makes their reality seem unreal. The rare doting middle-aged couple thus becomes either silly or suspect, and the result is perverse: happily married older people feel embarrassed about displaying the very devotion that is the goal of everyone who has ever gotten married in the first place.

So what? you ask. Who needs a public showing of other people's pleasure? We all do. If society benefits from knowing the truth about abuse and inequity in marriage, wouldn't it benefit even more from knowing that there are many kinds of successful unions, including dynamic, lasting relationships between people who are past their "prime"?

Lacking positive narratives and vibrant images of long marriages, younger folks tend to construct caricatures based on their general negativity about time and age. In most minds, age is associated with things that wear down, wear thin, and wear out, so how can that not be true of marriage, too? Young people cannot imagine that older people could possibly be having good sex — or sex at all. Are you kidding? With *those* bodies? And in this culture, any entertainment longer than a sound bite or a sitcom brings on an attention-deficit disorder, so how could something that lasts thirty years not be a humongous bore?

Now, if I want to refute those misguided assumptions, I run three serious risks: invasion of privacy, insufferable smugness, and the wrath of the Evil Eye. Anyone who writes about a happy marriage, especially her *own* happy marriage, risks sounding sappy and self-satisfied unless she reveals personal frailties and sex secrets that might balance her story at the expense of her spouse's right to marital confidentiality. With such obvious hazards, why am I even bothering to maneuver between this (writer's) Scylla and (wife's) Charybdis? Because no book on time and aging would be complete without some talk of how love and sex weather the years.

The Evil Eye

The fact remains that writing about my own happiness makes me nervous. Every time something good happened when I was growing up — if I got an A in school, or a compliment on how I looked — my mother was afraid someone might envy me. Envy was toxic; it meant the person wanted what you had, hated you because you had it, wanted to take it away from you. Envy was the work of the devil — the Evil Eye in my house — whose mission was to zap not only those who are vulnerable (remember the name change for the sick person) but anyone who might be getting too many goodies. So whenever the spotlight fell on something positive in our lives, whether it was an accomplishment or an accident of good fortune, my mother, who seemed to be on speaking terms with the Evil Eye, taught me to say "*kenna-hurra*," an incantation to ward off envy. She taught me to believe in God but also in demons. She saw all of life as a cosmic balance sheet, and if God gave you too much, the Evil Eye would try to even the score by taking something away from you. To avoid its deadly gaze and not attract its attention, the rule was, keep your happiness under wraps, don't focus on the good things, and don't enjoy life too much.

Someone who has never been the child of a superstitious parent probably cannot imagine how powerful such early teachings can be or how lasting their influence. Despite having grown into a chronic rationalist, there is a small, secret part of me that still guards against the Evil Eye, as if letting go of this remnant of my past would insult my mother's memory or, more likely, unleash the demon's wrath in spades. The result is, throughout my married life, I've been walking a tightrope, wanting to savor the pleasure my marriage gives me, but afraid to arouse the force that could bring a plague upon our house and ruin everything.

It's crazy, but it's my legacy and I know I am not alone. My Jewish friends often say things like "She had the baby last night and he's perfectly healthy, *kenna-hurra*." And my Christian friends knock on wood after they utter an innocent boast like "I've never gotten a speeding ticket" or "I'm pretty lucky at cards." It's hard to enjoy your good fortune if you're always checking over your shoulder to make sure nothing is going to spoil it or steal it from you. Because of the Evil Eye, even when I'm happy I'm not happy. I'm worried that *being* happy might attract a balancing dose of misery, or I'm sure that my happiness can't last much longer because I've had it so long, *kenna-hurra*, and one of these days, my zap will come.

Beyond this admittedly neurotic train of thought, there is a more obvious reason why being happy in marriage can be problematic: the more deeply we love someone, the more afraid we are of losing them. While I've been giving my other anxieties a run for the money, I can't seem to shake this one. Fear of loss has been one of my staples, and now it has intensified with age, which is only to be expected. The older we get, the more we appreciate the fragility of life and the harder it is to deny the real possibility that death could claim a spouse before his time. This raises contradictions that are the marital equivalent of "damned if you do, damned if you don't." If I follow my own advice and savor my marriage mindfully — enjoying the happiness while I'm lucky enough to have it — then I arouse my anxieties about the Evil Eye, envy, and loss. But if I don't enjoy my marriage consciously, if I don't really look at it, as Emily said in *Our Town*, and cherish it, then — like anyone who takes a good thing for granted — when I lose it, I will surely hate myself for having failed to live it to the hilt. Torn between fear of loss on the one hand, and commitment to mindful appreciation on the other, I now sally forth into this minefield to tell you about my husband.

Scenes from a Marriage

I've been lucky, *kinna-hurra*. It was nothing but luck that brought us together one summer Sunday in 1963 when I went to the beach with a date and Bert was among the guy's group of friends. It was just luck that I was wearing a yellow bikini that day; he appreciates yellow and bikinis even more (though I haven't had one on in years, alas). It was sheer coincidence that he was smoking Lucky Strikes at the time, my father's brand; and he's a lawyer, like my father; and when he was in college he belonged to my father's fraternity. And it was nothing but coincidence that his mother and aunt, like my mother and aunt, were old Lefties — their politics, not their handwriting — and he'd lost a parent and I'd lost a parent, and we turned out to be ethnic twins, half Russian, half Hungarian. I read somewhere that "coincidences are God's way of remaining anonymous." The Sunday we met, June 9, 1963, was my twenty-fourth birthday.

We were married six months later. "How did you know he was the one?" young women ask. "I just *knew*," I say stupidly, as millions have said before, many of whom are now on their third husbands. The truth is, I didn't know much. Neither of us can claim to have made a reasoned choice based on well-considered information. We hadn't lived together or tested our reactions in stressful situations or even gotten around to discussing whether we wanted children. But now, looking back over three decades, as I try to make sense of why this marriage never needed saving, I think it may be because our basic values and likes and dislikes are the same, while our temperaments are vastly different. In other words, where it really counts — moral judgments, sexual attraction, political affiliation, emotional availability, family commitment, sex roles, child-rearing, taste in pleasures like food, music, movies — we're shoulder to shoulder and eye to eye, but when it comes to behavior styles, we're yin and yang. Not along the lines of the traditional feminine/masculine split, but with a definite "opposites attract" quotient.

Our core similarities ensure that we don't have big things to argue about, and our differences, though they sometimes rub us the wrong way, have tended to work in our favor; for example, in the sense that he's a morning person and I'm a night owl, which made it easier to split the parenting, or that our different temperaments have permitted decades of worry-sharing. When it came to the kids' physical well-being, I've always staked out the external threats — natural disasters, freak accidents, fire, flood, earthquakes — while he worries about internal threats, such as infectious diseases and the American Cancer Society's checklist of danger signals.

The reason most divisions of labor run into problems is that couples tend to organize themselves according to gender stereotypes rather than their actual interests or skills. Or they think that someone has to be "the boss in the family," a cherished axiom despite reams of testimony to the contrary from couples who nearly foundered on the shoals of hierarchy, and despite countless studies indicating that the healthiest, happiest marriages are those in which husbands and wives hold equal power. In short, where both adults act like adults.

Perception and Reality

As I think about our patterns, I realize that it's not what Bert and I have done or how we've done it, but how we've *interpreted* our choices that has made this marriage "happy." Calling that conclusion profound would be like calling the *National Enquirer* literature, but it's the truth: our perceptions have *become* our reality.

Take the mail, for instance. We have always opened and read one another's mail. It never occurred to me to consider this odd until a friend happened to be visiting one morning when the letter carrier arrived. As I tore open a letter that was addressed to Bert, my friend was clearly shocked, horrified actually, as if she'd just witnessed a safecracker in action, or caught a relative's hand in the till.

"How *could* you?" she asked.

At first, I didn't know what she was talking about. Then she delivered herself of a lengthy peroration on the inviolate nature of personal mail, and how married people ought to guard their individual privacy and not invade each other's "space." The lecture was lost on me as it would have been on Bert, who often reads my correspondence before I get to it. He and I are respectful of each other's need for *solitude*, but privacy? Who needs privacy? Since we have no secrets from each other, what purpose would be served by drawing the line here? We don't interpret reading one another's mail as "invading privacy" but as "sharing in each other's lives." And therein lies the difference.

I tell you this to explain why "positive interpretation" is one of my answers to the question "What makes a marriage last for thirty-one years?" How spouses choose to interpret each other's behavior forms the attitudinal frame within which the marriage either flourishes or sours. Problems arise when one person's interpretations change over time. Say, she used to find his speaking style animated and commanding but now, twenty years later, though his voice hasn't changed, she has reinterpreted it as overbearing. Or he used to see her flightiness as adorable, but at fifty, he reinterprets it as infantile and insufferable. Or suddenly the couple's lifelong spending habits are reinterpreted by one spouse as extravagant and by the other as stingy.

The happiest long marriages surely are those in which reinterpretations have been kept to a minimum and both partners continue to share similar perceptions about whatever reality happens to be theirs.

Conflict

At midlife, when we are rethinking what matters to us, our love relationship is often the first thing that goes under the microscope. If both partners have evolved a constructive way to handle conflict, chances are the union will survive close scrutiny and be judged healthy enough to sustain another twenty or thirty years.

Arguments are inevitable in any relationship, but what interests me is how couples process conflict and cope with their disputes because that's where, over the long haul, hairline cracks in a relationship can become unbridgeable chasms. Obviously, conflict-resolution styles vary from one marriage to another depending on the partners' backgrounds, temperaments, and how much they want peace. Some long marriages seem to thrive on bickering, and other unions are almost suspiciously tranquil. I've known people whose rage drives their relationship to the brink every time they have a disagreement, yet when the smoke clears, they seem able to reconnect with affection and kindness. I've known couples who have nursed the same grievances for twenty-five years but prefer the sulk to the scream. Different strokes for different folks. If it works, why knock it; and if it doesn't, there's always couples therapy. Then, too, plenty of twenty-five- or thirty-year-old marriages have ended in the divorce courts, which is probably where they belong. A long marriage is not some icon to be protected at all costs. Relationships exist for our sake, not the other way around.

Bert and I don't fight often, but when we do, there's one way in which we're rather civilized about it. Although the conventional wisdom says, Never go to bed angry, when we have an argument we *always* go to bed angry. We like to let off steam, then retreat into silence and leave the dispute unresolved until the next morning, when we can view it in perspective and talk more calmly. We never force ourselves to kiss and make up before bedtime. We can't stand the idea of using sex to paper over what's bothering us. Sex is an act of love, not contrition. So after a fight, we climb into our bed, turn our backs to each other, and go to sleep.

I don't know if other people who handle anger this way feel good about it, but I find our behavior enlightened. Never go to bed angry has always struck me as code for "Woman: heal this marriage." (You don't see articles in men's magazines on the importance of making up with your spouse before bedtime.) Anger is a legitimate emotion; not one I welcome, but one every human being is entitled to. Just because the clock is about to strike midnight, I don't want to have to make nice or pretend that everything is okay when it isn't.

Never going to bed angry has become such a sacrosanct principle of marriage that I can well imagine it precipitating a major crisis between two people if, after a fight, one were to turn away from the other and dive into a deep sleep while the other was still in the throes of rage or insomnia. But because Bert and I think we're the soul of rationality when we go to bed mad, this habit has cleared the air for us for three decades.

More important, no matter how angry we are, we never give vent to the worst. The common wisdom dictates that couples should speak their minds to each other and "let it all hang out." Followed to its logical conclusion, however, this dictum could lead to disaster. In the name of candor, married people inflict terrible pain on one another; they say the unspeakable, spew hatred, and make threats that they assume can be recalled when things calm down. Other couples realize that certain words are corrosive enough to eat away at the strongest bonds, and some sentences keep bouncing off the walls of a relationship long after the fury that fueled them has passed.

"The one thing we have learned well in our marriages is how to hurt one another," writes Francine Klagsbrun in *Married People: Staying Together in the Age of Divorce.* "Always at the height of an argument, you have your finger on the weak spots. You can claw at those spots if you wish. Or you can protect them, maneuver around them. . . . In lasting marriages, even in moments of sheer hatred, an alarm sounds and you hold back from saying the very thing the other most dreads hearing."

Those who hold back — who put limitations on their marital warfare and manage to remember in the heat of battle that the person they hate for the moment is the person they love most in the world — probably are still married.

Why Marry?

Lest this chapter degenerate into a how-to guide or a lugubrious paean to wedded bliss, I should explain that while I believe in married love for myself, I don't think everyone should be married, or stay married, or that marriage necessarily is the ideal structure in which to wrap a romance. In some cases, marriage is the death of love and, for women especially, the end of independence. Innumerable critics have detailed why it can be a raw deal for women. In the sixties, while hippies disavowed coupled togetherness in favor of communes and free sex, Ti-Grace Atkinson and other feminist thinkers declared romantic love an opiate and analyzed how women get hooked. In the seventies, the human-potential movement promoted open marriage to air the hothouse of one-on-one commitment, and long-term monogamy was seen as that drab old thing one's parents did. More recently, of course, America discovered the flip side of wedded bliss: marital rape and domestic violence.

Gloria Steinem often says, "The cause of divorce isn't the women's movement; the cause of divorce is marriage." Yet, women themselves insist they like being married. According to a national poll conducted in 1987 by Research and Forecasts, Inc. for Lifetime Cable, 76 percent of American wives maintain that marriage is either *the* most, or one of the most, important things in their life, and 85 percent of them say that, if they had it to do over again, they'd remarry the same man.

Why this enthusiasm? What's so great about marriage per se? Why not just live together now that unwed couples can set up housekeeping openly, even in small towns, and there is little moralistic imperative to make it legal? People who don't want children, such as older lovers, have no need for a marriage license. Those who want children can take care of issues like paternity, support, insurance, and inheritance, leaving no reason for the state to sanction their union or "legitimatize" their kids. Lesbians and gay men can form long-term unions and establish themselves as families without benefit of clergy or judge. Why not heterosexuals, especially older people, who are supposed to be beyond caring what people think?

Again, I ask, so why marry?

Because it's good for you, say the social scientists who have determined that, over time, being married brings dramatic emotional, financial, and health benefits that are not consistent with single life or cohabitation. Linda Waite, a professor of sociology at the University of Chicago and an expert on family structure, says this is because cohabitants are more likely to assume that each partner is responsible for him or herself, whereas married people offer each other mutual support. Waite says wedded couples are generally more financially well off because they are much more likely to pool their money and invest in the future, meaning they spend their money on better medical care, healthier food, and safer surroundings. Summarizing a range of studies, including the broad-based National Survey of Families and Households, which has followed its subjects into the 1990s, Waite adds, "Marriage may provide individuals with a sense of meaning in their lives, and a sense of obligation to others, inhibiting risky behaviors and encouraging healthy ones." Though the married state seems to suit both sexes, men reap its greatest benefits, "because women tend to do the emotional work for the family." Most married men get nurturing, cooking, cleaning, and child care with the deal, and married men even *live* longer than bachelors.

In keeping with my midlife tendency to challenge all the givens, I don't want to just *be* married, I want to understand why I've stayed married, what I get out of it, and why the married state seems more fulfilling as I age. Would Bert and I still be together today had we remained cohabitants?

Would our lives be as thoroughly intertwined as they are had we never stood under the *chuppa* or taken out a marriage license? If not, why not? And if so — I repeat — why marry?

When I ask this question of other couples, they say they got married to formalize their commitment to each other, to make their togetherness official, to put it on the public record, to make sure "everyone knows," to establish that they're no longer available to others, and to make it hard to "just walk away when things get tough." (Since divorce is a lot more complicated than moving out of a live-in situation, marriage presumably discourages people from giving up too easily.)

None of these explanations quite does it for me. To my mind, the main reason to get married is the "until death do us part" part. What impresses me most about marriage is the *time* commitment it involves. And the inherent *optimism*. And the married mindset, which, despite all evidence to the contrary, puts its hope in *permanence*. I've come to realize that I like the whole ideology of lifelong *co*existence, the notion of braiding two lives together while never losing sight of each strand. I love making something from nothing and watching it grow, being present at the creation of an immutable "us" and giving it meaning and making it last. I know, I *know:* half of all marriages break up. But eight out of ten divorced persons remarry, and at least six out of those eight remarriages prove permanent.

At a friend's fortieth wedding anniversary, there were a good dozen couples who had been married nearly as long as the guests of honor. All had been through life's ups and downs and had reached what one man called "joyful accommodation" with their spouses. They testified to feeling more generous toward each other and more appreciative of one another's love than they were ten or twenty years ago. "At this age," said one of the wives, "you remember why you married this person in the first place."

I believe a marriage that lasts and improves with time — one that sinks its roots into the decades and gives shape to the years in the form of memories and children and traditions and history, one that takes joy in the notion of "together forever" — such a marriage can *make time tangible* and thus become humanity's best defense against the emptiness waiting for us at the end of the line.

A Brief History of Love

Here is what I mean: Not long ago, when we were celebrating our thirty-first anniversary, Bert started musing about being sixty and reminiscing about some of the highlights of our years together. Sitting across from him at the dinner table, taking it all in, I marveled not just at what he said but at how he looked as he spoke. He was so absolutely, quintessentially the man I know, the man I have always perceived as disarmingly attractive, yet he also seemed suddenly unfamiliar, like someone I was meeting for the first time. I noted, as never before, how age has softened the outlines of his jaw and neck and loosened the skin hooding his eyes. I saw that his hair, still curly and thick around the sides, is spare on top, and the stubble of his beard is gray. All this registered on me with something of a shock. Though I've looked into those eyes day after day for thirty-one years, though I've watched his face age as I've watched my own, I suddenly saw him as An Older Man.

My God, he's sixty, I thought. I'm actually married to a sixty-year-old man! And then, as I listened to him taking stock of our marriage, the lines in his face began to seem less a measure of his years than of our years together. Thirty-one winters is a long time, I thought, and the flesh is our witness. What I see today in my husband's face is, in large part, what *I* put there — my complaints and worries, my anger, my demands, my needs, my adoration and appreciation, they're all there, written on his skin. I am in my husband's face as he is in mine, in the laugh lines and the frown lines, and the light behind the eyes.

The actress Jeanne Moreau once said, "Age doesn't protect you from love. But love, to some extent, protects you from age." To be sure, being married all this time has protected me from many of the vicissitudes of age, notably loneliness and sexual dormancy, and maybe the truth about myself. I haven't had to drag my drooping bod into the cold, cruel world of singles bars and summer shares to test my powers of attraction. As one of Judith Viorst's poems warns,

> It's hard to be devil-may-care
> When there are pleats in your derriere . . .
> It's hard to surrender to sin
> While trying to hold your stomach in.

I haven't had to run ads in the Personals columns that say things like "I'm 55, look 45, feel 35, love Chopin, sushi, Susan B. Anthony." I haven't had to wonder who will be there for me when I'm sick, or scared, or in trouble.

Not long ago, one of my single friends and I were in an automobile accident far from home, and though we escaped without injury, we had to spend the night in a motel while a body shop pried the fender off the hood and coaxed the engine into working order. The first thing I did when we hit our motel room was to call Bert, who was waiting up for me. My friend pointed out that she had no one to call and felt pretty depressed about it.

"One of the oldest human needs is having someone to wonder where you are when you don't come home at night," said Margaret Mead. Yet 11 percent of all Americans between ages forty-five and fifty-four live by themselves; in the fifty-five to sixty-four age bracket, the proportion rises to 18 percent for women but goes down to 10 percent for men. Psychologist Lenore Tiefer says never-married women have the least problems adjusting to aging because they are accustomed to living alone. I know several never-married women in my age group who live alone and like it. They have active social schedules and seem to spend more time with their friends (most of whom are women) than married women do, which makes sense. They lead busy, stimulating lives. Yet, if they aren't lesbians, which most aren't, they invariably say they are lonely. They complain about the paucity of men — and no wonder: there are 14 million single women older than fifty-five in the U.S., and only 4 million single men.

Many of my single friends are indifferent to marriage — those who are financially independent consider it a bad bargain, and the others just want their independence — but they're still interested in finding a man to love or to sleep with. The ones who do have active sex lives are still looking for a lover who isn't self-centered, or impotent, or on the prowl for someone younger. "They all tell me the same thing," says fifty-two-year-old Lynn B. Goddess. "They say, 'Y'know, you're the oldest woman I've ever gone out with' — and they look so proud of themselves."

If a single woman were writing about love and sex over fifty, this would be a very different chapter in a very different book. As I've said, I don't know how it feels to be divorced, never-married, or widowed, although I tremble when Grace Paley says, "Men, in death as in life, have a sad edge over women," or when I read that 80 percent of all women outlive their husbands and the median age for widowhood is fifty-six. All I know is how it feels to be in love with one man for more than half my life, *kinna-hurra*, and how scared I am to lose him.

In "Late Fragment," written shortly before he died, Raymond Carver speaks for me when he says he got what he wanted in life:

To call myself beloved, to feel myself
beloved on the earth.

Sex and the Long-Married Woman

Margaret Mead, who said many smart things, said the only reason marriage worked so well in the nineteenth century was that people only lived to be fifty. Now, couples are living *together* for fifty years; not only that, they're having sex with each other right to the very end, which is exactly what I intend to do.

When I say something like that, or when I'm with a group of women and the talk turns to sex, I notice two reactions — embarrassment (the age thing), or curiosity, a relatively new phenomenon. I used to be the last person my friends would ask about sex. Now everyone wants to know what I think. I haven't changed; the world has.

Throughout the freewheeling sixties and seventies, when people talked about sex with the enthusiasm now reserved for new software, someone would inevitably point to me and laugh, "Don't ask *her* about sex, she's been monogamous forever."

Talk about caricature. I used to feel like a full gallery of "types." Either I was the monogamous matron who only *thinks* she's happy with one man because she has no idea what she's been missing all these years, or I was lying about the monogamy and cheating on the side, or I'd been duped by a husband who claimed to be faithful but must be schtupping women left and right. Otherwise, I was the erotic naïf who probably still was striving for simultaneous orgasms and thought the missionary position was as exciting as doing it from the chandelier, or I was the feminist goodwife who spent the Sexual Revolution selling raffles at a child-care benefit, or the quaint romanticist who believed in marriage when everyone knew better. Or I was kidding myself and what I'd been calling good sex all these years was just habit.

In my consciousness-raising group in the early seventies, we often tackled sexual subjects from every conceivable angle. At that time, the prototypical feminist was either an assertive sexual adventurer or a crusader against Phallocentric Man. I fit neither category. My groupmates talked about "men" as subject matter. I talked about one man as a lover, husband, and father of my children. On issues such as body image or erogenous zones, I had as much to say as anyone else. But when it came to talking about group sex, kinky sex, lesbian love, affairs with married men, or one-night stands, the other women (all single, separated, or divorced) told tales to rival Scheherazade while I just listened.

When we went around the room giving testimony, I spoke of marital satisfaction while my friends feigned exaggerated yawns or listened with affectionate tolerance. In fact, they were remarkably accepting, remarkable since the group included such sexual radicals and seekers of equal-opportunity orgasm as Betty Dodson, the legendary maven of masturbation, and Anselma Dell'Olio, who wrote "The Sexual Revolution Wasn't Our War" in the very first issue of *Ms.* I felt lucky to be able to listen to such high-octane sensualists and often took their esoteric erotica home to my marriage bed. Contrary to right-wing paranoia, none of my feminist friends ever tried to talk me into leaving my marriage. Not one badmouthed my husband or gave me lectures on male oppression or made me feel like a traitor to the movement just for being in a traditional relationship. They thought I was a rarity, but it was I who defined myself as a square.

Sometime in the eighties, though, AIDS stopped free love in its tracks and my sex life suddenly came into vogue. Now everyone wants to know the secrets of monogamy. How do you stay faithful to one partner? they ask. It's not even an issue, I answer, aware that I have no answers. Believe it or not, and many don't, I never think about "staying" faithful because I haven't wanted to sleep with anyone else since the day my husband and I met. Sure, I notice sexy men, but I notice them with aesthetic distance, the way one might appraise Michelangelo's David or Richard Gere. Or I notice them with an eye to fixing them up with one of my friends. I don't feel that hormonal quickening that led me around by the libido during the years I was single.

The only metaphor I can think of, and it's entirely inadequate, is to compare a good husband with a dream house. When I was young, I lived in many different places, my childhood room, my married sister's attic, several college dorms, various New York City apartments, with a roommate or alone, and since Bert and I have been married, we've moved three times. The last apartment, the one we bought and have lived in for twenty-five years, is my dream house. Since moving in, I've seen gorgeous penthouses and private estates far bigger and ritzier than our digs, but I've never lusted to live in them. I *have* my home. At some point in life, when you realize you've found what you're looking for, you stop moving.

In the nineties, people who are thinking about safe sex, or flirting with the "new traditionalist" lifestyle, want to know whether long-married couples ever miss the excitement of the chase or the variety of new conquests. Even though I've become a proponent of pursuing newness in other aspects of my life, in this case, my answer is no. I *have* all the variety I need; not in sexual partners but in sexual practices. That kind of variety can prove more satisfying over time, particularly for the older woman. In a long, burnished marriage, she doesn't have to worry about building trust or testing the relationship to see if it's safe to be vulnerable. She doesn't have to fear that she might be transgressing if she's more sexually assertive than women are "supposed" to be. Standing on a foundation of comfort, confidence, and trust, she has a lot of room to experiment and pursue the new within herself. As for romance, what long-married couples lack in the thrill of conquest, we make up in the joys of self-celebration. Like most older people we don't have sex as often as we once did, but we have more time and space to be playful.

"You can tell if a couple is happily married (or sexually satisfied, or still attracted to each other) by how often they have sex." People my age grew up with that guilt-inducing bunk. Years ago, I had a boss who was known to ask his married employees how many times a week they had sex; I was never sure if he was motivated by prurient interest or the need to compare his frequency rate to everyone else's. Nowadays, most fifty- and sixty-year-olds would agree with Eda LeShan, who says, "Having started my adult life feeling guilty about too much sex, I'll be darned if I'll end my days feeling guilty about too little sex."

Little doesn't mean lesser. More doesn't mean better. Some couples give each other plenty of orgasms but not much else. In the refined phraseology of Erik Erikson, "You could have a highly active sex life and yet feel a terrible sense of isolation." Yet the myth that "frequency equals quality" endures, casting sex as an Olympic event and putting pressure on people who are having good sex but whose lives may not permit them to have it often. I despise sexual score-keeping, but since everyone seems to wonder how often everyone else is "doing it," and since I promised you honesty in every chapter, I'll skate the thin ice of marital privilege and confess that once a week is the most we seem to manage these days, sometimes less. This puts us right in line with our age-mates. A poll of 6,000 people analyzed by the sociologist-novelist-priest Andrew Greeley found that 61 percent of married people in their early fifties and 37 percent of those over sixty have sex weekly. The 1992 Masters and Johnson report *Human Sexuality* found similar frequency rates for these age groups.

In October 1994, the National Opinion Research Center at the University of Chicago released a study of nearly 3,500 people between the ages of eighteen and fifty-nine that many have called the most important survey of American sexual behavior since the *Kinsey Reports*. Perhaps the most striking of its many startling findings was this: regardless of age, the people who are having the most sex (and the women most likely to have orgasms during sex) are married, not single, and the largest percentage of married people (47 percent of wives and 43 percent of husbands) are having sex "a few times a month" — meaning once a week or so, just like us.

As is true of millions of couples, Bert and I find that exhaustion and work stress often put lovemaking on the back burner. We don't have the energy. We have a million things on our minds. We have to prepare for the next day. We've been up too late. We have to get up too early. We haven't read the paper or watched the news. You get the picture. Sometimes, when it's been too long between trysts, we actually make a date with each other — we put it on our calendars and protect its priority to make sure it doesn't get preempted. I used to think sex wasn't sexy unless he swept me off my feet in some spontaneous seduction scene, but I've learned that the preplanned encounter adds the extra dimension of anticipation, and no matter how contrived, once it's underway, romance is as romance does.

Which brings up a *good* reason why we make love less often, a reason that should be underscored in connection with sex and aging. In plain words, we're doing it less but enjoying it more because we're letting it last longer, which makes the whole experience rather more interesting than the quickies of our youth. Now, our lovemaking is more ardent and embellished, less hurried and more savored, more of an event, and an event isn't special if you do it too often. Besides, who could find time for it? According to sex researcher Morton Hunt, the average time spent on sexual foreplay is fifteen minutes, and the average duration of intercourse is ten minutes. To me, twenty-five minutes sounds rushed.

I will confess one problem: when our kids come to stay overnight, I can't indulge. (Bert has embellished this story to the point where I have trouble making love when the children are anywhere in the neighborhood, but it's not true — it's only when they're in the house.) Somehow, the possibility of being heard in the act wreaks havoc with my libido. Obviously, their father and I made love behind closed doors throughout their childhoods, but that was different: I knew they were asleep.

One of the miracles of long-married love is that we don't lose our lust at the rate we lose our looks. Our eyes don't see the wrinkles or stretch marks; our hands don't feel the jowls or pot belly. We just see each other, and feeling secure in that attraction, we take the party with us wherever we go.

"I asked Elena whether she still loved me now that I am getting old," wrote Edmund Wilson in his diary. "She said, 'Old has nothing to do with it.'" Research shows that 90 percent of married older couples find their mates "very attractive physically." Nearly two-thirds report that they engage in frequent sexual experimentation, including making love out of doors and in swimming pools. "Sexual passion, pleasure and playfulness are not just for the young and beautiful," says Andrew Greeley. "The empty nest may actually be a love nest."

Helen Gurley Brown, guru of the single "girl" but herself a wife for nearly forty years, has called marriage "the bran muffin of sex." Presumably, that means she finds lovemaking healthy and filling though not exactly a taste treat. A muffin wouldn't be my metaphor of choice, but if forced to liken married sex to something in a pastry shop, I'd say fresh-baked bread, the staff of life, or — on our best days — the icing on the cake.

Infidelity

The low frequency and high quality of midlife sex may be surprising to some, but the real stunner is the truth about infidelity. I know several couples, men and women married as long as Bert and I, who've had extramarital affairs and either succeeded in keeping their dalliances a secret from each other or weathered the disclosure and managed to remain together. All these couples say they are now monogamous. (Whether due to lack of desire or lack of opportunity, I can't say.) The rest of my long-married friends say they've never strayed, and I have every reason to believe them. The notion that millions of randy middle-aged people are busy cheating on their spouses never rang true to me in the first place.

In 1994, my intuition was validated by the results of that landmark University of Chicago sex survey: 85 percent of married women and more than 75 percent of married men said they have always been faithful to their spouses. What's more, the happiest, most sexually satisfied couples turned out to be the monogamous couples, married or not. While this news may warm the hearts of Jesse Helms and Pat Robertson, my enthusiasm for monogamy is not based on the Seventh Commandment or a holier-than-thou morality. It comes from a rock-solid belief in personal loyalty, a deep need to trust those I love, and a loathing for betrayal. Just about everyone shares those values, but in my case, they're a bit obsessional and I have no way of knowing why. My parents fought World War II in their marriage, but infidelity wasn't one of their issues. Theoretically, I believe that cheating on one's spouse is not necessarily sufficient reason to break up an otherwise healthy union, but if it ever happened in my marriage, I know I could never survive the breach. To regain my trust in an unfaithful husband would be as impossible as trying to unscramble an egg.

In his book *Transformations: Growth and Change in Adult Life*, which was published in 1978, Roger Gould, a psychiatrist and expert on adult development, briefly posits what might happen to marriage in the future. "If monogamy and fidelity prevail, [marriage] could be at a higher level of maturity," he writes, and then illustrates the attitude with an "I" statement that emphasizes the importance of uncoerced faithfulness: "I choose [to be faithful] because it's the best way for me, not because I'm told it's the only way."

In our culture, adultery is familiar, having been well exposed on page and screen. Everyone knows how cheating feels — the thrill of the forbidden, the logistics of deceit, the first inklings of suspicion, followed by discovery, confrontation, anguish, and rage. But what we don't read about or see in the movies is how peace of mind feels, how it expands love's breathing space. Many people simply cannot imagine that this sort of peace might coexist with passion. For them, the possibility of infidelity is a direct consequence of the inevitability of sexual boredom; both are coded into their concept of marriage, and nothing anyone can say (or any survey shows) will change their minds. They've seen trust in friendship; *that* they believe, but romantic loyalty? Impossible! An oxymoron! An adolescent's dream!

In this cynical climate, the combination of love and trust can be made to sound drab, moralistic, and confining, which is unfortunate because, in fact, there is nothing more liberating. "How bold one gets when one is sure of being loved!" wrote Sigmund Freud. Bold, yes, and at the same time, serene. Certainty in love frees up all kinds of energy; you can enter your own life more fully when you know, and know absolutely, that the person you adore is not in someone else's bed. I can't count how many nights I've been away from home for lectures and book tours, sometimes for weeks at a time, or how many nights Bert's labor-law practice has kept him out until all hours, sometimes until morning, bargaining a union contract up against a deadline. Yet, never once in thirty-one years has either of us worried about the whereabouts of the other.

"Think of how much misery we've spared ourselves all these years," says Bert.

And how much time.

Those are the subjects people ask about most — division of labor, conflict resolution, sexual attraction, fidelity — yet none of them quite captures the essence of long-term love, which is the best-friendship. Passion fluctuates, anger comes and goes, children grow up and leave, but through it all, there is this constant, growing friendship, this wholeness, the continuing desire to be with that one person, the ongoing feeling of looking forward to having meals together, wanting to share a thought, knowing this person is on your side and desires only the best for you, watching for that face in a crowd, hoping for that voice on the phone, waiting for that key in the lock.

It's hard to make any of this sound fresh, yet it is. Ours is a seasoned marriage that feels new. "Honey, when I'm with you, I feel six feet tall," Bert kids me. He *is* six feet tall. The thing is, when I'm with him, I feel six feet tall, too.

10

Relationships at Midlife: Family, Friendship, and Solitude

> When you care about a person . . . you accept that this person is in your life, and for me that's it. . . . This person is a permanent part of me.
>
> — *Lynn Sharon Schwartz*

By now, thanks to the places we've been and the years we've lived, most of us are enmeshed in a sprawling web of intimate relationships. Whether children, parents, friends, or family, those nearest and dearest to us cannot help but be affected by the agitations and transformations that barrel over us in middle age and by the same token, these are the people who have the most profound impact on our midlife state of mind.

A 1990 poll found that the vast majority of Americans see middle age as a time of deepening relationships, increased closeness, and heightened compassion. Friendship comes to mean more to us than it did when we were focused on building a marriage or career and rearing children. As our kids become involved in their own worlds, we have more energy for outside relationships, and our friends move to center stage. We become less judgmental, more tolerant of their foibles, more forgiving when they disappoint us, more appreciative of qualities we once took for granted. As we grow older and loneliness looms, we become more grateful for their support, their loyalty, and their company — gifts we once took for granted. As we become more protective of our time, we may want to spend more of it with those closest to us, or we may expect them to understand why we want to spend more of it elsewhere, to make up for lost time, including time lost servicing *them*. As we grow into ourselves, we also may become more assertive about what we want or need from others, and though this honesty may deepen our relationships, it may also make us tough to take. Paradoxically, too, we may find ourselves fonder of some old friends, dead bored by others; committed to making new friends, or not sure it's worth the trouble; complacent about how well our kids turned out, or convinced they're the offspring from hell. This is sensitive territory, and nothing I say is to be considered binding on anything I might feel in the future. Nonetheless, it's clear to me that the fact that we're aging can alter the tenor and substance of our most meaningful human alliances, two of which I want to discuss here — the relationship with one's kids and that with one's closest friends.

Although I know some women in their fifties with much younger children, most of my generation, unlike women today, had our babies when we were in our twenties and early thirties, so the children I'm talking about are now in their twenties and thirties — which raises the following question —

How Do You Mother an Adult?

I have always been amazed that society lets us rear our offspring unattended when we have zero training or experience. People without background qualifications aren't allowed to run classrooms, countries, or companies, but new moms and dads are routinely left alone in the house with a helpless infant (in our case, two of them) and expected to bring it to adulthood without serious mishap. If parents manage this at all, it is usually because they came to the job with memories of how *their* parents managed it. Without that history, they improvise, and since my memories of being mothered are rather truncated, my mothering has been more improvisational than most.

On April 20, 1995, the fortieth anniversary of my mother's death, it dawned on me that I had now known my children twice as long as I knew my mother. When she died, I was in high school. My sister, Betty, was thirty and about to give birth to her fourth child. Over the years, Betty had watched her relationship with Mother develop into a richly nuanced friendship in which, among other things, they had motherhood in common. I went directly from teenaged daughter to motherless child and missed all the experiences I've heard other women talk about from a daughter's perspective. Since I've never been an adult daughter, I don't know how it feels to grow to maturity with a mother's love; or how it feels to break out of a mother's embrace or oppose her will. Never having been mothered as an adult, I'm not quite sure how to mother the three grown-ups who happen to be my children, and I have a hunch some of the rough air of recent years could have been avoided if not for that gap in my biography. When my kids were young, I had a general notion of how to respond to their emotional needs because I remembered what my mother did for me when I was their age. But at the point in their childhoods when I could no longer conjure up my mother's side of the equation, I was left without a compass. I could remember *being* nineteen or twenty-six, but I could only guess at what degree of involvement might be appropriate for the mother of such an adult. Too often, I guessed wrong and overplayed the role, albeit with good intentions: I was trying to *be* the mother I wished I'd *had*.

When the Kids Are on Their Own

"By the time they're old enough to be good company, they leave home," said an anonymous parent. I found my kids good company from the time they were three or four years old, so I felt a real sense of loss when they moved out of the house at twenty-one or twenty-two. No, let me amend that: desolation and emptiness alternated with an occasional wave of exhilaration ("They've gone! We did it! We're done!"), making mincemeat of my emotions. I understand why a woman in Westchester County formed a discussion group whose only criterion for membership was that you had to be the parent of a child who had *just* left home. "I'm not interested in anyone whose kids moved out a year ago," she said. "I don't want to hear their advice on how to get through it; I want us to go through it together." For me, going through it was especially problematic because my son, our youngest, graduated on the very day I turned fifty, and when he moved out, with him went my last excuse for hands-on mothering.

As I write this, David is twenty-six and single, Abigail and Robin are twenty-nine and married. Since they finished school, all three have lived on their own, held decent jobs, and supported themselves (*kenna-hurra*). The independence of one's grown-up children is supposed to be a measure of successful parenting, but for the first couple of years after mine left, I missed them terribly, confounding the notion that the empty-nest syndrome only happens to full-time housewives who make their kids their career. I missed them even though my work life was busier than ever and my sex life was benefiting from our newfound privacy. One of the clarities of age is this: I was not just missing my children for themselves but for what they symbolized — the idea of a houseful of kids with us at the hub dealing with their ups and downs and comings and goings, which, of course, is a basic definition of parenthood. *Young* parenthood. In part, I missed my children because they had kept me young.

"Don't you feel a little obsolete and purposeless?" a friend asked when my kids first left home. "Don't you long for the days when they were cute and manageable?"

Yes, but I long for so much more than the obedience or adorableness of childhood. I miss the dailiness of family life: I miss our dinnertimes — Bert and I once calculated that the five of us logged more than 6,000 hours at the table. I miss plopping down on the bed in one of their rooms and just schmoozing, with none of that hurried feeling I sometimes get now when I'm trying to catch up on their lives. I miss knowing all their friends. I miss the on-site enjoyment of Abigail's comical accents and imitations, Robin's incisive analyses of everyone's personal problems, David's winding narratives and wonderful cooking. I miss the sounds of childhood: guitars, radios, phone calls, fights. I miss the rituals, the metaphors of family intimacy; the litany, "Good-night, sleep tight, wake up bright, in the morning light"; the way we played Twenty Questions on long car trips, or sang Broadway show tunes in harmony, or decorated the front door to welcome home whoever had been away for more than one night.

When children leave for college, it's a gentle segue; most of their stuff is still in their childhood rooms and they still come home for vacations. But when they've gone for good, taking their books, their posters, their contact-lens cleaner, either you adjust to their departure or you find yourself a psychiatrist who knows how to treat posttraumatic stress. If learning to accept one's own aging is a long journey with a lot of landmarks, letting your children go is surely one of the major challenges along the route. Sure, I miss their childhoods. (That's another reason why I keep scrapbooks.) I'm glad I knew them then, but I think I enjoy them even more now because all I have to do these days is enjoy them. I don't have to raise them, feed and house them, or check their beds at 2 A.M. Of course, no matter how old they are, a hot meal, a listening ear, and an emergency loan will always be available to them at home. And as long as I draw breath, I will worry about them being struck by drunken drivers and flying cornices. I will call to make sure they got home safely. I will pray for their health and happiness, but that's not the same as being responsible for their lives.

Being the mature parent of mature children turns out to be a whole new trip with different challenges. I've discovered that the best way to adjust to physical separation and arms-length parenthood is to think of it as another kind of closeness. Paradoxical but true: the more independent they become, the more adult their concerns. The more adult their concerns, the more I have in common with them. The more we have in common, the closer our relationship. Ergo, separation yields closeness.

What Bert and I have in common with our children is that we work for a living and they work for a living. We file tax returns, so do they. They stock their own refrigerators, pay their own phone bills, and make their own dentist appointments, just like us. We share many of the same interests and laugh at the same things, so much so that their father and I sometimes forget they're the children and we're the parents. We have traded the authority role for a kind of equality that is the result of both *their* aging *and* ours. Without actually marking the moment of change, the five of us have altered the basic premise on which our relationships are founded. For the first time in our lives, we are dealing with each other from a position of mutuality and equivalence, a symmetry of status and sensibilities that does not make me less of a mom but does make me more of a friend.

During this wonderful window in time, when there is no dependency on either side, when the kids are no longer children and the parents are still healthy enough to keep up, we come together not just because we love each other, but because we like each other. The sad part is, I know it can't last. Down the road, the balance will tip in the other direction. Equals no more, we'll become "the parents" again, only this time, the children will be taking care of us. Until then, I agree with Jane Adams, author of *I'm Still Your Mother: How to Get Along with Your Children for the Rest of Your Life,* that these can be the best years — although "best" doesn't mean uncomplicated. These are also years of reassessment and realignment as the parent-child relationship adjusts to the seismic changes taking place in both our lives. This is the time when we try to figure out what may have gone wrong in the past and how to make it right from now on.

Taking the Blame

I admit it. Like many other mothers, I am overly involved in my kids' lives, even more so because of my own maternal deprivation. I tend to define mothering as staying close, *really* close. I harbor an exaggerated view of a mom's importance to her offspring. As a result, I probably transgress my children's personal boundaries: I ask too many questions about things that aren't my business. I offer advice before it's solicited, advice that comes across as criticism when I mean it in the spirit of concern. Since I value *their* counsel, I can't seem to get it into my head that they might want to reach their decisions without factoring in my opinion. And since I've spent forty years wishing my mother were available for consultation, it's not surprising that I would assume consulting to be part of my mandate. In my limited experience, a mother is someone who is always in your corner, so why wouldn't you want her advice? If you don't agree with it, you can always ignore it, I tell my kids, so what do you have to lose by listening?

Then again, for me it's all theoretical. If my mother had been offering her opinion all these years, I might feel as resentful as my friends who still have their mothers and are chafing at the bit. It's quite possible my mother would not have approved of my life as a single woman or of my pursuing a career once I had a husband and children (she was a traditionalist after all). What if she'd found fault with my involvement in the women's movement? Or my child-rearing methods? What if I'd had to fight every word out of her mouth? Maybe the way to avoid this with my kids is to hedge my bets and keep *my* mouth shut. Yet, whenever I pull back from my usual ways, I feel out of touch; I don't feel "like a mother." Then I worry that my kids might misinterpret the pull-back for indifference. So I start getting involved again — asking questions, tendering opinions, and wondering what else I might be doing wrong.

Self-criticism is agony for anyone but especially for parents who have not come to terms with their adult children — those who are struggling with old issues that have yet to be resolved or new issues that keep cropping up around differences in lifestyle, behavior, values, and disparate expectations of each other. I know parents and children who bicker constantly, can't communicate, get on each other's nerves, or aren't on speaking terms at all.

One friend complains that her twenty-nine-year-old daughter, who lives 2,000 miles away, is always calling home in tears, defeated by the smallest frustrations. "When is she going to grow up?" asks the mother, who is tired of all the "babies" in her life, all the needy adults who expect her to fix things. My friend takes the blame for having raised a child who can't cope, but as I see it, the daughter's behavior could be directly traceable to the mother's life stage. When her child moved out, my friend — like many people our age — became more involved with her work, friends, marriage, which made the daughter feel insecure about their connection. To assure herself that her mother still cares, the daughter is now dumping on Mom's doorstep, testing Mom's love, using a child's misery to attract a mother's attention.

Our children have the power to deny us what we want most: their own happiness. If they are in distress, they know we will spring into action and do what mothers do — worry, care, comfort, stay connected. But if they're okay, if everything is copacetic in their lives, they think we may conclude that our jobs are over. Sometimes grown-up children act like babies to keep us acting like mothers.

I know a woman who can't bear the way her twenty-six-year-old son talks to her — his belligerent tone, his disrespect, his foul mouth. Why does she put up with it? Because she feels guilty about having divorced his father when the boy was in his teens, and she's still trying to make it up to him.

I know another woman who frequently criticizes her daughter's housekeeping habits; she knows she's going too far and she dreads the arguments that follow one of her "suggestions," but she can't seem to help herself — probably because *her* mother raised her to believe cleanliness is next to godliness and now she wants her daughter to have a seat in heaven. Plus, she's old-fashioned enough to fear that her son-in-law might leave her daughter if there's dust on the baseboards and his socks aren't pressed.

Still another mother has issued a new family rule — "You're out of the house by forty." It seems her grown-up children keep moving back home whenever their lives collapse, causing an upheaval in the parents' neat and orderly lives, not to mention a strain on their finances. There are 22 million "boomerang kids" in America, young adults whose marital or financial problems keep sending them back under their parents' roof. "If these parents didn't have homes," says Congresswoman Pat Schroeder, "their kids would be homeless." At the kids' end of the axis, the strain is compounded because, on top of the hardships that sent them home in the first place, they experience their return trip as a sign of failure, an admission that they still need Mommy and Daddy's help. Afraid of being sucked back into their childhood roles, they become hostile toward the parents to whom they were forced to turn for help. It's a no-win situation: you're heartless if you turn your kids away, not that you'd want to, but if you take them in, you're infantilizing them.

Parental pain knows no age limit or cut-off date. The distress of grown-up kids — those who can't find work, are in the throes of a nasty divorce, or in debt over their heads — weigh on parents even more heavily than the crises of a young child who lost a beloved pet, couldn't pass algebra, or didn't make the team. To love your children with all your heart and not be able to help them when they're in trouble has to be one of the greatest sorrows in a world with no shortage of suffering.

In extreme cases, children's problems have very nearly destroyed their parents' lives. Older parents have become chronic victims of their violent offspring, a phenomenon so common that it has been given a name: elder abuse. Some parents have been robbed of their savings by children who are supporting a drug habit. A friend's son — who has somehow turned into a twenty-seven-year-old drug dealer with unsavory companions and a girlfriend and baby he has abandoned — threatened to kill his father when the man reported to the police that the boy had a gun. Family businesses have become generational battlegrounds on which every operational decision becomes a power struggle until one day, parents and children end up in court, speaking through lawyers and trying to take each other for all they're worth.

Often, in these situations, you hear mothers and fathers asking one another how what began in the delivery room with such innocence and hope could possibly have come to this. Parental pain is compounded by memories of that sweet once-upon-a-time beginning — images of the smiling baby reaching out to us from her crib, the trusting little boy sliding his hand into ours — and by the unavoidable feeling that the mess of the moment is all our fault. We did something wrong, or didn't do something right, or should have known, or must have seen, or could have prevented the problem if only. . . . And as parents and children get older and matters don't improve, it becomes clearer with each passing year that the way things are is probably how they will always be — unless they get worse.

Competing with One's Children

"She's jealous of her daughter's figure." The "she" was a woman my age, and the sentence, spoken by a mutual friend, nearly bowled me over. How could a fifty-six-year-old woman even begin to compare herself to a twenty-three-year-old girl? How could a mother be envious of her own daughter? Well, it turns out that mothers can, and fathers aren't immune either, and parental jealousy of the same-gender child may in fact be the dirty little secret of my age group.

For men, the contest usually revolves around something monetary, intellectual, or physical (think of *The Great Santini*), because that's where the turf battles of masculinity are acted out. One friend tells me that he hated playing tennis with his sons when they were young because they were inept and he was impatient, but after a few years, when the boys got good enough, he was glad to have such strong partners, and he played with them every chance he got. Now that they're expert players, *they* won't play with *him*. Though he's proud of their skills, he also admits that watching them on the tennis court makes him jealous. It makes him long for his youth — then realize that he was never that good a player, even when he was younger. Envy overtakes his pride, then guilt, then sadness. "I wish I could just enjoy watching them," he says. "But it ends up being about me."

Another father had trouble accepting his son's doctorate with appropriate enthusiasm because something inside him kept nagging. "How can he be smarter than you? It's not right for a son to be smarter than his father." Instead of taking pleasure in the accomplishments of his own flesh and blood, he felt his son's Ph.D. diminished him and his paltry B.A. He thought he might now appear smaller in his wife's eyes. He was competing with his son for her admiration.

Perhaps the darkest domain of father-son competition is the area of sexual conquest (think of *Damage,* in which Jeremy Irons's character seduces his son's fiance), while for mothers and daughters, competition around beauty and sexuality often happens in the light of day, with mothers overtly struggling to recapture the allure of youth. Not long ago, Carly Simon told the startling story of growing up in a privileged household in "an atmosphere of erotica" created by her mother, Andrea. "The sexual haze was so thick you could cut it," the singer tells Marie Brenner in an interview in *Vanity Fair*. "As the Simon sisters grew up," writes Brenner, "there was a bloom of adolescent sexuality in the house. In the opinion of Lucy [one of Carly's siblings], Andrea so identified with her daughters' burgeoning sexuality that it was difficult for her to perceive their need for independence." When the girls were teenagers, Andrea, then in her mid-forties, began a long affair with a twenty-year-old student she had hired as a live-in companion to her son. (Think of *Class,* in which Jacqueline Bisset's character has an affair with her son's prep school roommate.) The young man, named Ronnie, was a member of the Simon household for the next eight years. Brenner writes, "It is Lucy Simon's belief that Ronnie unwittingly set off a sexual competition among the sisters and their mother, a tangle of rivalries for male attention."

A friend of mine describes a mother whose sexual competitiveness was more wily and manipulative: "Once, when my mother was going to the drugstore, I asked her to fill my prescription for birth control pills. I was in my thirties at the time, she was in her fifties. When she came back, she bragged that the druggist thought the pills were for her. She always had to let me know men found her young and attractive, the implication being that she was *more* attractive than I am. Later, during the same visit, I asked her what contraceptive method she had used when she was young. 'I didn't have to worry about that sort of thing,' she answered in an unbelievably superior voice. '*My* husband took care of it.' Meaning, of course, that my father loves *her* more than my husband loves me."

Some people despise aging to the point where, at some level, they blame their kids for being old enough to make the parents' age undeniable. They try to obliterate the generational line by narrowing the difference between parent and child, and beating the kids at their own game, whether it's sports or sex appeal. In effect, these parents are refusing to *be* the parent, and in doing so, they leave their kids confused about how much growth is permissible. If sons in normal situations are reluctant to supersede their fathers — as many are — imagine the burden of the son whose father is pathologically invested in winning. The boy may decide to lose on purpose, thwarting his own growth to retain his father's love.

Some parents say they are not jealous of their children but only of their youth, to which I'd say, pick somebody else's youth to be jealous of, if you must; or direct your jealousy to youth in the abstract, but don't think you can separate your children from *their* age any more than you can separate yourself from *your* age — which is what fueled the problem in the first place.

When a woman told me she envied her nineteen-year-old daughter for her youth, I pursued the issue and asked her why.

"Why *shouldn't* I envy her?" replied my friend. "Every night, the kid has a quick bite and then she's out the door having fun."

"You could do the same thing," said I.

"Are you kidding? What would Fred do for dinner? What would Fred think?"

Youth-envy was the catch-all excuse for her desolation, but youth had nothing to do with her discontent with the confines of her own life.

Not every parent goes through the jealousy phase. I can honestly say I have never felt competitive with my daughters. When my kids excel, or when something good happens to one of them, I walk on air. My reaction is not a matter of good character but of good fortune; having been lucky in my life choices, I don't begrudge my children their successes. I'm not sure I would feel this way had I been frustrated in my own aspirations.

A friend of mine makes a similar point with reference to her twenty-four-year-old daughter: "Walking down the street with her the other day, I was suddenly aware that every man coming toward us was looking her up and down and clearly appreciating what he saw.

"When I told this to my psychiatrist, he asked, 'How does this make you feel?' And my answer was, 'I had my shot. Now it's her turn.' "

"If you really feel that way," said the psychiatrist, "you're a very healthy woman."

Parental Regrets

I can't imagine that there is a parent alive today who doesn't have regrets. "Regret is guilt without the neurosis," writes Jane Adams, meaning, I suppose, that guilt is normal at this stage of our lives when the verdict on everything we've ever done or not done is up for grabs. We look back and see our parenting errors in bas relief, especially those most poignant of all regrets, the might-have-beens that can never be again. One can regret missing the circus when it passed through town, but there's always next year. One can regret having eaten the whole banana split, but there's always the StairMaster. Parental regrets, however, cannot be undone because no one gets a second chance at her children's childhood. It's too late to undo the past and for anyone grappling with time and mortality, no phrase cuts to the quick like "It's too late."

A friend of mine regrets that her daughters, born eighteen months apart, shared a room until they left home. "We should have gotten a bigger place," she says. "We could have afforded it, but we didn't think it was that important. In fact, we liked the idea that our girls were so good about sharing their space and belongings."

When the daughters were in their twenties, they told their mother how miserable they had been in that room. The younger one had always resented the lack of privacy and to this day is hungry for solitude and gets upset when she feels closed in. The older one said she loathed having to share a desk and bookshelf with her sister and having to turn off her light when her sister went to bed. "God knows how all this is going to play out in their marriages," says the mother.

Another friend wishes she had demanded more of her son around the house. "I made all the classic mistakes," she recalls. "I taught my daughter to clean up after herself, prepare meals, do the laundry, and make the beds. All my son had to do was walk the dog. Now he's twenty-nine and, quite frankly, he's a spoiled brat. I can't blame his girlfriend for refusing to live with him. He'd make her into his housekeeper. The way he sees it, that's what women do, because that's what his sister and I did when he was growing up."

Regrets roll across a parent's horizon like storm clouds: "If only we'd had more mealtimes together." "I should have been more alert to his mood swings." "I should have taken it seriously when she had trouble making friends in the third grade." "Why didn't I teach them to manage money?" "I wish I'd exposed them to more art and music when they were young." "If only we had done more talking . . ." This is nostalgia's sad face, the face that sees the time wasted, the moment missed, gone, never to return.

One of my regrets stems, ironically, from Bert's and my commitment to treat all three children equally. I don't mean we saw them as indistinguishable from one another, but rather that we wanted them, the boy and the two girls, to have the same opportunities, the same broad selection of toys and activities, the same chances, choices, stimulation and exposure to the world, the same amount of our attention. In principle, I still believe this to be the right policy; in practice, it could have benefited from some fine-tuning.

We were *too* evenhanded. Maybe we were blindsided by the fact that our first child was children. When you begin parenthood with twins, you get used to simultaneity — feeding and bathing them together, going places together, bedding them down at the same time, all of which tracks you into a groupthink approach. Then, too, we were philosophically opposed to sex separatism, which meant that our family didn't divide up into male and female squads but hung out together as a team no matter what the activity. Dad and son weren't out washing the car while Mom and the girls baked a cake. We wanted all three to experience *everything,* so we all went to the ballet, or we all played touch football, five at a time.

In recent years, of course, we've gotten together in all sorts of combinations, one parent with one child, two parents "double-dating" with a daughter and son-in-law, or spending the weekend with whoever happens to be free. But back in the years when we had the children to ourselves, we did everything together so no one would feel left out. I wish we had thought less about equality and more about intimacy. I wish we'd put less emphasis on family activity and more on the pleasures of unstructured

band. If I did not want to lose her, I knew that I had better find a way to accept him. The next day, she and I had a pizza together and I told her that however she resolved the religious issues was her business, not mine. I said I was sorry I'd let my feelings intrude. I said my relationship with her mattered more to me than any "issue." I told her I would learn to love him. Then I flew home and cried my eyes out.

A month later, they broke up. When she moved back to New York, she didn't explain in so many words why she had left him, but I got the sense that religion had been one of many incompatibilities. Maybe my willingness to accept her choice of mate allowed her to stop fighting *me* and start examining her own feelings, or maybe I had nothing whatever to do with her decision. In any case, after those agonizing nine months, it was clear to me that my relationship with Abigail had passed into another phase and would be different from then on, not worse for wear but *different*. At fifty-two, I learned how to be the mother of an adult. I discovered that my most cherished beliefs are not as important as my daughter's happiness and my need to stay connected to her life, to her energy, to *her*. For her part, she had succeeded in doing things her way. She had challenged my thinking, made her own decision, separated, and come back as her own person.

Robin's declaration of independence, not having been aroused by a crisis, has been more gradual and ongoing. She found her voice by using it to tell me exactly who she is — and the message was, she isn't me. She has made it plain that, although both of us are writers married to lawyers, that's where the resemblance ends. Okay, I get it. I see why she needs to affirm her individuality, although I'm rather pleased when she confesses to certain habits, good or bad, that I recognize in myself. It makes me feel I have a soul mate. I know she is different from me in a thousand ways, but I like it that we're both workaholics and we both like to give dinner parties and neither of us can throw out old newspapers until we've read them all. It makes me happy to know that we both think we stink at board games, find most TV a bore, love country auctions, and hate small talk. I savor our similarities and feel a special bond with her because of them. She emphasizes our differences and uses them to define the boundaries between us, boundaries that are necessary to her identity.

In the last couple of years, thanks to several deep and difficult conversations, our relationship has evolved dramatically from what it was as recently as when she was in college. We are less intense and less enmeshed but probably more honest with each other. Among other things, I have come to understand that Robin needs to *not* need me — which I consider an age-appropriate goal for me as well. In the postparenthood stage, mothers should not need to be needed by their children. The strange thing is, the more autonomous and self-governing Robin becomes, the more *I* lean on her. I trust her reactions to my work, her analysis of problems and personalities, her advice. When there are logistics to be taken care of — plans to be made, things to be picked up, people to be called — I usually turn to her. Recently, I've realized that this is how Robin and I have managed to both separate from one another and continue to remain close. She doesn't need me the way a child needs a mother, but I need her the way one adult needs another. I am the mother but we are both grown-ups.

The realignment of my relationship to my daughters wasn't easy for us, but I've come to understand that it was necessary. In order to become fully themselves, they did not have to separate from me entirely, thank God, but they did have to loosen the connection, and I had to let them.

I think I also understand why no comparable realignment took place between me and my son. He played no role in the mother-daughter-mother-daughter sequence and thus could loosen his links to the family without threatening my definition of myself as a mother. He did his separation number rather dramatically in his teens, testing the limits in school, slacking off on his studies, staying out until all hours, and drinking too much on occasion, all of which scared the daylights out of his parents, though he never disdained us or tried to cut his ties. While extremely close to Bert, and more comfortable with father-son affection than most young men, David has never felt the need to measure himself against his father's life choices — only against Bert's moral and ethical standards. When the dust settled, David had chosen a totally different route from anyone else in the family: he went to culinary school, became a cook in a four-star restaurant, and is now in restaurant management. He has always been his own person, against the grain, with the grain, marching to his own music — which I sometimes find unlistenable — traveling far afield but never too far for his parents to reach him.

Between David and me, there is only our own history, the push-pull of mother-son love. Between Abigail, Robin, and me, however, there was my mother's unfinished symphony. I tried to complete it by being the mother *I* wanted, but that wasn't always the mother my daughters needed. I am not claiming that, had I known then what I know now, I would have been able to do anything different, but I will be interested to see if my daughters find a better way when they become mothers. I hope they can come up with answers to the questions that continue to confound me and other mothers of girls: How can a mother communicate her values without prescribing her way as the only way? How can a daughter reject her mother's choices without rejecting her mother? How do our daughters learn from us without feeling the need to become us? And how do we help our daughters grow up strong and free without growing away from us altogether?

I've pondered these questions for years, and the only honest answer I've come up with is, we can't and they can't, and that is as it should be. We cannot communicate our values — about women's place in the world, about justice and equity and decency and fairness, about self-respect and high aspirations — unless we do it with full conviction, not as a casual menu of either/or possibilities. And that full conviction is bound to be construed by our daughters as pressure until such time as they are old enough and strong enough in themselves to find their own way. But when that time comes, they will have our standards as their checklist, a starter sampler of ideals and precepts from which they can buy in or opt out; accept, adapt, or decline. We may experience their choices as rejection — a daughter cannot refuse her mother's beliefs without repudiating a part of the mother — but that very experience is what forces mothers to see their daughters as distinct and separate individuals and, with new clarity, to enter into a relationship of equals.

The mistake we feminists made was to assume the process could be avoided. Since most of us preferred not to follow in our mothers' footsteps, we assumed our rejection of our mothers was a function of the constricted choices represented by their lives. We thought that if we opened up the world to our daughters and showed them by example that all things are possible, they wouldn't have to pull away from us, they could just forge ahead. We thought we would spare them the struggle and spare ourselves the rejection. But we didn't realize that the struggle is a process that cannot be skipped because, like growing pains, with all their stress and soreness, the process itself is the reward. For the daughters of feminists, as opposed to the young women of previous generations, there is one important difference: the challenge is to pull away from a feminist mother without rejecting the freedoms she stands for.

As my children consult the checklist that is their mother's life, I sometimes feel I am being overdefined, my outlines etched too sharply, as in, Mom is a dyed-in-the-wool liberal; Mom's enthusiasms are over-the-top;

Mom is a hopeless romantic; Mom is a sucker for everything Jewish; Mom thinks feminism can do no wrong. These broad strokes deny me my own ambivalence. I don't always like the woman they describe; she is without nuance. I tell my children when they've got it wrong — I will not oversimplify myself even for *them* — yet I think I understand why they need me to be unambiguous, like North on a compass, the fixed orientation point from whence they can wander and return, the baseline against which they can compare and contrast themselves.

As much as I am enjoying my children's adult selves and all that we now share, sometimes I get a little wistful about how it used to be when our relationship was simple — no layers, no subtexts, nothing to decode. I remember when they were little and we were big, and we had a lot of fun together and they thought we hung out the moon, and sometimes I long for that simplicity. This, I am told, is why people have grandchildren.

Waiting for the Next Generation

I'd like to have some, too, preferably before I'm sixty. In 1900, the average grandparent was sixty and had twelve to fifteen grandkids scurrying underfoot. Today, the typical sixty-year-old grandparent has only three, and is less likely to live in the same town, never mind the same house, and is more likely to be trying to have a meaningful relationship with each grandchild, which is exactly what I'm hoping to do as soon as someone provides me with a subject.

A friend's needlepoint pillow reads, "Had I Known Grandchildren Were So Much Fun, I'd Have Had Them First." I'm Jewish, female, and fifty-five, so it's not news that I'd like some grandbabies right about now. In fact, I've been fantasizing for months about one of my daughters getting pregnant and giving birth in time for me to write about the experience in this book, because all my friends who are grandparents tell me it has been the single most satisfying event of their middle age. No such luck. Besides, while I want to *be* a grandmother, I have trouble imagining myself actually functioning in the role, which I associate with my Grandma Jennie the way I associate the role of Scarlett O'Hara with Vivian Leigh. Since Grandma Jennie wore her hair in a bun, stayed home every day of her life, spoke mostly Yiddish, and was welded to her apron, I'll have to cast myself against type. The other problem is, even when I manage to see myself as a grandmother — albeit one in a ponytail and a leotard who buys her grandkids multicultural toys and anatomically correct dolls — I can't quite envision my daughters as mothers. This, too, I'm told, is normal. "It doesn't seem possible that your baby can have a baby until she does it," a friend promises. So, I'm waiting . . .

Not long ago, Abigail had a dream that *I* was pregnant. "What do you think it means?" I ask, casually.

"That I see you as vibrant and young," she answers — clever girl. But if you ask me, the dream is saying, "Don't hold your breath, Mom. If you want a baby so much, have it yourself."

Generational matters have been rubbing me a little raw since a year or so ago when my mother-in-law died. She was our children's last grandparent. Her death reminded me for the millionth time of how tragic it is that my children never knew my mother. It also occurred to me then that the next grandma in our extended family will probably be me.

Bert's mom was both a one-of-a-kind character and a classic Jewish mother. Like my Grandma Jennie, she made rugalech, wore an apron, sang Yiddish songs, and baby-sat on request, but she was also a tough cookie, a politically savvy ex-Communist, a voracious reader, and the life of the party whenever there was a party in her life, which was never often enough to satisfy her. And she was a wonderful grandmother.

When the kids were small, we'd go about once a month for an overnight visit to her house in Roosevelt, New Jersey, where Bert grew up and where his childhood room still contained bits and pieces of his childhood — paydirt for a nostalgia addict. I remember how my mother-in-law would turn the place over to her grandchildren, letting them litter the living room with toys, seemingly oblivious to the Lego pieces in the candy dish, the peanut butter on the TV knobs, and the Matchbox cars underfoot. Will I be as relaxed, I wonder?

Thanks to her many years as a nursery school teacher, and the broad scope of her interests, she had a talent to amuse. She taught our children nursery rhymes, labor union songs, and Yiddish standards like "Tumbalalaika," and played Woody Guthrie and Pete Seeger records on the phonograph. She set the kids up at the kitchen table with paint, glue, sprinkles, and pipe cleaners, and couldn't care less if the gold stars got stuck to the place mats. In nice weather, she had them out in her garden planting seedlings and watering flowers, or trudging through the woods behind the house collecting rocks. On rainy days, she gave them free access to her clothes closet and jewelry box for dress-up play, and didn't even flinch when a flamboyant gesture impaled her sequined sweater on a rhinestone earring. Will I be as patient? Will I remember the lullaby my mother taught me? Will I remember how to play Red Light, Green Light? Or will I bore my grandchildren to tears?

When our kids got older, their grandma played Scrabble and Boggle with them (and hated to lose). She came to all their school plays. She kept track of their boyfriends and girlfriends and asked even more invasive questions than I do. She told them stories of her girlhood, regaled them with her views on current events and cultural happenings, and gossiped with them about each other, which is how she always knew what everyone was up to. For my kids to have had such grandmothering until their late twenties was a great bonus; and for Bert's mom to have seen five grandchildren to adulthood, and been around to dance at two weddings — that wasn't bad, either. She was the hub of the family wheel, Action Central, the undisputed expert on who was doing what, including the sons-in-law. Will I live long enough to meet the people my grandchildren marry?

My mother-in-law was fifty-three when Bert and I first made her a grandma. My mother was fifty-three when she died, but she already had three grandchildren and a fourth on the way. At fifty-five, my sister was presented with the first of her six grandchildren. I'm fifty-five and I have none, and not a pregnancy in sight. While I don't expect my kids to time their families to suit me, I'm hoping they won't wait until I'm too old to be active in the part. I want them to know I'm ready anytime they are. And I just remembered how to play Red Light, Green Light.

Friends and Age

Children and grandchildren may claim the lion's share of our concern at this stage of life, but it is usually friends who claim most of our free time. Once the kids are launched on their own, friendship tends to fill the gap. But while midlifers have more energy for friends, these relationships are often complicated by problems attributable to age and aging.

I will never forget how sad I felt when I realized that all the people attending the funeral of the elderly father of my friend Sarah were *her* friends, not her father's. I could only assume that the man had been some sort of scoundrel. Why else would nobody show up to say good-bye?

Because they were all dead, that's why. Later that evening, Sarah spoke of how her father had been the last of a tightly knit group of friends, all contemporaries, who had passed away one by one when they were in their seventies, leaving him to his eighties, alone. Casey Stengel is relevant here: "Most people my age are dead at the present time."

Research shows that, on the average, each of us has four to seven people in our lives whom we consider close friends, and the most noticeable thing about these pals is that they tend to be just like us — same gender, race, religion, social class, marital status, *and age.* I am no exception. I didn't plan it this way and I'm not pleased about it, but the truth is, my dearest friends are within four or five years of my age.

This fact violates my sense of myself as a person who appreciates diversity. It implies that I screen birthdates before deciding whether to like someone. It tells me I'm cheating myself of other perspectives that would enrich my life. It makes me realize that, since all my pals are around the same age, they could die off around the same time, leaving me friendless if I should happen to outlive them. "Life without a friend is death without a witness," wrote George Herbert, but sometimes, death without a witness is merely evidence of longevity. And since every woman has a strong chance of being widowed in her later years, I could end up like Sarah's father, with no one but my children and *their* friends to bid me good-bye.

There are obvious reasons why most of us gravitate to people who are like us: they're the peers with whom we learn, live, and work, and therefore have the chance to get to know. School friends are almost always our age, give or take a year. Workplace friends tend to be similar ages because occupational hierarchies usually parallel years of on-the-job experience. Many activities, from sports to PTA meetings, attract age mates. Housing developments often concentrate people of similar ages. And while age solidarity separates older people from the mainstream and may contribute to ageism, it is necessary for identity politics, which, in turn, bond age mates together in a shared cause.

In addition to all these reasons why we tend to have friends our own age, there is some question as to whether younger or older people are interested in making friends with us.

On the beach one summer afternoon, I observe the following exchange between two little girls sitting several yards from one another.

"Come play with me," says the six-year-old in the pink polka-dot bikini, who seems to be digging a hole to Beijing.

"Why should I?" asks the three-year-old in the red tanksuit, looking up from the mud pies she's squashing with her Ninja turtle.

"Because I like you," replies the polka dots.

"Okay," says the tanksuit, skipping across the sand, Ninja turtle forgotten.

If only it were that easy to cross the age barrier now.

I have meaningful acquaintances who are in their sixties and seventies, and two in their eighties — vibrant, active women who set an example of constructive aging and the well-lived life — but I don't know them well enough to tell you what goes on in their minds and hearts; I don't know what hurts them or makes them happy. Likewise, I have many acquaintances in their thirties and forties, but if not for my friendship with my daughters, I wouldn't know the emotional reality of younger women's lives. I'm not close enough to be useful to my younger friends who may be having problems with things like motherhood, mentoring, or menopause.

I want younger friends who can be counted on to stay alive into my old age, but more importantly, I want friends who can open a window on the world, keep me tuned to the changing culture, stop me from getting stuck; friends I can help and nurture and kid around with. The problem is, unlike the little girl in the pink polka dots, people my age can't always get younger folks to play with us. (I can see why a fifty-five-year-old might appear uninteresting to a thirty-five-year-old, since I have made the same assumption about seventy-five-year-olds despite knowing several old women in space shoes and support hose who are fascinating people.)

Regardless of all indications that friendship across age boundaries is good for us, there remains the indisputable fact that most people seem genuinely to prefer friends their own age who provide a special kind of nourishment. For one thing, familiarity breeds comfort; we relax in the presence of whatever we know best. We like to talk in shorthand with others who've lived through the same events from the same general perspective. We get a little testy when our cultural references meet with blank stares. Alice Furland writes in a "Hers" column in the *New York Times* of becoming slightly unhinged when she discovered that young friends of hers had never heard of Pierre Boulez, Jerome Kern, the duke of Windsor, Sinclair Lewis, and Socrates — until she was covering the Cannes Film Festival and had to confess that she'd never heard of Robert De Niro, Barbara Hershey, or Mickey Rourke, and couldn't name a single Michael Jackson song "even under threat of slow torture."

For another thing, same-age friends enjoy the advantages of parallel lives. When my mother-in-law was battling cancer in the retirement residence where she had lived for the last six years, I noticed how several of her fellow residents provided substantive friendship and served needs that were unmet by her relatives, loving as we were. The family members were between ages twenty and sixty and presumably more energetic than the senior citizens, but we could only visit her after work or on weekends, some having to travel long distances. Meanwhile, her friends — people in their seventies, eighties, and nineties — popped in throughout the day, brought her chocolates, magazines, a new blouse, a bit of gossip. Then, too, while the relatives were distraught at her suffering and depressed by her prognosis, the older people were always talking to her about future community projects that awaited her input. It was these friends, age mates all, who preserved a sense of normalcy in my mother-in-law's life and kept her hopes high to the end.

The superiority of same-age friendships has been suggested by any number of studies showing that, in midlife and beyond, people feel better about their appearance, accomplishments, and physical condition when they socialize with their own generation than when they spend their time with younger friends who may make them feel inadequate by comparison. In addition, age similarity eliminates some of the flashpoints of friendship, the disputes that stem from the disparate needs and financial resources of people of different ages or the different amount of time they make available to one another, which in turn is related to life stages and the time demands that go with them.

So much that seems to be about other things ends up being about time, and friendship is no exception. "To have a friend takes time," said Georgia O'Keeffe. Friendship can't be rushed. It needs hours, not minutes. It needs years. It needs space and leisure, long evenings, long walks. I keep saying I want to widen my friendship circle, but I have absolutely no surplus social energy. In addition to my "four to seven" closest friends, I have dozens of other people whom I care about and enjoy spending time with yet see too rarely. How can I add another special person to my life when I've already been stockpiling friends for fifty-five years? Like books, or houseplants, or anything else one can cherish yet accumulate in such abundance, the fact is that the few lose out to the many. One of these days, I say, I must consolidate, cull, prune and make room for new titles.

Ogden Nash wrote that middle age occurs "when you've met so many people that every new person you meet reminds you of someone else." I have that experience frequently, which may be a sign that I have too many acquaintances, which in turn may explain why I don't have enough time to deepen my real friendships or cultivate new ones. As some tough customer once put it, "Middle age is when you can't make a new friend until an old one dies and opens up a space."

But it is important to make new friends at our age because we are different people now than we were ten or twenty years ago. We've outgrown some old friends, others have outgrown us, or we bore each other in both directions. "Sometimes you have to get to know someone really well to realize you're strangers," Mary Tyler Moore once said. I've had that experience, too, but when I think about culling the friendships that have seen better days, something stops me. My own history, to be exact. How can I summarily "dump" someone I've known since high school just because she might have grown a trifle tedious? Doesn't time have its privileges? Suppose this woman and I remember each other's prom dresses? Suppose she was there the night I drank my first martini? I ought to be able to tolerate a little tedium to keep such a witness in my life and to serve as a witness in hers. So the answer is, I don't cull; I keep the old books, and once a year or so I dust them off and thumb through them for old time's sake.

Losing People

"Before the flowers of friendship faded friendship faded," wrote Gertrude Stein. Sad as it is, the death of a friendship is nothing compared to the death of a friend.

Recently, I transferred the contents of my ten-year-old address book to an electronic organizer and, in so doing, realized how many of my friends have died in the past decade. Middle age is when the losses start mounting up, and here was written evidence of it — the crossed-out names of Gloria (cancer), Jean (stroke), Leonard (heart attack), Bern (heart attack), Martin (heart attack), Tobi (cancer), John (cancer), Marguerite (cancer), Ellen (suicide), Marshall (cancer), Morry (plane crash). As I read through the X'd out names, my thoughts linger on each friend who passed away, one in her early forties, one in his late seventies, the rest in between and all of them too soon.

Death is friendship's final closure. It crushes us as at any age but more so when it strikes in the prime of life, adding existential terror to our loss.

When a friend dies, there is Self and Other in our grief. We mourn the end of the friend's life and the end of our life with the friend. We weep for what we will never get to do together, and for all that we never said. Death teaches us that some wounds never heal. To be a whole person we must accept that we are gouged; pieces of ourselves have been torn away and each empty space is now a part of who we are. Our losses help define our wholeness.

From now on, when friends die, my electronic organizer would make it all too easy for me to delete their names from my screen. But for the moment, I hold in my hands the old address book with its messy pages edited by death — a friend, a friendship, a life, crossed out forever.

It was only seventeen months from the time my friend Tobi keeled over in a Columbia University ladies' room until her brain cancer finally killed her. She was fifty-three, married for thirty-one years, the mother of three kids in their twenties. Just two years earlier, she had enrolled in law school, and now she was looking forward to a plum job, clerking for a judge. At a fiftieth birthday party given by her family, her husband had toasted her resilience, her adaptability, her capacity to make a new life for herself time and time again. Everyone listening knew she had followed him across the globe for the sake of his career, sometimes getting lost in the shuffle, sometimes angry at the world, but always springing back and inventing herself anew in each location, taking on a job, a project, a plan, trying to be a distinct, functional human being in the shadow of a prominent husband. Now Tobi's time had come. With a roomful of her friends, I raised my glass to her and my eyes filled with tears.

That jubilant moment came back to me many times during her sick months, the fighting-back months, when the doctors tried everything and her body swelled like a waterlogged doll, and she lay in a hospital bed, bald, with a screaming scar across her skull, talking about how her law clerk job was being held for her and how she was trying to stay up to date on her coursework. I remember when she walked around with a scarf on her head, how odd it was to see her move so slowly, 33⅓ after a lifetime at 78 r.p.m., and soon afterward to see her in a wheelchair, and how it hurt me in my heart to look into her eyes, and smile and nod and make enthusiastic noises as she talked about the three of us, she and I and Sarah, taking a trip up the Hudson to scout the villages along the river. I listened. I wore hope on my face. I made the right noises. I watched her die.

She was not the easiest person in the world to get close to, but she had shared her frustrations with me, and I had felt her struggles so acutely and rejoiced so genuinely in her self-discovery that by the time she died, I was devastated. The cruelty of her dying, the unfairness, the dashed dreams, the randomness, the irony, all of it overwhelmed me with sorrow. I was forty-eight. Other friends have died since then, but that death stays clear and cold in my mind.

Tobi's husband has since remarried, to a lovely woman who herself has become a friend. Tobi's children are incredibly successful, and I know she would have been bursting with pride — though I suspect she'd be pushing them to get married by now. I think of her whenever I hear that a woman has gone back to school in her fifties. I think of her whenever I see a bald woman, a woman fighting cancer in a scarf.

I know a fifty-five-year-old man who says he thinks twice these days before postponing a get-together with a friend. "It's not that I'm morbid, I'm just aware that we're not going to live forever." When you pass fifty, this awareness hovers over you like the branch of a tree, and in its shade, human attachments seem more precious. Lately, social scientists have confirmed the importance of human relationships to one's physical and emotional health. A University of California study of 7,000 men and women found that those with the fewest social ties were twice as likely to die as those with the strongest connections. Data from a Swedish study of fifty-year-old men revealed that the subjects who lacked friends and family support were three times as likely to die from events associated with stressful lives than those men enduring similar stress who had adequate social support systems. And we've already noted that married men live longer than bachelors.

This sort of information makes me worry a little about Bert. He has close family ties, but his friendships are, by and large, superficial and situational, a pattern that precisely parallels the traditional behavior of American men of his generation, which doesn't make it healthy.

Men, Women, and Midlife Friendship

Social science research quantifies the pattern, but no one needs an expert to tell us what we see around us every day; that men tend to get together around an activity — a working dinner, a tennis date, a ball game — whereas women get together just to *be* together; we don't have to *do* anything but talk. As a rule, men friends don't schmooze for hours on the phone, they don't meet each other for lunch unless they have an agenda, they don't nurture friendship, don't cultivate, don't irrigate. Women are the farmers of the social landscape, the caretakers who make the dinner dates, remember people's birthdays, send get-well cards. Male friends rarely talk about personal matters; they discuss politics, sports, law, sex, and money, while most of women's talk centers on relationships, people, and feelings. A man's idea of an intimate conversation is a woman's definition of a casual chat.

Morton Hunt asks himself, in an "About Men" column in the *New York Times*, "How is it that after having been friends for twenty or thirty years (and in some cases much longer) we are only now becoming intimate?" He writes of longtime friends in their sixties and older who have just now "taken the mask off" and started confiding in each other; men who had "never revealed our insecurities, weaknesses or hopeless yearnings."

What happens at the outer edge of middle age — at least to those men who let it happen — is that they see time running out and they recognize that something important and meaningful is missing from their lives. So they open up; they start letting other men know who they really are, and they discover to their amazement that they can survive the exposure. "What seems strange is how easy, comforting, and natural it is to do so now that we all know we are in the last act of the drama and before long the curtain will fall," Hunt writes. "How fortunate that we can be intimate now, when we need to be. How sad that we never could before."

My husband is unusual in that he talks to our children several times a week and keeps abreast of the goings-on in their lives. But he doesn't divulge his innermost thoughts to anyone but me, which is flattering but foolish. I hate to think of how emotionally isolated he would be if I weren't around anymore. I wonder if he will ever know real closeness with a friend. And if he doesn't, who will comfort him if the curtain falls on me first and he has to go through the last act alone?

I can't believe I'm actually thinking about this. You know you've entered a new phase when you start worrying about your husband's friendships after you're gone — but men's problem with intimacy is worth discussing because it's very real and very common. In most marriages, if the wife doesn't make the social arrangements, the couple doesn't see anyone; if she doesn't get the theater tickets, they stay home; if she doesn't keep in touch with their friends, the friendships wither. Lately, I've challenged Bert to examine his behavior in this regard, and he concedes that there's a problem. "When I'm dead, you're going to be mighty lonely," I say. "Why won't you pick up the phone and call X, just to see how he is?" "Why not take in a movie with Y next Wednesday when I'm away?" "Did you ever think of asking Z for lunch since he lost his job?" Bert still resists taking that sort of initiative, but he has shown some progress. He has reached the point where he dislikes small talk almost as much as I do, and he finds lately that his conversations with certain men are going deeper. Often, but not always. The other night at the gym, he met a friend who had just broken up with the woman he'd been seeing for two years.

"How does he feel?" I asked Bert when he came home.

"I don't know, I didn't ask."

"You didn't *ask*?"

"Well, I didn't think he'd want to start talking about it in the middle of the shower room."

As for my own friendships, while I'd wish for more variety, I have no complaints about intimacy. I feel well nurtured, and also more nurturing, and appreciative of those dear to me. Sometimes I catch myself looking long and hard at my best-loved friends, or I conjure their faces in my mind and cherish them. Sometimes I even find the words to tell them what they mean to me. In the last few years, since the mindfulness set in and the cherishing picked up steam, I've told my friend Selma, who was my college roommate, how grateful I am that we weathered our stormy periods and how much her big, sunny, loud, loving friendship lights up my life. I've told my friend Gale how I admire her incredible focus, the way she makes every friend feel like number one, the way she notices *everything* and can describe it to the last detail — people, places, movies, and now, the college courses of her so-called retirement. My friend Sarah knows I love her for being so passionate about social justice and political issues, for her incredible generosity, for taking in strays and making them into friends and sharing all her friends with all her other friends. I've told my friend Phyllis I love her for being so wise, so dependable, so solid, and so smart. I've told Marcia, my sister-in-law, that I love the fact that we are family but also close and loving friends. My friend Barbara knows I find her both funny and profound, that she makes me laugh and makes me think and that I love our walks because it gives us one full hour of uninterrupted schmoozing. I've told my friend Jane how much I appreciate her unfailing kindness, her loyalty, her fabulous cooking, and her willingness to forgive me for being so much less available to friendship than she is.

I don't find it hard to say what I feel though sometimes my listeners seem less than comfortable hearing it. In a world of critics and complainers, we don't always know how to accept a compliment from a friend.

Discovering Solitude

No matter how much I understand about friendship, certain contradictions seem irreconcilable: I want new friends, but I don't want to shortchange those I already have. I'd like to have younger friends and older friends, but so many of my concerns are related to the vicissitudes of middle age, and I need to share my ups and downs with people who are going through the same stuff at the same time. I sense the increasing importance of friendship in my life, but I'm also discovering something brand-new: how much I enjoy my solitude.

In the past, I saw only two alternatives — being happy with people or being lonely alone. Now there's a third possibility — being happy alone. As much as I love good conversation, lately I can take long walks without company, because there seems to be so much to look at and think about, so much to wonder at and plan and worry over and try to figure out. For the first time in my life solitude seems to have its own fullness. I am satisfied to be by myself, alone, burrowing into time.

Then, too, I have noticed myself becoming more responsive to spirituality and prayer. I've found pathways to transcendence that circumvent the patriarchal institutions of traditional Judaism. I am more open to the power of dreams and other extracognitive, nonlinear journeys that I might have ridiculed in my younger days. I feel more connected to my heritage, my ancestors, and, for want of a better word, cosmic time.

Solitude and spirituality are among my most surprising new pleasures, but there is still another unexpected development: suddenly, I love quiet. Absolute stillness. I hear silence as never before. I prefer small sounds to bombast. The music I enjoy most these days is produced by fewer instruments — Beethoven's piano sonatas rather than his symphonies, Chopin's polonaises and nocturnes, Mozart's sonatas instead of the concertos. In my ears, less has become more. I hear the hum of the refrigerator motor, the creak of the stairs, a squirrel scurrying through dry leaves. I notice the wind. Maybe it's part of the midlife reassessment process. While taking everything apart and questioning where each piece fits into my life, I've become interested in the pieces themselves, in the details, those tiny sparks that together illuminate the big picture.

I know it sounds like a cliché, but I also seem to be developing a new appreciation of nature. One finds beauty and solitude in nature, so what's not to like? But the fact is, I had always been apprehensive in the great outdoors — its hidden brambles and unpredictable skies represented everything unknown and frightening to me, everything that threatened to make me feel out of control and unmask my physical weaknesses. Instead of sylvan glades and meadow paths, I used to prefer walking on city sidewalks, where one can always find a pay phone. But now I'm actually eager to get out of town and into the woods. I am newly captivated by the perfection of tiny pine cones, of birds crossing a shaft of sunlight, of moss-shrouded rocks tossed about the forest floor like hassocks in green velvet slipcovers. I am discovering another world.

Maybe this is why I've been devouring the works of the late May Sarton, high priestess of solitude, the feminist Thoreau, a poet and writer who lived alone in New Hampshire and then on the coast of Maine, and who made of solitude an art and a way of life. Reading her journals, I enter her modest life as if it were a Tolstoy novel — waiting with her for the delphinium to flower, worrying when the woodchuck eats the hollyhock and the rain batters the daffodils, admiring the monarch butterflies, sharing her days and nights as she turns seventy or fights her way back from a stroke or goes visiting. I wrap myself in her words about time and aging, her tributes to old friends, her patient tending of relationships, her honesty and rage about growing old inside a failing body, and her enduring passion for peace and quiet.

In *Journal of a Solitude,* she writes, "I am happy to be alone — time to think, time to be. This kind of open-ended time is the only luxury that really counts and I feel stupendously rich to have it."

It is completely unlike me to be interested in this sort of prose, yet lately I cannot seem to get enough of it. Partly, I suppose, this is related to my new habit of *noticing;* I'm seeing time, people, events, in a new light; why not solitude? Why not nature? Then again, maybe it's primal. Nature nourishes and renews, which might explain why I'm drawn to it now, in my fifties, when nourishment and renewal are harder to come by. Or maybe this sudden attraction to the quieter side of life is part of some grand master plan that is preparing me to spend some portion of my future alone, a plan that my unconscious has hatched to answer the unspeakable question "What will I do when he's gone?" Of course, it could simply be another ordinary step in the aging process that people forget to tell you about. For all I know, it happens to everyone. In any case, it's happening to me. I want friendship and solitude in equal measure. Not either/or. Both.

I had assumed that from fifty on, everything would change for the worse, but what I've just described — acceptance of my children's independence, renewed commitment to friendship, finding pleasure in spirituality and solitude, heightened perceptions of the natural world — all have been life-enhancing changes. I have chosen to make a fuss about them because any positive transformation that happens to us at this point in our lives strikes me as a marvelous thing. "The moment of change is the only poem," wrote Adrienne Rich. I am beginning to understand its poetry.

11

Doing Life

It's never too late to be what you might have been.
—*George Eliot*

Contrary to the laws of good breeding, I do not consider it impolite to ask people what they do. The question offends, presumably, because we are supposed to be interested in who someone *is*, not what they *do*. To me, that's nonsense. There is no *being* without *doing* unless you're comatose. People *are* what their actions and passions say they are. People *are* what they do with their life and their time. That the question has been interpreted solely as an inquiry into occupational status is not my problem; it's a problem for a society that reduces all doing to what one does for money.

When I say you are what you do, I don't mean you are your job, although that might be a partial truth if, in fact, your work life matches your private commitments. Some are lucky enough to get paid for work they would do for free. Others make a living doing things they find meaningless but use their own time for other kinds of doing: doing things for children, for sick people, for art, for fun, for the growth of their minds, or the good of the planet.

Working side by side in a charitable or community organization, one doesn't always know what one's fellow volunteers do for a living but only that they care enough to give their time to something they believe in. That's what they *do*.

At the MacDowell Colony, a retreat that provides brief residencies for writers and artists, newcomers always get acquainted with one another by asking, "What do you do?" The answer is, "I'm a poet," "I paint," "I'm a composer," though, in fact, most of these people have other money-making jobs back home. They teach, they work in offices and bookstores, they program computers, but in their minds, where it matters, they are artists.

"A man must do. A woman need only be." The proverb is the proof. To *be* is passive. To *be* is to sit there, empty. In that sense, to be is *not* to be. There is no being without doing: thinking is an act, so is meditating or listening or praying. To do is not necessarily to move around or make money or material objects; to do is to make meaning out of time.

It is that effort, those acts, those choices, that use of the time within one's control, that I think of as "*doing life*," the doing that gives purpose to one's existence. And because I believe this, I'm still asking myself, in the deepest, broadest sense, what do I want to do for the rest of my life?

Inspiration and Impediments

Since turning forty, I've been collecting stories of well-known people who produced great work in their middle years and beyond. When I'm feeling stale, it heartens me to know that Michelangelo hit a lull at forty but bounced back to produce the Medici Chapel at age fifty-five. Tchaikovsky thought he had run dry when he was forty-one, but at forty-eight he wrote his fifth symphony and at fifty-three, his sixth. Beethoven slid into a five-year funk at forty, then went on to compose his seventh, eighth, and ninth symphonies and all his late quartets (from Opus 130 on). The prima ballerina Margot Fonteyn danced brilliantly until she was fifty-eight. Julia Child started her TV career in her fifties. Bella Abzug first took her seat in the U.S. Congress at fifty. Sarah Vaughan was able to say at sixty-three, "My voice just keeps getting better and better." Beverly Sills sang her last operatic role when she was fifty-one, then "retired" to a second career in opera management. (Staggering thought: had John F. Kennedy lived and been reelected, he would have finished his second term at fifty-one, with the rest of his life ahead of him.) The sculptor Louise Bourgeois was over seventy when her work was first recognized with a one-woman show at the Museum of Modern Art, and now, at eighty-three, she is at the height of her powers. "People are stunned that someone of her age can be so contemporary," says Beatrice Parent, the curator of a major Bourgeois retrospective held in Paris in 1995. "One has the impression that the older she gets, the younger and more energetic she becomes."

Writers, naturally, are my main inspiration, especially women writers, for, as Carolyn Heilbrun observes, "we live our lives through our texts." I've never forgotten that Tillie Olsen was fifty when she wrote her first book, *Tell Me a Riddle*, a novel that remains well read more than thirty years later, or that poet Amy Clampitt didn't publish her first book until she was sixty-three and by the time she died at seventy-four had left a significant body of work and a decisive mark on American letters.

Along with grand tales of public glory, I'm moved by many stories of ordinary people who do what they love and love what they do. I admire people who pursue a passion in midlife whether it pays or not, whether they excel at it or not, whether or not it's easy—people who write what they must, lawyers who open restaurants, teachers who restore old houses, retired corporate types who give pro bono advice to fledgling businesses, a friend in New Zealand who took up both airplane gliding and auto racing in her fifties. I admire people in their sixties and seventies who work in senior centers and nursing homes, because, as one seventy-eight-year-old volunteer put it, "the old folks need a helping hand."

But when I hear their stories, it sometimes makes me think I should try something completely different myself, say, run an antique shop, since I love old things, or open a bookstore. I worry that I may be stagnating, or that I might have a calling that has yet to make itself known and, if it does, I won't hear it in time to pursue it. I think maybe I should remain a writer but try a different genre, something other than nonfiction, maybe short stories, a play, that novel I keep talking about. Eventually, I calm down and opt to keep doing what I do but try to do it better, and with less sturm und drang.

People assume that after twenty-five years, writing ought to be a piece of cake. Well, maybe a seventeen-layer cake that takes weeks to whip up and looks as if it got caught in the rain and tastes like glue if you don't watch it every minute. I'm always amazed that, no matter how long I do it, writing never gets any easier; in fact, it gets harder because, as we grow older, our critical standards rise but our talent doesn't necessarily rise with it. While trying to figure out why I still shudder at the sight of a blank page, or why it frightens me to switch genres at this age, I thought about Ralph Keyes's wonderful book *The Courage to Write,* and all those writers' fears that I mentioned earlier, and it occurred to me that writing as a profession has much in common with the themes I have set forth in this book.

Mortality tremors? "One of the most fundamental of human fears is that our existence will go unnoticed," Keyes says. "We'd all like to have it recorded somewhere. What better way to achieve this goal than by writing? Long after maggots have had their way with my corpse, my name will still be on the spine of books in the Library of Congress. I'm *on the record*."

Mastering one's fears? Writers convert their anxiety into essays, books, and poetry—and get paid for it. Mindfulness? Noticing is what writers do, what they *must* do: listen, watch, ask questions, pay attention to the details, the smell of a waxed floor, the plant on the windowsill, scuffed shoes, silk cushions. Time obsession? "Proust regarded an hour spent in the company of others as an hour lost to writing forever." Hemingway believed good writers "must face eternity, or the lack of it, each day;" Virginia Woolf spoke of "the exalted sense of being above time and death which comes from being in a writing mood." And, says Keyes, "Many authors enter a trancelike state as they write. . . . After what seems like minutes, writers glance at the clock and see that they've been working for hours." Self-exploration and the search for authenticity? It was George Santayana who said, "I write to find out what I think." And *feel*. Embracing new risks? "As a writer one has to take the chance of being a fool," said Anne Sexton. "That perhaps requires the greatest courage."

Sometimes my courage fails me, and I wonder, yet again, if I'm in the wrong trade.

How odd to fulminate over such matters at fifty-five, an age when I would have expected to be luxuriating in the warm bath of professional certainty. (If not now, when?) Yet, fulmination is appropriate when one is really asking not "What do I want to do next?" but "What do I want to do *with the time I have left?*" And how much time can it be? Maybe twenty years with full use of my faculties, then a few more for good measure. Lydia Bronte, author of *The Longevity Factor*, studied people over sixty-five who are still actively working and found that 85 percent of them had no real physical problems, but who's to say you or I will be so fortunate. And even with luck, what's twenty years? A blip on the time line, the blink of an eye. Looking back, I can remember twenty years ago as if it were yesterday, and as for tomorrow, well, we all know the future happens much sooner than it used to.

While I'm giving myself a spiritual migraine worrying about what I want to be doing next, I'm aware that many people my age haven't the luxury of thinking about meaningful work because they can't find a job at all, or one that pays a livable wage. Here's the lead paragraph of a recent trend story in the *New York Times:* "Despite a decade-long push by private and government organizations to market older people as reliable and mature workers, advocates for people fifty-five and older say their efforts have largely failed. They say that employers continue to view age not in terms of experience or stability but as deterioration and staleness." Reams of research have proved that older workers are more reliable, have higher productivity rates, are just as easy to retrain as younger people, and are absent from work less frequently than employees under age twenty-five, but these findings never seem to sink in at the management level. Federal law prohibits discrimination on the basis of age, but that hasn't stopped many employers from deducing applicants' ages from their gray hair, wrinkles, graduation year, or years of work experience, and then acting on their biases anyway.

"Everybody saw them as reliable, like a Saint Bernard," Martin Sicker, an employment analyst, told the *Times* about older workers. "[Companies] love them but they won't hire [or promote] them. . . . They use words like 'mature' and 'dependable' but they don't look at individual skills and characters. They lump older workers together in a way they don't younger ones. . . . It does just come down to 'ageism' and we haven't found a way to crack it."

A 1990 Louis Harris survey found two million nonworking Americans between fifty and sixty-four years old who are willing and able to work but can't find jobs because of age discrimination and employers' attitudes. The Equal Employment Opportunity Commission says there's been a 30 percent jump in age-bias complaints since 1990, and the complainants now include people in their forties as well as those in their fifties and sixties. This does not bode well for older women who need a job for their financial security or their sanity.

In 1979, for her book *Women of a Certain Age: The Midlife Search for Self*, sociologist Lillian Rubin interviewed 160 women including this one who yearned for purposeful work after decades of homemaking: "Twenty years of kids and doctors and chauffeuring and PTA and bridge and all that talk, talk, talk about nothing, is enough. I got so I knew I couldn't stand another afternoon of that talk. Enough! There's got to be more to life than hot flashes and headaches." For such a woman, finding a job might be as lifesaving as finding water in the desert. Another housewife told Rubin, "Yesterday I was picking up some clothes to put them in the washer, and suddenly I realized that I was doing the same work now that I was doing twenty-nine years ago when I first got married. *It's like never growing up.*"

Once upon a time not very long ago, women weren't permitted to grow up; they were treated like children in that most were dependents of men, with no money of their own, no autonomy, independence, or decision-making power, and, supposedly, no aspirations. Today, any woman who embraces that sort of passivity is committing economic suicide.

Paying Our Own Way

Probably the only midlife fear that can compete with the specter of illness and death is the fear of spending one's last years in poverty. Yet many women my age belong to the era Lillian Rubin wrote about: they did not work outside the home for most of their lives, believing they could be safely dependent on their husbands. Now they are economically stranded by widowhood or divorce. As Flo Kennedy once put it, "A housewife is a woman who is one man away from welfare."

By the same token, many employed women are not much better off. Victims of sex and age bias in hiring, promotion, and pay scales, they haven't made enough money to amass big savings accounts, and most remain strangers to the concept of planning for their old age—which explains why some of my most successful friends have nightmares in which they see themselves ending up as bag ladies. For single and divorced women, this is not as far-fetched as it sounds; without the safety net of a husband's income and pension, countless older women are struggling to make ends meet, often having to decide between food, rent, and medicine.

Labor analysts project that 76 percent of women between forty-five and fifty-four and nearly 50 percent of women from fifty-five to sixty-four will be in the workforce by the year 2000—most of them by necessity. Unless things change radically in this country, the combination of ageism and sexism is likely to remain a serious impediment to older women's earning capacity (not to mention their self-esteem). A recent study by the Older Women's League found that the economic gap between the sexes widens with age. In 1994, wage-earning women between ages twenty-five and thirty-four earned 83 percent as much as men in the same chronological group, while women between fifty-five and sixty-four earned only 66 percent as much as their male counterparts. Among retirees, the gender gap has actually worsened in the last twenty-five years. Back in 1970, women received 78 percent of men's Social Security benefit; in 1995, women's average monthly benefit was only 76 percent of that of the average man—$538 as opposed to the males' $858.

Since so many women are now spending decades in the workforce, the number of us who are entitled to Social Security based both on our own employment records and that of our husbands has increased dramatically from 5 percent of all female recipients in 1960 to 25 percent in 1993. However, because we still earn far less than men, and are far more likely to work part-time, or to have left the workforce for several years to raise children, our Social Security benefits remain low. Women who get their benefits as *wives* receive an amount equal to half their husbands' monthly check, which is more than they would get as workers, even though they paid into the Social Security system in their own right. This is why the percentage of women choosing to draw benefits based on their own (as opposed to their husbands') employment records has dropped from 42 percent in 1970 to about 36 percent in 1993. Most women who have worked outside the home and contributed to the Social Security system for years get the same benefits they would have received had they never held a job at all.

Many commentators render women invisible by talking about "senior citizens" as if everyone were in the same circumstances when in fact the two sexes have vastly different prospects. Older women are three times as likely as men to be poor, and a major cause of female impoverishment is widowhood—loss of spouse being far more common to women than men. In 1993, women over sixty-five had a median annual income of $8,499, which was only 57 percent of the $14,983 median income of older men. A scant 13 percent of these women had a pension to fall back on, compared to 33 percent of the men. The mean pension income for men was $7,468; for women it was only $3,940. These numbers tell us why, even within the same socioeconomic class, older women fear aging more than do older men, and why middle-aged women have every reason to worry about their economic futures.

Those of us who will *become* older women must ensure that we have adequate income as we age, which means taking responsibility right now for planning our financial futures, even if we presently have a husband who is willing to make those decisions for us. "Don't bother your pretty little head about it" is the sort of attitude that left Doris Day in bankruptcy after her husband died, and left millions of ordinary women wondering, at sixty-five, why they can't afford a sandwich. Whether we have to consult with a financial planner, accountant, or bank officer, or read a how-to book that walks us through every step necessary to ensure our comfort and security in old age, every woman must assume this responsibility before it's too late—and understand what's in store for her if she doesn't.

Justifiable Paranoia

Though self-employed and immune to the indignities of a corporate layoff or midlife job search, I am as troubled as anyone by what those age-bias studies tell us about prejudice against workers over fifty, and by extension, against work *produced* by people over fifty. The EEOC findings, plus anecdotal evidence from every occupational field, can't help but feed the depression endemic to aging and stimulate a condition I call "has-been paranoia" — the fear of becoming passé that many midlifers harbor as a result of having witnessed the price others have paid for aging on the job.

At a certain point, no matter who you are or how well you are doing, your age is all they see. Witness the press coverage of the Rolling Stones' ballyhooed world tour. Their concerts were sell-outs, their music judged first-rate by most critics, yet virtually all the media hammered away at the age thing with comments like these, taken from just two stories in the *Times* (August 1994): "The Rolling Stones won't grow old gracefully." "The band members are now in their 50's with well-creased faces." "[Mick] Jagger has figured out ways to conserve energy inconspicuously as he roams the huge stage." "The Stones, who are not getting any younger, are showing some wear." "Charlie Watts has silver hair." "The set started with a vow of persistence, 'Not Fade Away.' "

Entertainers may be no more prone to ageism than workers in factories and offices, but as its most visible victims they help us by publicizing the scourge. Actresses of the caliber of Faye Dunaway, Lauren Bacall, and Meryl Streep openly complain about the paucity of roles for midlife and older women, a situation that puts the biggest names out to pasture in their prime. Streep almost didn't get the part of Francesca in *The Bridges of Madison County* because Warner Bros. at first insisted on testing a flock of much younger actresses. Director Clint Eastwood said certain powers at the studio strongly opposed his casting Streep as his leading lady, though at forty-six she was just a year older than the book's Francesca, while Eastwood, at sixty-five, was thirteen years older than the character he plays, Robert Kincaid.

At the "Fabulous Palm Springs Follies" — where the minimum age is fifty and the current chorus line ranges from fifty-seven to seventy-eight — the dancers are working professionals who put on ten shows a week that one critic has called "vital, vibrant, even sexy." Veterans of the Folies Bergère, the Latin Quarter, and the stages of Reno and Vegas, they had no place to strut their stuff despite their enduring competence and desire to work. Until an impresario had the idea to tap this mother lode of dormant talent, they'd been considered washed up.

No one escapes. Older designers say they detect a bias in favor of younger designers. Ditto for older chefs, photographers, and filmmakers. The common wisdom is that physicists and mathematicians do their best work in their youth, which doesn't account for Einstein but does explain this poem by Paul Adrien Maurice Dirac:

Age is, of course, a fever chill
That every physicist must fear.
He's better dead than living still
When once he's past his thirtieth year.

A literary agent says she is pursuing a promising young writer but doubts he'll come into her stable: "Why would someone who's thirty want to be represented by someone who's sixty?" she asks, anticipating his assumption that she won't be in the business much longer. "I was quick to tell him that I plan to work until I die — and my mother lived to be ninety!"

Among writers, who have famously vulnerable egos to begin with, it's hard not to feel like a has-been when magazine editors claim they are looking for writers with "style" or "edge," and what they really mean is youth. Says novelist Mary Tannen about meeting with agents and editors, "How could I convince them that my ideas were young and fresh if my face was old and worn?"

It's pernicious — the euphemisms and mendacity on the one side and on the other the fear of becoming passé. Held captive by the way we look or the date on our birth certificate, we worry that someone else's ideas about age will prevent us from doing our work. "I can still see, thank God," wrote Eudora Welty in her later years. "I see the mail coming, and the laundry, and friends coming. I want to keep on writing as long as I can think."

For the better part of my adult life, I've been able to do my thing: speak and be heard; write and be published. It hardly bears contemplating, but all that could stop, dry up, disappear. Friends of mine have known the desert, fellow scribblers whose market has vanished. Like showgirls without a stage, they have no way to do what they love because there are no takers. Having seen such loss, one learns to fear it. Especially if work is an important part of one's life.

Passion

The truth is, I'd rather work than play — so much so that I often overdo it, sitting at my desk for hours, oblivious to the world, tangled up in paragraphs or roaming around in my head searching for a clearer way to say it, whatever "it" is. I wish I could find a way to explain this passion without coming off as a raving fanatic or sounding sanctimonious, but since I can't, I'll let others make the case. Mark Twain said, "Work and play are words used to describe the same thing under differing conditions," and proved it with Tom Sawyer's fence-painting gambit. Thomas Carlyle, the Scottish historian, flatly declared, "Blessed is he who has found his life's work, let him ask no other blessedness." Also using religious terminology, the social reformer Antoinette Brown Blackwell wrote, at fifty, "Work, alternated with needful rest, is the salvation of man or woman." Following her own counsel, she lived to ninety-six, speaking and writing to the end. The artist Kathe Kollwitz was another rhapsodic workaholic: "For the last third of life there remains only work," she said. "It alone is always stimulating, rejuvenating, exciting and satisfying."

Obviously, such passion is the privilege of those for whom work is not menial drudgery, but a challenge and an opportunity for self-expression. Because my work gives me that, I want to be able to keep doing it until I'm too old to lift a finger. But here's the crazy part: when asked what I'd do if I had only six months to live, my answer is, I'd travel; I'd "do" Europe in 180 days in the company of the people I love. This raises an obvious paradox, one of the many I am learning to live with as grown-ups must: For the past quarter-century, most of my waking hours have been spent doing the work I love. Yet, were I told death was imminent, I wouldn't write another sentence or attend another meeting, nor, for that matter, would I curl up with the complete works of Martin Buber or Virginia Woolf. It embarrasses me to admit it, but when push comes to ultimate shove, activism and intellect be damned. If the end were around the corner, all I'd want is to head off on that farewell voyage and go out in style.

Even without an impending death sentence, I've noticed myself trying to program more and more travel into every year, searching for new and different destinations and prodding Bert, whose schedule is not as flexible as mine, to use more of his vacation time. This is not to say I've been weaned of my compulsive productivity, but I have started two-timing the work ethic and succumbing to the attractions of pure pleasure as never before, courting the good life like a new love, mining the delights of the arts, food, and travel as if my days were numbered, which, of course, they are. I intend to remain a useful citizen for as long as I live, but after decades of worrying about everything from nuclear war to putting three kids through school, I don't want to feel guilty about reaching the point where I'm ready to lighten up.

On the bathroom wall in a downtown restaurant is the scrawled imperative LIFE IS UNCERTAIN; EAT DESSERT FIRST. If people my age are thinking about dessert more often these days, does it mean we're hopelessly sybaritic? Is it a sign of terminal self-indulgence? Are we wrong to want to coast a bit after so many years at full throttle? Right or wrong, this sudden attack of pleasure-seeking does seem symptomatic of middle age.

Living Well Is the Best Revenge

Because we feel the time crunch so much more keenly now, many of us are choosing to dedicate whatever disposable income we have to buy experiences rather than material things. This rings right to me. Past the age of fifty we need something exciting to look forward to as a counterweight to the apprehension of an unknown future. Pleasure is an amazingly potent tonic, an antidote for mortality tremors, a pick-me-up for downhill jitters, a detour from the slide, and the best revenge against aging that I know. Pursuing our chosen delights allows us to feel *new* when it is no longer possible to feel young. Newness is, after all, what youth is about. Just by being alive, young people have fresh experiences from which they grow every day, while we who are in midlife must *create* newness, struggle daily against inertia, and push ourselves to keep growing, a task that gets more difficult as we become more set in our ways. Doing life means finding an equilibrium between the familiar and the new for the familiar satisfies our need for security, while the new makes us feel alive.

Kicking the habit of retreat into the familiar doesn't necessarily require a lot of cash, it just takes mindfulness, a conscious, purposeful effort to elevate the ordinary in ways that make it *feel* new. We can decide to eat

carves out a small portion to master and lets the rest go by the boards. I told her I had opted out of disciplines like molecular biology and Sumerian civilization with absolutely no regrets, and she, too, would decide eventually which islands of erudition to leave unexplored. This seemed comforting enough for the moment, and she grew up just fine, but I have never forgotten our conversation, because I've been run over by the same freight train while trying to continue my education into middle age. It seems clear to me that I stopped studying Hebrew because I couldn't see my way to the end.

Nothing is quite as thrilling as the voyage from darkness to light, from "I can't" to "I can," which is the essence of learning in childhood. Until recently, I'd always assumed that, if I applied myself, I could elect to take that journey whenever I felt like it and learn whatever I put my mind to, an assumption rooted not in arrogance but sheer naïveté. Lately, however, optimism has bowed to realism. The fact is, I will probably never get any better at all the things I've been doing badly for years — like skiing, ice-skating, baking, sewing, playing tennis, chess, or poker. Moreover, certain bodies of knowledge (microbiology and Sumerian civilization among innumerable others) will remain altogether beyond me. I know enough not to blame this on aging; there were plenty of things I couldn't master when I was young, too, but the pain of facing my limitations cuts deeper now than it did then. Now, I've accepted that there are some things I will *never* learn. It's the finality that hurts.

When we decide to focus our attention on what we really want to do with the rest of our life, when we force ourselves to consider our options and choose among them with mindful awareness of our limitations and the limitations of the life span, then the layers of self-deception fall away like scales from the eyes and a kind of clarity results. Thinking about the importance I place on learning and how to translate it into "doing life," I have come to realize that my favorite educational experiences are those that offer instant gratification. I like it when someone teaches me something and I get it on the spot. Tell me what to listen for in a symphony, and I'm all ears. Send me through an art museum with a well-informed docent. Show me how to fix a bicycle tire, or make the perfect omelette. Sign me up for a panel discussion on ethnic identity, a conference on women's health, a briefing on the Middle East, where I can build on my existing knowledge, and I'm a happy camper.

This helter-skelter, lecture-loving learning style is just one of many ways people my age pursue their interests. I know a sixty-year-old businessman who saw a group of people staring at the sky one morning, became curious about what they were looking for, and in the process of finding out, identified seventeen different birds in his own backyard and got hooked on birding. A fifty-one-year-old woman is learning belly dancing. Another man has seen hundreds of old films since he assigned himself the task of taping and cataloging the classics that run on TV. My friend Annie, fifty-five, whom you may remember from my birthday lunch, is taking guitar and voice lessons. Carol, fifty-five, another guest at the lunch, is taking courses to learn how to be a theatrical producer. And the more systematic of my acquaintances have formally enrolled in college, where more than one in ten students is over fifty.

My sixty-year-old husband began windsurfing when he was fifty; now he's learning to type. He also wants to take up in-line skating, though thus far, he's been deterred by memories of a recent attempt at skateboarding. In five seconds, he was on his back on the sidewalk, and the bruise, which turned every color of the rainbow, ached for weeks. Years ago, fear of injury wouldn't have stopped him, but at this age, when there's a chance of broken bones or strained muscles and the specter of a long period of immobility — making it hard to work and impossible to exercise to counteract one's retarded metabolism — caution becomes the better part of passion.

Why so much learning fervor at this time of life? Lots of reasons: The *use-it-or-lose-it* theory. The desire to follow wherever curiosity leads in keeping with the "growth spurt" of middle age. (If I'm learning, I'm growing, and if I'm growing, maybe I'm not dying.) The idea of exploring new options to fill whatever void retirement may leave in one's life. The decision to pursue a lifelong interest that we always intended to get to someday, and now, of course, someday has arrived. It may not be the End of Days, but the End of Procrastination has come. It's now-or-never time, we tell ourselves. The mind is a terrible thing to waste. The learning curve needs time to make it around the bend, so get going or forever hold your peace.

"I grow old learning something new every day," said Solon, the Athenian statesman, but he had nothing on my sister and brother-in-law, Betty and Bernard Miller. Retired from their careers in education — she was an English teacher, he a high school principal — the two of them, now seventy and seventy-five respectively, have enrolled in more Elderhostel trips than I knew existed. This marvelous travel-study program offers people fifty-five or older a choice of more than 2,000 academic institutions in forty-nine countries that offer short-term courses in everything from "Hispanic Writers" to "Medical Ethics" to "The Romance of Archeology" — and Betty and Bernie are working their way through the catalog page by page. For the last ten years, they have also been blazing a trail around the globe, learning about other places, people, and cultures, with the zeal of a pair of roving reporters from *National Geographic*. With reams of research poking out of their portmanteaux, wearing sensible shoes and trudging through every site you've never heard of, they stay away for weeks at a time, usually on a budget, learning, looking, listening, then come home with an infectious enthusiasm and enough folk art for a small museum.

Re-Tiring People

Mentioning my peripatetic relatives brings me to that idiosyncratic life form known as retirement. Betty Friedan says she hates the word because it "helps reify the age mystique, it suggests we are retired from society, it defines us only as objects of care to be walled off in retirement communities." All of which is true, of course, but the word has assumed a different emphasis lately because of some retired people I know — friends who have retired not as listless old dropouts but as people who are *re-tired* and ready for action. They've exchanged their old wheels for a new set and they're on a roll.

Gale Robinson and Marshall Goldberg, close friends of ours, retired a few years ago and couldn't be happier. Gale, a former filmmaker, went back to school, where she's taken courses on women's journal writing, Italian, and the philosophy of aesthetics; I haven't seen her this excited about anything in years. Marshall, a retired business owner, devotes his time to causes that interest him, above all, Project Return, a rehabilitation program for ex-offenders and former drug abusers. To say the two of them are in retirement is a misnomer, but I know no other word for the postcareer activities that rev people up in their middle or later years. Call Marshall a volunteer and it sounds as if he drops around now and then to stuff envelopes. Call Gale a reentry woman and you miss the passion in her pursuit. The Goldbergs are not "working" in the traditional sense of the word, and they're not "retired" the way one imagines people on golf carts and porches. They're in overdrive, they've got their second wind, they're doing life.

My sister and brother-in-law have made a science of visiting relatives, mapping a route around the United States that takes them to every town where Betty has unearthed a great-aunt or a second cousin — someone who is invariably overjoyed to have been discovered — thereby raising the pulse in what would otherwise be a moribund bloodline. When nearly a hundred people turned up at a family reunion three years ago, Betty and Bernie knew them all. Besides their many travels, they attend plays and concerts, fuss over six grandchildren in three different states, take in Fresh Air kids every summer, and work as AIDS respite caregivers. By me, this hardly qualifies as retirement.

The Millers and the Goldbergs have become my role models for the future, but for now I cannot imagine not working at all and neither can Bert. I'm counting on us sustaining parallel attitudes in this regard, because I know life can get complicated when spouses are on different time tracks. I'm thinking of one couple, call them Pat and Mike, who may be on a collision course. Mike is sixty-two, a businessman and an avid golfer; Pat, fifty-four, had dropped out of the job market to raise their children, then twelve years ago, found a position she loves. After forty years at the grind, Mike is ready to wind down, retire, and move South, but Pat is just beginning to hit her stride; her job has just been expanded, she's up for a raise, and she doesn't want to budge. It won't be a marital picnic if neither one gives an inch.

Compromise is possible for Pat and Mike: She could make the effort to find a comparable job wherever he wants to relocate. He could settle for golf links closer to home, maybe join a different country club to give himself a fresh start. She might ask her company to let her cut back to a four-day week so they can have long weekends together. Or they could try a "commuting marriage" — say, he moves South, she stays to do her thing, and they get together once or twice a month at either end of the axis. To afford the travel costs, they might have to live in smaller digs in both locations and economize on other things, but scaling down may be worth it if both people are able to do life in the way that makes each one happy. Plus, I'm told, those reunions can be pretty romantic.

By focusing on possible compromises, I don't mean to minimize the difficulties of asymmetrical retirement. Typically, it's the husband who quits first, because he is generally older and has been working longer. When he retires, the wife, if she's at home, suddenly has to adjust to having him around the house twenty-four hours a day. If she's employed outside the home, she has to learn to live with his disengagement, the lessening of his worldly status, and, often, his frustration when he can't find enough to do. Indeed, many men discover they are lost without their jobs to give purpose and order to their lives; others find their friendships wither when there is no longer a workplace to serve as the binding force and focal point of their social life.

Lillian Rubin, who became a college freshman at thirty-nine and eight years later left the campus with a doctorate in sociology and postdoctoral training in psychology, says "if a couple has a history of respect for one another's needs, they already understand that mutual adaptation is the only solution. It's not a simple shift," Rubin warns, speaking both as a working therapist and a wife whose husband retired years ago. "It's hard for a woman raised in our culture to accept weakness in a man and come to terms with his waning powers. It requires a *re-visioning* of who your partner is. Women often get angry when the guy takes over the household. They didn't marry a man to have a househusband. They don't like being sole or major support of the family. They wanted to work for gratification and meaning, not a necessary wage. Their complaints are the same as men have had about stay-home wives, only the gender pronouns have changed: 'He's become boring.' 'All he wants to do is talk and after eight hours at work, I'm sick of talking.' 'He expects me to come home and make his life interesting.' 'I know I should do more around the house, but then I think, why should I? I work hard enough all day.' " Ah, how familiar it all sounds.

Even when the couple has no money problems, a husband's retirement forces a woman to confront the reality of aging, a fact she may have been trying to finesse. Whether or not she's near his age, once he retires, she can no longer deny time and mortality a central place in her life.

Helen Bennett wrote in a "Hers" column that besides being resentful about suddenly having to share her turf with her stay-at-home husband, she felt a "gray sadness. . . . I hated my husband's retirement because it made me feel old. Out of it. Diminished in an unexpected way." Her core identity had been linked to her husband's work life, and when he retired, he pulled the plug on that vital energy source, sinking her into old age before her time. When two people have a close marriage, they often identify with each other at an organic level: you feel his arthritis in your joints; he carries your disappointments as his own. Even economically autonomous, independent-minded partners can feel attached at the hip when it comes to the vicissitudes of aging, and when something happens to one member of a couple — retirement, say, or menopause — the other member can feel older by proxy. This, I'm sure, is why a friend of mine felt depressed during her husband's convalescence from a broken ankle. The bone didn't set properly and he hobbled around on a cane for months, and she hated seeing him with that cane more than he hated having to use it. It's also why I overreacted to Bert's slight hearing loss. Any change in him reminds me of where I'm headed. Fortunately, on the issue of retirement, he and I are in lockstep for the moment. But despite my unequivocal wish to continue working, I must confess that work is not enough.

Are We Having Fun Yet?

Some people think having fun over fifty is an oxymoron. I think it's as necessary as air. Time flies whether you're having fun or not, so you may as well have it, make it happen, go for it. The mother of all clichés comes to mind here: *we only live once*.

My friend Nadine Markova, who would sooner try to fit a thunderstorm into a thimble than adapt herself to anyone else's mold, nonetheless got skittish when she turned fifty because of all the unfun images associated with aging. "How do I act now that I am old?" she asks in one of her letters. "Should I start acquiring a taste for celery soda and mashed carrots? Ought I carry a jar of stewed prunes in a paper bag? Need I learn to like melba toast and drink tea in a glass? Is it time to stop flirting, roller skating, and wearing jeans? Do I have to cut my ponytail? Must I dye my hair pink, buy some harlequin glasses and move into a trailerpark with my small dog?"

Separating the "musts" from the "want to's," I've tried to rid myself of the garbage that can pollute a perfectly pleasant middle age. Lately, for example, I've sworn off judgmental people. I am trying not to give a fig about other folks' views of age-appropriate behavior, and to steer clear of those "friends" who presume to know better than I do how I ought to behave. Feeling judged is distressing at any age but particularly in transitional periods like the teens and the fifties, when we are struggling to redefine ourselves and shape an authentic identity. It should go without saying but it doesn't, so I'll say it: how we live our lives, how we fill our time, who we spend it with, where our money goes, how we dress, where we live, what we do for fun — our *lifestyle*, for want of a better word — is no one's business but our own. The reason this fundamental proposition needs reiterating is that self-styled critics are always telling people to "act their age," a phrase that pushes my buttons whether directed at me or anyone else. I want to know what it means to act one's age and who authorized whom to define what's appropriate?

Is a forty-eight-year-old woman who wears her hair like Alice in Wonderland and rides a motor scooter acting her age? How about a woman of fifty-seven who travels the world on a steamer, or a man of fifty-two who sports a ponytail and a gold stud in his ear? Is it any skin off our noses if someone wants to take up surfing at sixty or be a "Deadhead"? Are such midlifers Generation X wannabes? Or do they simply want to be themselves?

The people I have just described aren't eccentrics, they are ordinary folks who have chosen to follow their passions. I can vouch for that, since I happen to know everyone mentioned — and I'm the one on the motor scooter. A hybrid vehicle whose size, weight, and horsepower fall between that of a motorized bike and a Harley Davidson, a motor scooter offers fun in the saddle and an economical urban conveyance that slips through traffic jams and always finds a parking spot. In my twenties, I owned a silver-gray Lambretta 150. I loved tooling around the city or cycling through the countryside with the wind in my hair (though helmet laws have tempered this exhilaration). But when I got pregnant, I acceded to Bert's wishes and gave up the sport to keep his children's mother out of harm's way, resolving to return to it when my kids were grown; which I did. For my forty-fifth birthday, I bought myself a Yamaha Riva and I would have it to this day had it not been stolen from the streets of Manhattan, as was the Honda 350 I got to replace it. I've resisted buying another, only to replenish the thieves' supply, but I'm still crazy about scooters, and during the years in my late forties when I drove one, I took a lot of heat for it. Friends used to call me "the Wild One" or "the geriatric Hell's Angel," though my shiny red scooter was hardly heavy metal and there was nothing remotely wild about the sight of me driving it in business clothes with a briefcase strapped to the back fender.

The concept of "age-appropriate" behavior makes sense in child development — parents have reason for concern if their babies don't walk and talk at a normative age, and teachers want teenagers to stop acting like rambunctious ten-year-olds — but for adults, the idea of acting one's age is utterly meaningless. "One thing is certain, and I have always known it," writes May Sarton, " — the joys of my life have nothing to do with age." I have dozens of friends in their fifties and sixties who do everything younger people do; I don't just mean run marathons or play squash, I'm talking about scuba diving, helicopter skiing, river rafting, and Outward Bounding. How could any category of fun be wrong for their age if it's right for them?

When I decided not to care about "how it looks" and "what people think," I felt truly liberated and a step closer to my authentic self. How did I learn to stop caring? First, by reminding myself that this is my life, my one and only life; no one else can live it for me and no one else will be with me on my deathbed tallying up my regrets. Second, by remembering how much of my mother's energy was dedicated to conformity and the satisfaction of other people's expectations; before she had the chance to do what she wanted, she was gone. And third, by focusing solely on *my relationship to my own delight*. Once I kept my eye on the pleasure, I stopped noticing how many of my friends were ribbing me and started noticing how many of them wanted rides.

Risk-Taking

Besides the pressure to conform, other kinds of garbage clings to us from childhood — girl garbage, for instance, meaning in my case, fear of the physical world. As I've said, I was raised with traditional, almost caricatured notions of femininity, so I grew up to be cautious, unathletic, and assertively unadventurous. The most I ever risked was a fine for an overdue library book, and to this day, I tend to rank a trip on a Ferris wheel right up there with skydiving. Rising to the slightest challenge can make me feel like the Bionic Woman.

I hate to admit it, but my timid approach to risk-taking is consistent with female sex stereotypes. It's the absolute antithesis of the male approach. Most men were taught physical confidence from infancy, when they were hurled in the air and played with more vigorously, and later, when they were encouraged — some might say pressured — into sports. Because boys are called "sissy" at the slightest sign of fear, many grown men still feel the need to prove themselves through daredevil adventures and athletics.

Today's young women have infinite opportunities to test themselves, take on physical challenges, and live on the edge, if that's what makes them happy. No one would dream of faulting them for building muscles or breaking a sweat. But most women of my generation were reared with far narrower notions of femininity. Warned of the world's many perils ("Be careful, it's dangerous"; "You'll get dirty"; "Nice girls don't . . ."), we were taught that the ultimate expression of womanhood was to play it safe. With this boring background, it should be clear why, as my forties wound down, I was asking myself some pretty basic questions: Am I in a rut? Do I want to go through life without taking a single risk? Will I ever try to reach beyond my grasp? Feeling comfortable is great as far as it goes, but adventure was said to have its charms, too. A few of my friends actually made the joys of sport and risk-taking sound appealing. Would I ever know that side of life or would fear forever stop me at the gates?

Isaac Abrabanel, a fifteenth-century thinker, believed that fear is an unavoidable emotion—not a sign of cowardice or weakness, but simply a dimension of the human condition. Fear cannot be overcome, he said, it can only be dealt with through action. Mark Twain said courage was "resistance to fear, mastery of fear—not absence of fear." I decided to attempt to master my fears in twentieth-century fashion by choosing to go on a completely out-of-character holiday—not a culture-oriented sightseeing tour or a hotel with a quiet beach, but an activity vacation. For the first time ever, I would challenge fear with action and see what my body could do.

Friends of ours asked us to join them for a summer biking trip in the Loire Valley. Although it represented the height of daring to me, the trip was hardly the Tour de France. We were to pedal along the banks of the river on paved cowpaths, cover less than thirty miles a day, stay overnight at storybook châteaux, and have our luggage transferred from town to town by a van. Nevertheless, I inquired if I might be permitted to rent a motor scooter. You'd have thought I'd asked to bring a Big Mac to a vegetarians' convention. "Absolutely not!" replied the tour leader. "This trip isn't about getting places easily, it's about being close to nature and using your body!"

That's what I was afraid of. Just imagining myself on a bike for eight days was giving me terminal stress. I knew how to ride, but how could I possibly pedal such long distances, so many hours, for eight solid days? *You can't,* said the voice inside me, the one that always reminds me of my flaws. *You won't be able to keep up. You'll probably fall and hurt yourself. You'll get tired. You'll get lost in the middle of nowhere. You'll ruin everyone else's fun.*

Despite these apprehensions, I literally browbeat myself to say yes because the catalog made the trip sound so inviting — charming villages, great food — and I wanted to share this vacation with my husband and our friends. If I can actually pull this off, I told myself, maybe I'll feel less depressed about my age. That June, I would be forty-nine.

The weather was idyllic the day we met up with the group. Each of us was given a mountain bike equipped with a water bottle, air pump, lock, and repair kit, equipment that was both reassuring and intimidating. I mounted up and began pedaling. Beset by my usual fears and low self-esteem, I started out tentatively, trying to summon the child within, as they say — the little girl who once rode her beat-up old Schwinn bicycle all over the neighborhood. After the first three hours, I was as amazed by my own stamina as by the glories of the French countryside. By the end of the week, despite an aching fanny, quaking quadriceps, and a congenital inability to pedal uphill, I'd had such a marvelous time that I readily agreed to return the following summer for a bike tour of Burgundy, which, in fact, became the keystone of my fiftieth birthday trip. That second time around, I felt no fear, heard no naysaying voices, experienced no shaky resolve, just pure pleasure, and the unfamiliar sensation of spending an entire week without one negative thought about my having turned fifty.

The dictionary defines risk as "the possibility of loss or injury . . . hazard or danger." Unfortunately, even after the lesson of two successful bike trips, those scary possibilities kept squelching my interest in further adventure. The successes didn't stick to my psyche or change my view of myself as a world-class weakling, nor did they whet my appetite for other sports; they just made an exception for biking. For everything else, I still had to start from square one.

Take skiing. (Please!) Bert already loved the sport when I married him and he convinced me to join him in it a dozen or so times over the last three decades. By now I can do the intermediate runs — which are designated by blue circles, as opposed to the advanced trails marked by signs with black diamonds — though rarely without my heart in my mouth. After the two bike trips, I expected my newfound gutsiness to rub off on my skiing. No such luck. The next winter, when I pushed off the chairlift at the top of one of the mountains and found myself mistakenly on a black diamond trail, I looked down at the steep incline, the swelling moguls and shiny patches of ice, and heard the same old put-down voices: "You can't do this"; "It's too hard for you"; "You'll get hurt." Just to propel myself down the slope — well, not exactly down but in lateral zigzags — I had to keep repeating that old feminist mantra FEEL THE FEAR AND DO IT ANYWAY . . . FEEL THE FEAR . . . DO IT ANYWAY!

Listen up, fellow midlifers, here's another surefire way to increase your awareness and slow time to a crawl: all you have to do is ski beyond your ability, in treacherous conditions, on a trail named "Whipcord" or "Jaws of Death," and I can assure you, mindfulness comes naturally. Whoever said "Nothing concentrates the mind like fear" must have skied behind me that day at Mount Snow. Never has panic yielded greater vigilance. I paid attention to every detail of that mountain as if my life depended on it, which it did. Bottom line: I got down in one piece and proved to myself that I can feel the fear and do it anyway, but frankly, at this age, I need no death-defying risks to keep me alert. Life itself is a death-defying risk, a black diamond trail meant only for the advanced skier.

As you can gather, unlike biking, skiing has yet to reveal its euphoric potential to me, and I can honestly say I'm not having fun yet. That's why I was so happy when I discovered a "sport" I could handle — walking. In fact, my new ability to walk three miles a day struck me as such a major accomplishment that I felt ready to spend a week hiking in Utah. I planned the trip as a gift for Bert's sixtieth birthday, but it was fueled by my hope that if we really took to it, we would integrate some hiking into all our future vacations, maybe even do Yosemite or the Alps. I even imagined that, after thirty years, I might give my husband the gift of a nonwimpy wife. However, as often happens with me and physical endeavors, I fantasize well and perform badly.

The first morning in Utah, I wake up in a terrible funk, anxious to the point of nausea. That day's hike is listed as seven miles long. At home, I have never done more than three miles. Panicking, I decide I won't be able to keep up with the group; the climb will be too steep, the pace too fast, my feet will ache, I'll get tired, cold, hurt, lost. Bert keeps reassuring me I can do it. "Runners have this axiom," he tells me. "They say people can easily run three times further than whatever distance they cover in regular training. That means you could do nine miles this morning with no sweat." (Yeah, right, I think, trying to keep down breakfast.) Should the formula not prove out, he promises to keep me company at my pace at the rear of the group.

I stuff my backpack with Vaseline (to prevent blisters), Band-Aids and antiseptic cream (for anticipated falls and scrapes), a fresh pair of socks, bottled water, fruit, celery and carrot sticks (in case I get lost in the desert), and off I go, hating myself for starting our vacation on such a sour note. My cowardice weighs on me more heavily than the backpack. Why must I be such a colossal party pooper? Why do I always imagine the worst? How could I be afraid of a seven-mile hike, yet comfortable dodging New York City traffic on two wheels with no armor or doing TV talk shows or lecturing to large audiences? Simple: I trust my mouth and my machines a lot more than my body. Fear of weakness, of loss, of bleeding, of dying — it doesn't take a rocket scientist to see the connection.

The group has gathered for some prehike stretching exercises. Looking around, I'm taken aback by everyone else's high spirits; they're as frisky as pups waiting to be released from a pen. How can I be afraid when all these people are raring to go? Bert's coaxing plus the specter of public humiliation eclipses my fears long enough to permit me to put one foot in front of the other as the group forges out onto the prairie, like a gung-ho squad of Marines, with me attempting to lose myself in the conversation of my fellow travelers. Minutes later, our hardy band is trudging through the vast scrub desert, with no one in sight but us — sixteen hikers encircled by snow-capped mountains and massive boulders the color of terra-cotta, picking our way through shadowy chasms and sprawling desert ravines gilded with sunlight and dotted with early spring flowers. About a half mile into our journey, I realize with astonishment that my anxiety is gone, replaced by a feeling I can only call ecstasy — a big, billowing lightness unlike any I've ever known. My legs float in front of me as we traverse the wide-open spaces that I recognize from Hollywood Westerns, and before long we are clambering along a rough, rock-tumbled trail and up the craggy cliffs until we come out, high above it all, on a mesa in the sky.

"The fear is worse than the ordeal itself," goes the old adage, but this is no ordeal, this is heaven with a dazzling blue sky, and to think I'd almost talked myself out of experiencing it. Bert's running axiom proves true. I have no trouble keeping up, whether rock scrambling or moving along on level ground, where I feel myself pulling ahead, buoyed by the realization that I am not only going to be able to complete the seven miles, but do it effortlessly. I walk at my treadmill rate, filling my lungs with the soft April breeze, amazed as I watch myself amble easily past women and men who are ten, twenty, and thirty years younger, until I am actually at the front of the line of hikers, striding alongside the leader, which is where I stay every day for the rest of the week. Instead of fragile, I feel solid and strong. Instead of fear, I know something close to rapture. For the first time in my life, I feel what an athlete must feel — huge reserves of energy, an eagerness to keep on going, and, miracle of miracles, faith in my own body.

Two months later, when Bert and I were in San Francisco for a family wedding, we left our hotel on Octavia Street at 9 A.M., walked down to the waterfront, past the Palace of Fine Arts, across the Golden Gate Bridge, and into the city of Sausalito — a distance I've been told is close to ten miles. I was so pleased with myself, you'd have thought I'd done the decathlon. When I was twenty-five, I could not have walked ten miles in two and a half hours if my life depended on it. We ended our journey on the outdoor deck of a Sausalito restaurant, where we gazed across the Bay at the San Francisco skyline and identified the exact spot where we'd begun our trek. At that moment, relaxing with a Bloody Mary in hand, enjoying the triumph and the tingling in my leg muscles, it seemed absolutely beside the point that I had just passed my fifty-fifth birthday.

I had a similar attack of self-satisfaction after we trekked a good portion of the length of Fire Island, the barrier-beach community where we met more than thirty summers ago when I was a certifiable noodle. (Incidentally, self-satisfaction is one of the few perks of middle age, and we should revel in it freely, since we aren't likely to get many strokes from other quarters. Only *we* know our limitations well enough to know when we've overcome them, so who else has a greater right to feel satisfied than the self.) The beach walk, which included some heavy slogging through surf and wet sand, took many hours, and when we reached our destination, my pedometer said twelve miles, a new record.

Hiking has been a revelation, a new way of seeing the world and its wonders. I've become thoroughly enamored, rushing out to buy local trail maps, books describing hikes in nearby states, a pair of hiking boots, and a pedometer. Whether I walk in the mountains, in Central Park, or on a measured track, I wear a pedometer at my waist and gaze adoringly at my mileage total. I still can't believe I'm the person producing all this forward motion. And I can't get enough of it.

I'm not saying hiking changed my life, and I don't yet count myself a card-carrying risk-taker, because I already know from the bike trips that a few breakthroughs are not enough to undo a lifetime's conditioning, or lack of it. However, since Utah, we actually have taken two hiking vacations, one in Costa Rica and one in Italy, and at this point, I only hope I can keep pushing myself to the other side of fear, the side where the rapture is. Familiar voices still admonish me ("You can't do it, Kiddo, this is too hard for you") but lately, I've been drowning out the naysayers with some new voices that cheer me on and remind me that growth may lie in a place I've never been.

"In the destructive element immerse," advises Joseph Conrad in *Lord*

Jim, which is a more literary way of defining the behavior of "counter-phobics," Otto Fenichel's term for people who inoculate themselves against anxiety by engaging in the activities they find most frightening. Counter-phobia is my next goal. Little by little, I hope to stare down all my terrors, deconstruct them as though each was a blood phobia, until there is nothing left to be afraid of. I shall take them on, one at a time, in a duel to the death, which is where it all ends anyway.

"You gain strength, courage and confidence by every experience in which you really stop to look fear in the face," writes Eleanor Roosevelt, one of the voices that I have newly chosen to heed. "You are able to say to yourself, 'I lived through this horror. I can take the next thing that comes along.' You must do the thing you think you cannot do."

Eleanor's mantra was, "Courage is as contagious as fear."

This is precisely what I keep telling myself, but I wish someone had taught it to me sooner, and I wonder what I, and every woman raised with the same learned helplessness, might have been capable of had we started earlier in life. Yes, I know: it's never too late, but it is too bad. All that time wasted. . . . When I think of how much I've missed — the adrenaline rush, the self-respect, the beauty of the outdoors, the sheer fun — I feel cheated. Nevertheless, the fact that I have finally begun to fight back and to witness myself growing stronger with age pleases me — no, that's too mealy-mouthed; it thrills me. And now I have some catching up to do.

Generativity

The repair of the self is a hollow enterprise unless it comes with a commitment to do one's part to repair the world. Fortuitously, according to many social scientists, a generosity of spirit and a conspicuous impulse toward helping others seem to be developmental hallmarks of my age group. A 1990 poll showed that "most people experience midlife mainly as a period of caring rather than crisis," according to John Pollack, who surveyed 1,200 men and women, 84 percent of whom agreed with the statement "At middle age a person becomes more compassionate to the needs of others." George Vaillant, a psychiatrist, found an increase in altruism, nurturing, and mentoring in Harvard men as they aged. Between the ages of forty-five and sixty-five, the men in his sample became more tender, more involved with their grown children, and more likely to commit acts of kindness — to coach Little League, help a church group get off the ground, advise and support younger colleagues.

Erik Erikson, the dean of American psychoanalysts, coined the term "generativity" to describe this critical life stage when human beings show an increasing concern for "establishing and guiding the next generation" and passing along what they know. In a mature person, these expansive feelings are not directed solely toward one's progeny but extend "to the Care of the creatures of this world and to the Charity which is felt to transcend it." Thus, childless people, including those in religious communities where procreation is prohibited, also experience midlife generativity. Erikson's term is a favorite of mine because it saves one from having to use words like caring, and nurture, which have been discredited by cynics and drained of their meaning by overexposure. Generativity synthesizes all those corny benevolent feelings and gathers them into one starched and stately word that allows us to discuss our best impulses without sounding like Jerry Lewis introducing his telethon.

Paradoxically, Erikson attributes midlife selflessness to a kind of self-interest, emphasizing that generativity is a two-way street serving both generations: "The fashionable insistence on dramatizing the dependence of children on adults often blinds us to the dependence of the older generation on the younger one. Mature men [and women] need to be needed, and maturity needs guidance as well as encouragement from what has been produced and must be taken care of."

For a woman, generativity may be nothing more than a broadening out of normal female nurturance. For a man, though, it usually represents a significant change in behavior and values that may well be rooted in a midlife phenomenon some have called "role relaxation." Psychologists have found that, in middle age, each sex moves gradually toward the gender role behavior that formerly was the province of the other sex, crossing paths at a point that I would consider Utopian, the women growing more assertive and independent, the men more family-oriented and nurturant.

The impulse to stop taking and start giving back, to leave a mark on the larger continuum of time and to make improvements in the world, is a very old story.

About 2,000 years ago, Honi the Righteous was journeying on the road when he saw a man planting a carob tree.

"How long will it take for this tree to bear fruit?" Honi asked.

"About seventy years," replied the man.

"Are you certain you will live another seventy years so you can enjoy this fruit?" inquired Honi.

"I found carob trees in the world when I got here," said the man, tapping the soil around the seedling. "As my ancestors planted those for me, so I, too, plant these for my children."

The generativity impulse may be inspired wholly by benevolence, or partly by a bid for immortality, which isn't necessarily a bad thing. Desire for lasting fame is an expression of power and ego, but it also may be as good a way as any of motivating people to leave something constructive and beneficial to the world — though such people usually require a plaque for doing it. Or the generativity impulse may arise out of our need to be needed at a point in life when we may be feeling less useful and less sought after. Whatever its cause, generativity yields all sorts of wonderful results both in terms of good works and personal rejuvenation. Interacting with young people restores and renews the life force and connects us to a prior age in ourselves. As the Psalmist says: "The righteous bloom like a date-palm; they thrive like a cedar in Lebanon. . . . In old age they still produce fruit; they are full of sap and freshness . . ."

Acts of generativity — what other generations called benevolence or loving-kindness — have the potential to produce sap and freshness and to upstage age by moving the mind off one's personal problems and redirecting it to broader concerns. In the grip of generativity, we become less concerned about making a place for ourselves in the world and more interested in making the world a better place. Betty Friedan offers examples of generativity in action: older people who volunteer as foster grandparents to help abusive mothers learn to care for their children; retired Columbia professors who offer their expertise to organizations in the surrounding Harlem community; the Senior Concert Orchestra of New York, an assemblage of musicians retired from major U.S. orchestras who give free concerts in high schools and colleges; the Seasoned Citizens Theater Company, which presents plays at nursing homes, senior centers, and hospitals — and whose motto is "We do not stop playing because we grow old. . . . We grow old because we stop playing."

When I think about generativity in action, what pops into view is the image of a clown I read about years ago in a magazine for seniors. She looks like a lot of other clowns — big red nose, orange scare wig, whiteface makeup, patchwork suit — and she does all the wacky things clowns do. The difference is, unlike most professional clowns, who started as kids, Betty Cozzens didn't enter the field until she was sixty-five. At age sixty-nine, with arthritis and a bad leg, her calendar was full of benefit dates for groups like the Cystic Fibrosis Foundation, and gigs at hospitals for sick or handicapped kids.

12

Death and the Future — Not Necessarily in That Order

> We shall not cease from exploration
> And the end of all our exploring
> Will be to arrive where we started
> And know the place for the first time.
>
> — *T. S. Eliot*

Some friends of mine have already bought their cemetery plots, so I guess it's time to talk about death. I've been skirting the issue for the last eleven chapters, and now there's no avoiding it even if I wanted to, which I don't, although I've noticed that a lot of people have a way of discussing death without ever mentioning it. When the subject comes up, a man I know, an octogenarian, says, "Let me put it this way: I don't buy green bananas."

The redoubtable Doris Day once quipped, "The really frightening thing about middle age is the knowledge you'll grow out of it." The poet Edna Frederikson writes,

> The trouble with being old is
> There's so little future in it.

Joseph Epstein, the cantankerous essayist, mentions mortality by name but only to complain that "it might be useful to place death somewhere other than at the end of a person's life so that he or she wouldn't have to spend so damn much time thinking about it."

After all the time I've spent thinking about it, pushing it under the rug, fearing it, I'm surprised at where I stand on the subject as I bring this book to a close.

Death Perceptions

Woody Allen, not my favorite source of aphorisms, once said, "I don't want to achieve immortality in my work, I want to achieve it by not dying." What upsets me — and I claim no uniqueness here — isn't the thought of dying, or even of being dead (underground, up there, wherever), it is the idea of not being *here* anymore. The tragedy is not that death is our final exclamation point, but that it appears at the end of such a short sentence.

In his seventies, sick and lame, Edmund Wilson found it daunting to absorb "the thought that I shall presently be extinguished."

At fifty-five, "presently" is probably overstating it but eventual extinction crosses my mind on cat's paws however vehemently I shoo it away. There is always that moment, usually around Labor Day and usually at sunset, when I wonder — the thought is so palpable that it may as well be sitting in my palm — whether I and everyone I love will still be alive next Memorial Day to see another summer. Have you ever had such a thought? And have you ever wondered who will pass away between now and then? Imagining the death of my loved ones is excruciating for me, too painful, too scary, too devastating. But thinking about my own death has been a most illuminating exercise. When we entertain the idea of our own extinction, we ponder who will miss us when we're gone, who will remember us, and for what, and how long. Not very long at all, we realize, and that makes us wonder what it's all for or why we put so much energy into living in the first place if everything ends and all is forgotten. "There is no remedy for death," said a woman at my local coffee bar to no one in particular.

Jean-Paul Sartre, where are you when we need you?

Take existentialism seriously and strange insights will zing you at odd moments. For instance, I suddenly realized how absurd it is to buy big-ticket items after a certain age — a thought inspired by my friends' immense new home and the knowledge that they had spent lavishly for the property, paid major money to an architect, built it with the best materials, and filled every room with gorgeous antiques. Is the house beautiful? It's breathtaking. Can they afford it? No question about it. Still, morbid old me couldn't help thinking how irrational it was for them to spend so much on a house when they'll soon be dead.

The fact of the matter is, my friends are not yet seventy. They could easily have ten or fifteen years left, which is more time than most people live in any one house regardless of their age. So the irrational thing was not *their* expenditure, but *my* reaction. I seem to have picked up my mother-in-law's deathbed penuriousness: "It's a shame I'm dying," she said. "I just bought a new dress."

Lately, I find myself studying the obituary page with more than passing interest, as if the ages of the deceased carry a clue to my destiny. No wonder I laughed out loud when I saw the *New Yorker* cartoon showing a man reading an obituary page on which the headlines over the death notices say, "Two Years Younger Than You." "Twelve Years Older Than You." "Exactly Your Age." "Three Years Your Junior." "Five Years Your Senior." "Your Age on the Dot." That's what goes on in my head every day when I open the paper to see who died.

If you happen to be similarly obsessed, take my word for it, January 21 and 22, 1994, were days of surpassing reassurance. Except for a precocious seventy-two-year-old, all the deceased reported in the pages of the *New York Times* were between the ages of eighty-two and ninety-nine. There were no thirty-four-year-old AIDS victims, no sixty-year-old men felled by heart attacks on the tennis court, no fifty-year-old women carried off by ovarian cancer, no flash floods to claim a child's life. Just reasonable, seasonable deaths at ripe old ages — ages sufficiently remote from mine to allow me to turn the page without first biting my lip and sighing, "There but for the grace of God . . ."

"If we didn't fear death," says my friend Nadine, "who would put up with agony?" The opposite rationale is just as compelling: who would put up with agony if we didn't love life and weren't willing to gamble that the payoff for suffering will be lots more life? Like everyone else, I am afraid of dying badly, of spending time in hospitals, in surgery, under anesthesia, in chemotherapy, in pain. I'm afraid that suffering will transform me into someone else, some tormented figure who eventually will displace all memories of the previous me. I don't want my final summation to the jury to be a moan. I don't want to be remembered in anguish.

So who does? Nobody; however, I am making myself explicit here to underscore my belief that if we can't die in our sleep while we're still healthy, we should be able to arrange our death to suit our life. Lately, more and more people are retaining control of their last days through the making of a "living will," a document that lets us leave instructions as to whether doctors should take extraordinary measures or pull the plug, and whether we prefer to meet our maker in a hospital, a hospice, or our favorite chaise longue at home. I see myself, wrapped in a cashmere coverlet, breathing my last in front of the fireplace in my own living room, which will require someone to go out and buy me a cashmere coverlet for the occasion. Dealing forthrightly with terminal matters while one is still riding on all cylinders requires a certain panache, otherwise the people who love you are apt to get depressed. I know this because I can't bear it when Bert talks about providing for me after his death, though I can easily discuss my insurance policy or where I want to be buried when the time comes. (Believe it or not, in Roosevelt, New Jersey, the town where Bert grew up; in its friendly little cemetery on a hill.) I've even indulged some random thoughts about my funeral: Two rabbis, please — Mychal Springer, a young woman who understands what it means to be a feminist Jew; and J. Rolando Matalon, who has made my Judaism joyful. It would be lovely if a tape of violinist Nadia Solerno-Sonnenberg playing Rachmaninoff's "Vocalise" could be playing in the background as people take their seats. And I'd like my immediate family to deliver the reminiscences, not eulogies, with a specific request to Bert to be his normal funny self even if it seems indecorous, because that's how I want to remember him.

It's not easy to face one's incredible shrinking future and imagine one's own end, but by George, I've done it, and you must admit that, for someone who began this book cowering in the shadow of the Sleeping Giant, I've come a long way. If I sound almost sanguine at this point, it's because I've calmed down about dying — not about being dead, but about dying. I can't say whether being dead consigns one to emptiness or eternal afterlife, but I can say that dying doesn't scare me the way it used to. On the theory that engaging one's most toxic fear is the best antidote for it, I've managed to wrap my brain around the idea, thanks to a metaphor that has made the subject thinkable: I imagine dying as my final fainting spell, the one I don't come back from, the big blackout that solves all my time problems by putting an end to real time, thereby giving me nothing left to lose. I've fainted often enough to know that conscious isn't the only way to make it through the day. Unconscious is rather a lovely state as well, and you slip into it without actually realizing you've left everyone behind — until you return and see their horrified expressions. The worst of it is, when you come to, you feel you've been gone for days, and wonder what you've missed or whether you've done anything disgraceful in your absence. The best of it is that, much as a good nap can feel like a full night's sleep, a good faint can leave you marvelously well rested, which one hopes is how death feels if it feels like anything at all.

Of course, metaphors have their limits. The final faint has me fading out but not coming to, so I must linger in the dark, trying to rewrap my brain around the idea of being gone for good, trying to conjure metaphors for that perfect permanence. It's like you can't go home again, *ever*. It's like checkout time, last call, bye-bye, no exit, The End. It means life goes on without you, as it did in your old neighborhood after you moved away, and when you visit, you find things have been humming along just fine in your absence; hardly anyone has noticed you're gone, and only the candy store man remembers your name. Not apocalyptic, just sad; to think that the essence of death is Not Being Missed. And that somebody can be nobody to everybody else. And that each death matters — matters enough for abject misery and mourning — to so few people.

But I can live with that (in a manner of speaking), because I'm not living for posterity or counting on an afterlife, I'm living for right now, for this minute, this remarkable, irreplaceable minute. Thinking it through, I understand as never before that the reason I will always fear death is my passion for life, and the reason I will never have enough time is that I cannot have forever. The sentence demands its exclamation point, short as it is.

Reconsidering my middle years in these pages, I've begun to recognize this, in Frank Conroy's words, as "the clearest and sweetest time of life," because I can see *everything* from here: where I've been and what I've left behind; where I'm going and who I wish to be. I've named my fears and overcome a few, swallowed my regrets, focused on what to cherish and what to change, and tried to accept the things I cannot help. Time, once tight as a turtleneck, has begun to give a little, making room for love and friendship, meaningful work, caring, repairing, and more pleasure than I used to feel I deserved. Solitude is elbowing for more space. My body is less of a stranger to me than it was in my youth, when I took it for granted, and my mind astounds me by what it remembers as well as what it forgets. Yesterday and today are learning to play in harmony with the new kid on the block — tomorrow.

Conroy said the fog lifted for him in middle age when he was no longer a captive of youth's narcissism and constant self-assertion. It lifted for me when I realized, about two-thirds of the way through this book, that I was no longer afraid of the future. I set out to contemplate time and aging, and seem to be ending up in a state of benign optimism with some clear notions about how I want to live the rest of my life. The great wordsmith Casey Stengel warned, "Avoid prophecy — especially about the future." I'm plunging ahead anyway, if not with prophecy, then with some vows and wishes that can't be all that different from yours, if you're past fifty . . . and counting.

The Woman I Will Not Be

I don't expect to grow out of middle age for another ten years or so, but I've started thinking about what I might grow into, and what I do *not* want to be when I grow up, or older, or — let me spit it out — old. I do not want to become a pain in the dork, a burden to my children, or invisible.

The first wish is the most within my control. If I keep my wits about me, I should be able to monitor my behavior sufficiently so as not to let age transform me into a crashing bore or a crotchety curmudgeon. This is not to imply that all old people are boring or crabby, or that old people are more likely to drone on or be hypercritical. However, while such behavior is rarely permitted to the rest of us, old people who act this way are often humored and indulged simply because they are old. As a result, they lose their grip on interpersonal etiquette and end up being demanding, grouchy pains in the dork whom you wouldn't choose to spend Sunday with if you had an alternative like root canal.

I don't want to be one of those sour old women, and I don't think it's ageist to say so. In fact, it may well be a form of ageism to indulge old people's antisocial behavior — as though one were saying the behavior doesn't matter because old people don't matter. As I get on in years, I know I won't always feel as good as I do today, and when I'm sick or miserable, I plan to be honest about what ails me, and I expect to be treated with kindness and understanding whether my problem is arthritis or depression. Illness-induced unsociability must be forgiven at any age. But when it comes to normal situations, I hope to be held to normal standards of social demeanor and congeniality rather than be merely tolerated. I don't ever want to be an obligatory visit on my loved ones' calendars.

Watching my daughter Robin with her husband's eighty-year-old grandmother, I've seen what happens when an older person is a positive presence in younger people's lives. Whenever Robin and Edward visit

Grammy Gert or invite her over to their place, they do so with no sense of duty. They look forward to spending time with her because of her warm, upbeat disposition and because she is interested in everything around her, not just herself.

Inspired by examples like Grammy Gert, and guided by my past antipathy to one or two nameless, negative, self-absorbed old people I have known, I think I should be able to avoid such obvious pitfalls as conversing at length about bodily functions, guilt-tripping my relatives, and having nothing good to say about anything or anybody. By keeping these tendencies in check, I would hope to offer agreeable company to my friends and relations for however long I'm around.

As for my second wish — not to become a burden to my children — that may be more complicated. Good fortune and attention to financial planning has made it unlikely that I will end up among the women over age sixty-five who comprise 70 percent of the elderly poor. If all goes well and our pensions keep pace with inflation, Bert and I should not have to turn to our kids for ordinary day-to-day support. Our goal is to stay healthy and vigorous or, as David Mahoney of the Dana Foundation puts it, "to die young as late as possible." But suppose we die old and age badly, suffer catastrophic ailments, grow helpless and fragile, yet stay alive year after year while the medical bills keep mounting? How do we avoid becoming that kind of burden?

My fears are prototypical: a 1991 survey found that two-thirds of American adults want to live to be one hundred years old but are afraid of spending the extra years in a nursing home or dependent on relatives. Even pensions and health insurance are no guarantee against the exigencies of long-term physical helplessness. Most of my friends are providing support or care to at least one aged parent, or did so until their parents died. Many are now wrestling with the issue of nursing home care. Bert and I should live and be well, as they say, but the chances are that, at some point in the future, if we live long enough, we'll become too frail, ill, or disabled to fend for ourselves. I subscribe to the social contract that expects each generation to take responsibility for the other, and I'm sure our kids would rise to the task lovingly and generously, but I don't want them to have to mortgage their lives to take care of us. Nor do I want their father and me to be deposited in a nursing home with God knows what kind of behavior passing for caregiving once the family leaves the visitors' lounge.

Though not worthy of a panic attack, the statistics are sobering: One in seven people over sixty-five can expect to spend a year or more in such a place. In 1990, only 2 percent of those between sixty-five and seventy-four, and 6 percent of the seventy-five to eighty-four age group, were in nursing homes — not to be treated for illness, just to get basic care — but the figure rises to 23 percent for people over eighty-five. If you hang on, the carrying costs at the average nursing home — estimated at $30,000 a year in 1990, and far higher in regions like New York — can eat up a lifetime's worth of savings in no time at all. The cost of private caregivers can do it even faster.

At this writing, the likelihood of increased public support for long term care of the elderly is nil, even for something as simple as a visiting aide to watch over a wandering Alzheimer's patient. In this punitive conservative political climate, those community programs that do exist are being cut to the core or eliminated altogether under a cloud of rhetoric about "family responsibility," which, in most cases, means daughters will shoulder most of the custodial care at the expense of their own lives. Right now, about 7 million Americans are unpaid caregivers to the elderly, and three out of four of these caregivers are women — average age, fifty-seven. More than half of these women are also holding down full-time jobs. Men care for parents, too, but studies suggest that they tend to keep in touch by checkbook and phone, or to assist on legal or financial matters, whereas women provide the hands-on, 24-hour-a-day caregiving, including cooking, bathing, dressing, feeding, lifting, administering medicine, and taking the elderly to their doctors' visits. Bottom line: the average American woman will spend seventeen years taking care of children and eighteen years caring for aged parents.

Since neither Bert nor I have living parents, caretaker burnout isn't something I worry about for myself, but I've started to view the whole mess from our children's perspective: twenty-five years from now, Robin and Abigail will be fifty-five — my age today — and David will be fifty-two. If we're still around, I'll be eighty, Bert will be eighty-five, and I don't want our kids to have reason to regret it. I want them to be able to enjoy their middle years just as we are enjoying ours today. I want them to look forward to the rewards of their careers and *their* grown children without worrying that taking care of me or their father will sap their resources or their spirit. I don't want to become the burden on our kids that is every parent's worst nightmare.

Experts say ours is the Age of Aging, since people eighty-five and older are increasing more than three times as fast as the population as a whole, and the over-100 club, now a constituency of about 45,000, is projected to rise to 120,000 by the year 2005. With this new staying power, increased costs for long term care are unavoidable. In my opinion, this is the price a developed society should be willing to pay for the gift of longer life. But, in fact, the super-old are not the problem. According to the *New York Times*, gerontologists have found that "the oldest old fare better, and in some ways more cheaply, than one might expect. Those in their nineties and above may in fact be a healthier group overall than people twenty years their junior [survival of the fittest], and when they die, they generally do so quickly, without the same degree of costly lingering that can accompany the death of those in their, say, sixties or seventies. . . . The amount lavished on a person's last two years of life — medically the priciest years of all — is only $8,300 for a person who dies at ninety, but $22,600 for the one who dies at seventy." All the more reason for us to live longer.

James Lubitz and his colleagues at the Health Care Financing Administration have calculated that the economic impact of our improved life expectancy will be relatively small — $98 billion in the next twenty-five years, a mere 3 percent of the projected increase in Medicare expenses — and this rise will be the result of sheer numbers (those aging baby boomers again), not increased costs per person. Class warfare is passé, but generational warfare may well become the next combat zone as people with age-related miseries are pitted against at-risk babies, poor pregnant women, and young people with AIDS, and as the growing mass of helpless older Americans compete for ever-shrinking resources.

Although most health policy analysts agree on the need to restructure Medicare to encourage increased use of managed care and to impose greater efficiencies and eliminate fraudulent claims, controversy rages over how to squeeze additional savings from the health insurance program without endangering the sickest, weakest, and poorest older Americans. Out-of-pocket costs for health care are already a burden on most Medicare recipients, yet at this writing, Congress has proposed changes that would increase the monthly premium old people now pay for doctor and outpatient services and would impose a 20 percent copayment for users of home health care services, which, by the way, constitute the largest single out-of-pocket expense in the system. In a time of job shrinkage and overstressed women, full-time care of the sick or frail elderly is not a problem that individual families should be expected to solve alone, but rather a collective problem that we must address as a society because of its impact on all of us. According to the Dana Foundation, Alzheimer's disease has already cost our national economy $89 billion dollars, making it far from a *private* family issue.

As with any policy issue, the question is, what are America's core ethical standards and are they being reflected in our spending priorities? Congress always finds enough money to support bloated military budgets, to fund weapons we know we will never use, to produce a B-2 bomber that even the Pentagon believes is a mistake, yet they cry fiscal crisis and deficit reduction when it comes to finding money for babies and old people. If Medicare is gutted to provide tax cuts for the wealthy, or is chipped away in the frenzy to balance the budget by the arbitrary date of 2002, it will be clear that the American social conscience is dead, for how children and elders are treated when they are unable to care for themselves is a fundamental barometer of a people's decency.

Words like "national ethics," "family values," and "traditional morality" are hollow hypocrisies if they cannot encompass something as basic as this: after our older citizens have given their all to their country — their labor and loyalty, their ideas, their offspring, their creativity and spirit — health care is not something to begrudge them, but something we as a people should *want* to provide as a gesture of recognition and thanks. If veterans of war are entitled to federally funded educational and health benefits for having defended America, veterans of life deserve federally funded long term care for having built, populated, and enriched our nation.

My third wish — not to become invisible — simply means I believe no one should have to accept nonbeingness as a consequence of aging. I want the words "older woman" to evoke an image of a strong, wise, self-confident female, not a hag or a nobody. Earlier in this book, I took issue with those who claim that being unseen in middle age offers a woman relief from years of ultravisibility as a sex object, an opinion I equate with praising the veil for protecting Muslim women from the male gaze whether they choose to be out of sight or not. For me, there is no such thing as positive invisibility. Fade into the crowd if you want to, but don't ask others to disappear with you.

It turns out women and men are in this disappearing act together. (Need I say, I never meant to achieve gender equality this way.) Older men also sense themselves vanishing, though for different reasons. Whereas women are erased when we are no longer seen as young and sexual, men are erased when they are perceived as inconsequential and powerless, when age does to them what color has done to black men of all ages. They become Ralph Ellison's *Invisible Man.*

In a thoughtful essay, Robert Coles, the psychiatrist-author who usually studies youth, writes about "the dismissal or rebuff or lack of regard" that older people routinely experience in their daily lives. He recalls a former professor, a man in his mid-sixties, posing this question to his medical students in the 1950s: "Who notices whom, and for what reasons?" After an animated class discussion about the influence of race and class on who gets noticed and who gets ignored, the professor brought up age as a factor, though it had occurred to none of his students. He confessed that, as he had grown older, he increasingly felt himself unnoticed; people in shops and restaurants no longer responded to him with respect or attention. In "real life," he was white, male, and a professor at the Harvard Medical School, but when he was just another stranger in a crowd, none of those attributes could correct for the invisibility of age.

Coles also tells the story of a seventy-year-old woman who found herself standing in a store, credit card in hand, holding merchandise she wished to purchase, while the salesman looked right through her, walked by, and offered help to a younger customer who was only browsing. Though cowed into humiliated silence, the woman vowed she would never again tolerate such treatment. "If I start thinking of myself as some of those people think of me, then I'm through," she said. "*Nothing doing.*" She wasn't shrill or bitter; she didn't become hostile to young people, but she did need to steel herself against future attacks of dismissiveness. So she learned, as Coles puts it, to "build up her own resources of mind and heart" by constantly reminding herself of her own worth, thinking about people her age whom she admires, and mobilizing in herself "a certain fighting humor." Plus she learned to talk back, and a few months later, when another salesman treated her as if she weren't there, she proceeded to make herself impossible to ignore. "He looked up at me — the first time he'd done so — and he even smiled a bit," she recalls. "So did I."

The things I don't wish to become — a pain in the dork, a burden to my kids, invisible to the world — all refer to the older person's impact on others. But there is also the woman I do not wish to become to *myself:* depressed, aimless, spiritless, self-pitying. I cannot predict the circumstances of my life when I'm seventy, eighty, or ninety — whether I'll be living alone, have money worries, suffer from illness or pain — but if I am alive and not incapacitated, I hope I will have sufficient inner resources to allow me to do more with my days than wait for death. I do not want to be like the irascible old matriarch in Albee's *Three Tall Women* who, when asked what was the happiest time of her life, replies, "Coming to the end of it. . . . When it's all done. When we stop." I don't ever want to *want* it to stop. I think I'd rather die than live long enough to reach that point.

The Woman I Hope to Be

The last part was easier. To say what sort of older person I hope not to become, I had only to describe some of what I see around me — old people who make other people miserable, old people unacknowledged and overlooked, old people who have no reason to keep on living. But to set down what I *want* to be is like writing a fairy tale in which all the queens are kind and all the witches are witty. Since I haven't witnessed a prior generation teeming with self-actualized older females, I've had to let myself dream.

It may not yet be possible in this society for a woman to *have* an ideal old age, but it is possible to imagine one. "I have in mind a pastel confection of the perfect old woman," wrote Natalie Angier in a 1988 "Hers" column. "She is wise and dignified, at peace with herself and quietly proud of the life she has forged. She doesn't waste time seeking approval or cursing the galaxy. Instead, she works at her craft. She is Georgia O'Keeffe painting, Louise Nevelson sculpturing, Marianne Moore writing." Add Martha Graham dancing, and Katharine Hepburn doing anything at all, and what else is new? What woman hasn't imagined herself aging like those high priestesses of art and elegance? When the 1994 Clinique survey asked, "Which of the following women would you most like to age like: Barbara Bush, Lena Horne, Katharine Hepburn, Joan Rivers, Elizabeth Taylor or Barbara Walters?" Hepburn got 37 percent of the vote, and for the best of reasons: "She is very strong and well-respected." "She was able to get out of life what she really wanted." "She did not try to hang on to youth. . . ." "She enjoys life and is not concerned about what others think." "She is dignified and has aged gracefully." Katharine Hepburn is a great choice, but where are the other women, the *new* paradigms of older women? We know they're out there but their light is buried under a bushel of negativity and neglect, leaving the role models of my generation with no role models for themselves as they age.

It is difficult for women to support and inspire one another if we can-

George Sand wrote, "The old woman I shall become will be quite different from the woman I am now. Another I is beginning." This is a remarkable assertion when you stop to realize the woman Sand already was. Under her pseudonym, she had published widely and exercised many prerogatives reserved for men as well as having been married and divorced, given birth to two children, amassed a distinguished coterie of friends, Franz Liszt and Honoré de Balzac among them, and dallied with some stellar lovers, including Frederic Chopin and the poet Alfred de Musset. I can't imagine what "different" old woman Sand had in mind, but I love the idea that she could still conjure up "another I."

I want to believe I could yet blossom into someone else if I choose to. My newfound faith in the transformative power of time may yet lead me to give birth to "another I." Or maybe I will just be myself but better at it for having worked at understanding who I already am.

When I ask myself what sort of woman I want to be, the woman I am now seems fine for now. This is not a paean to stasis but a definition of happiness: if I can continue feeling that the woman I am is fine for now, it will mean that I have accepted change, because whatever the present is when I'm sixty, seventy, or eighty will have become as valuable to me as life is today.

The anthropologist Ruth Benedict wrote, "Our faith in the present dies out long before our faith in the future." I want to keep both faiths alive. What I wish for myself and for all of us is to feel until the very end of life that each day is a gift of time and possibility, and to fill each day with less self-criticism and more self-knowledge, fewer grievances about age and more gratitude for life, more time and the wisdom to enjoy it.

In legends, the hero always leaves home to search for the meaning of life or the secret of eternal youth. In the real world, we read books and consult experts, looking for answers "out there," spending years at it, too many years, before we discover that we don't need youth if we have time, and that meaning is made, not found, in the crucible of one's own wondering soul.

Bibliography

Adams, Jane. *I'm Still Your Mother: How to Get Along with Your Grown-Up Children for the Rest of Your Life.* New York: Bantam Doubleday Dell, 1994.

Albee, Edward. *Three Tall Women.* New York: Dramatists Play Service, Inc., 1994.

Allen, Jessie, and Pifer, Alan, eds. *Women on the Front Lines: Meeting the Challenge of an Aging America.* Washington, D.C.: The Urban Institute Press, 1993.

Amery, Jean. *On Aging: Revolt and Resignation.* Bloomington: Indiana University Press, 1995.

Anderson, Marilynn Foss. "Embodying the Crone: Facing Age with Wisdom, Truth and the Spirit of Love." *New Directions for Women,* July-August 1992.

Auerbach, Sylvia. *How to Be Smart Parents Now That Your Kids Are Adults.* San Diego, Calif.: Silvercat, 1995.

Bailet, Emily. *Caring for Older Adults: A Handbook* (1993). Available from the National Council of Jewish Women, 53 West 23rd Street, New York, NY 10010. 212-645-4048. $4.00 per copy.

Baldwin, Christina. *Life's Companion: Journal Writing as a Spiritual Quest.* New York: Bantam Books, 1990.

Banner, Lois W. *In Full Flower: Aging Women, Power and Sexuality.* New York: Vintage, 1993.

Barbach, Lonnie. *The Pause: A Positive Approach to Menopause.* New York: Dutton, 1993.

Bart, Pauline B. "Depression in Middle Aged Women." In Vivian Gornick and Barbara Moran, eds., *Woman in Sexist Society.* New York: Basic Books, 1971.

Bartoldus, Ellen, Gillery, Beth, and Sturges, Phyllis J. "Job-related Stress and Coping Among Home-Care Workers with Elderly People." *Health and Social Work*, vol. 14, no. 3, August 1989.

Belsky, Janet K. *Here Tomorrow: Making the Most of Life After Fifty.* Baltimore: Johns Hopkins University Press, 1988.

Ben-Lesser, Jay. *A Foxy Old Woman's Guide to Traveling Alone Around Town and Around the World.* Freedom, Calif.: The Crossing Press, 1995.

Blaker, Karen. *Celebrating 50: Women Share Their Experiences and Insights on Becoming 50.* Chicago, Ill.: Contemporary Books, 1990.

Bordo, Susan. *Unbearable Weight: Feminism, Western Culture, and the Body.* Berkeley: University of California Press, 1993.

Borenstein, Audrey. *Older Women in 20th Century America.* New York: Garland, 1982.

Breines, Wini. *Young, White and Miserable: Growing Up Female in the Fifties.* Boston: Beacon Press, 1992.

Broner, E. M. "Blessing the Ties That Bind." *Ms.*, December 1986.

Bronte, Lydia. *The Longevity Factor: The New Reality of Long Careers and How It Can Lead to Richer Lives.* New York: HarperCollins, 1993.

Brown, Judith K., et al. *In Her Prime: A New View of Middle-Aged Women.* South Hadley, Mass.: Bergin & Garvey, 1985.

Budoff, Penny Wise, M.D. *No More Flashes—and Other Good News.* New York: Warner Books, 1984.

Butler, Robert N., and Gleason, Herbert P., eds. *Productive Aging: Enhancing Vitality in Later Life.* New York: Springer, 1985.

Butler, Robert N. *Why Survive?: Being Old in America.* New York: Harper & Row, 1975.

Carter, Rosalynn. *Helping Yourself Help Others: A Book for Caregivers.* New York: Times Books/Random House, 1995.

Chase, Marilyn. "The Baby Boom Hits 50: Their Bodies." *Wall Street Journal*, November 1, 1995, p. B1.

Chopra, Deepak. *Ageless Body, Timeless Mind.* New York: Harmony Books, 1993.

Cline, Sally. *Women, Passion and Celibacy.* New York: Carol Southern Books, 1993.

Cole, Thomas R. *The Journey of Life: A Cultural History of Aging in America.* New York: Cambridge University Press, 1992.

Coles, Robert. "On Feeling Invisible." *New Choices,* March 1989.

"Consumer's Guide to Long-Term Care Insurance." Pamphlet available from the Health Insurance Association of America, 1025 Connecticut Ave., NW, Washington, DC 20036.

'Copper, Baba. *Over the Hill: Reflections on Ageism between Women.* Freedom, Calif.: The Crossing Press, 1988.

Cutler, Winnifred B., and Garcia, Celso, Ramon-Garcia. *Menopause: A Guide for Women and Those Who Love Them.* New York: W. W. Norton, 1993.

de Beauvoir, Simone. *The Second Sex.* New York: Vintage, 1974.

Delaney, Sarah, and Delaney, Anna. *Having Our Say: The Delaney Sisters' First Hundred Years.* New York: Farrar, Straus & Giroux, 1993.

Doress-Worters, Paula B., and Siegal, Diana Laskin, with the Boston Women's Health Collective. *The New Ourselves, Growing Older.* New York: Touchstone, 1994.

Downing, Christine. *Journey Through Menopause: A Personal Rite of Passage.* New York: Crossroad Publishing, 1987.

Downs, A. Chris, and Harrison, Sheila K. "Embarrassing Age Spots or Just Plain Ugly? Physical Attractiveness Stereotyping as an Instrument of Sexism on American Television Commercials." *Sex Roles,* vol. 13, nos. 1 & 2, 1985.

Downs, Peggy, et al. *The New Older Woman.* Berkeley, Calif.: Celestial Arts, 1996.

Dychtwald, Ken, and Flower, Joe. *Age Wave.* Los Angeles: Jeremy P. Tarcher, 1989.

Earle, Richard, and Imrie, David. *Your Vitality Quotient.* New York: Warner, 1989.

Eliot, T. S. *Four Quartets.* New York: Harvest/HBJ, 1988.

Epstein, Joseph. *With My Trousers Rolled.* New York: W. W. Norton, 1995.

Erikson, Erik. *Identity and the Life Cycle.* New York: International Universities Press, 1959.

Faludi, Susan. *Backlash.* New York: Crown, 1991.

Fine, Irene. *Midlife: A Rite of Passage* and *The Wise Woman: A Celebration.* San Diego, Calif.: Woman's Institute for Continuing Jewish Education, 1988.

Fisher, M. F. K. *As They Were.* New York: Vintage, 1983.

———. *Sister Age.* London: Chatto & Windus, 1984.

Freedman, Rita. *Bodylove: Learning to Like Our Looks—and Ourselves.* New York: Harper & Row, 1989.

Myerhoff, Barbara. *Number Our Days.* New York: Touchstone/Simon & Schuster, 1978.

Miller, Sigmund Stephen, et al. *Conquest of Aging: The Definitive Home Medical Reference from a Panel of Distinguished Medical Authorities.* New York: Collier /Macmillan, 1989.

Ms. magazine, special issue on body image, September 1977.

Nachtigall, Lila, M.D., and Heilman, Joan Rattner. *Estrogens: A Complete Guide to Reversing the Effects of Menopause Using Hormone Replacement Therapy.* New York: Harper & Row, 1986.

Nachtigall, Lila, M.D., Nachtigall, Robert D., M.D., and Heilman, Joan Rattner. *What Every Woman Should Know: Staying Healthy After 40.* New York: Warner Books, 1995.

National Institute on Aging. *Menopause.* Washington, DC: National Institutes of Health Publication No. 92–3466, 1992.

Neugarten, Bernice L., et al. "Age Norms, Age Constraints, and Adult Socialization." *American Journal of Sociology,* 1965, 70.

Newsweek. "The New Middle Age." November 1992.

Nuland, Sherwin B., M.D. *How We Die: Reflections on Life's Final Chapter.* New York: Vintage, 1995.

Okimoto, Jean Davies, and Stegall, Phyllis Jackson. *Boomerang Kids: How to Live with Adult Children Who Return Home.* Boston: Little, Brown, 1987.

Olsen, Tillie. *Tell Me a Riddle.* New York: Dell/Delta, 1961.

Orange, Wendy. "On Turning 50." *Sojourner,* October 1995.

Orenstein, Rabbi Debra. *Lifecycles.* Woodstock, Vermont: Jewish Lights Publishing, 1994.

Paige, Judith, and Gordon, Pamela. *Choice Years.* New York: Villard Books, 1991.

Painter, Charlotte. *Gifts of Age: Portraits and Essays of 32 Remarkable Women.* San Francisco: Chronicle Books, 1985.

Pollack, Sandra. "On Growing Older." *New Directions for Women.* September/October 1991.

Porter, Nancy. "The Art of Aging: A Review Essay." *Women's Studies Quarterly,* Spring/Summer 1989.

Posner, Richard A. *Aging and Old Age.* Chicago, Ill.: University of Chicago Press, 1995.

Rand, Lillian. "Crowning the Crone." *New Directions for Women,* July-August, 1992.

Reitz, Rosetta. *Menopause: A Positive Approach.* New York: Penguin Books, 1977.

Robey, Bryant. *The American People.* New York: E. P. Dutton, 1985.

Roundtree, Cathleen. *Coming into Our Fullness: On Women Turning Forty.* Freedom, Calif.: The Crossing Press, 1989.

Rubin, Lillian. *Women of a Certain Age: The Midlife Search for Self.* New York: Harper & Row, 1981.

Sand, Gayle. *Is It Hot in Here or Is It Me?* New York: HarperCollins, 1993.

Sang, B., et al. *Lesbians at Midlife: The Creative Transition.* San Francisco: Spinsters Book Company, 1991.

Sarton, May. *Journal of a Solitude.* New York: W. W. Norton, 1973.

———. *As We Are Now.* New York: W. W. Norton, 1973

———. *A Self-Portrait.* New York: W. W. Norton, 1982.

———. *At Seventy.* New York: W. W. Norton, 1984.

———. *After the Stroke.* New York: W. W. Norton, 1988.

———. *Encore: A Journal of the Eightieth Year.* New York: W. W. Norton, 1993.

Scarf, Maggie. *Unfinished Business: Pressure Points in the Lives of Women.* New York: Ballantine, 1988.

Schafer, Edith Nalle. *Our Remarkable Memory: Understanding It—Improving It—Losing It?* Washington, D.C.: Elliot & Clark, 1992.

Scheiner, Ann. "My Face-lift: A Cautionary Tale." Ms., November 1986.

Sheed, Wilfred. *In Love with Daylight: A Memory of Recovery.* New York: Simon & Schuster, 1995.

Sheehy, Gail. *The Silent Passage: Menopause.* New York: Random House, 1992.

———. *New Passages: Mapping Your Life Across Time.* New York: Random House, 1995.

Shelley, Florence D. *When Your Parents Grow Old.* New York: Harper & Row, 1988.

Shore, Wilma. "Pages from a Widow's Journal," p. 59, and "A Little Accident," p. 123. *Women's Studies Quarterly,* nos. 3 & 4, 1989.

Silverstein, Brett, et al. "The Role of the Mass Media in Promoting a Thin Standard of Bodily Attractiveness for Women." *Sex Roles,* vol. 14, nos. 9 & 10, 1986.

Simpson, Eileen. *Late Love: A Celebration of Marriage After Fifty.* New York: Houghton Mifflin, 1994.

Smith, Page. *Old Age Is Another Country: A Traveler's Guide.* Freedom, Calif.: The Crossing Press, 1995.

Somers, Tish, and Shields, Laurie. "Women Take Care: Consequences of Caregiving in Today's Society (1988). Available from Older Women's League, 730 11th St., NW, Suite 300, Washington, DC 20001.

Starkman, Elain Marcus. *Learning to Sit in the Silence: A Journal of Caretaking.* Watsonville, Calif.: Papier Mache Press, 1993.

Steinem, Gloria. *Moving Beyond Words.* New York: Simon & Schuster, 1994.

———. *Revolution from Within.* New York: Little, Brown, 1992.

Taylor, Dena, and Sumrall, Amber Coverdale, eds. *Women of the 14th Moon: Writings on Menopause.* Freedom, Calif.: The Crossing Press, 1991.

———. *The Time of Our Lives: Women Write on Sex after 40.* Freedom, Calif.: The Crossing Press, 1993.

Taylor, Nick. *A Necessary End.* New York: Nan A. Talese/Doubleday, 1994.

Teubal, Savina. "Simchat Hochmah: A Crone Ritual," in Dianne Ashton and Ellen Umansky, eds., *Four Centuries of Jewish Women's Spirituality.* Boston: Beacon Press, 1992.

Thiriet, Michele, and Kepes, Suzanne. *Women at Fifty.* New York: Schocken Books, 1987.

Trien, Susan Flamholtz. *Change of Life: The Menopause Handbook.* New York: Fawcett, 1986.

Utian, Wulf H., and Jacobowitz, Ruth. *Managing Your Menopause.* New York: Prentice Hall/Simon & Schuster, 1990.

Vickers, Joanne F., and Thomas, Barbara L. *No More Frogs, No More Princes: Women Making Creative Choices at Midlife.* Freedom, Calif.: The Crossing Press, 1993.

Viorst, Judith. *Forever Fifty and Other Negotiations.* New York: Simon & Schuster, 1989.

Wade, Betsy. "For Adventurers 50 and Older." *New York Times,* Travel Section, April 16, 1995.

Wade-Gayles, Gloria. *My Soul Is a Witness: African-American Women's Spirituality.* Boston: Beacon Press, 1995.

Walker, Barbara. *The Crone: Women of Age, Wisdom, and Power.* San Francisco: Harper & Row, 1985.

Weed, Susan. *Menopausal Years.* Woodstock, N.Y.: Ash Tree, 1994.

Weeks, David, and James, Jamie. *Eccentrics: A Study of Sanity and Strangeness.* New York: Villard, 1995.

Weideger, Paula. *Menstruation and Menopause.* New York: Alfred A. Knopf, 1975.

Weintz, Walter, and Weintz, Caroline. *Discount Guide for Travelers over 55.* New York: Dutton, 1985.

Wilder, Thornton. *Our Town.* New York: Bard/Avon Books, 1975.

Wilson, Emily Herring. *Older Black Women of the South.* Philadelphia: Temple University Press, 1983.

Wilson, J. *Women, Your Body, Your Health.* New York: Harcourt, Brace, Jovanovich, 1990.

Wolf, Naomi. *The Beauty Myth.* New York: William Morrow, 1991.

"Women and Aging," special issue of *Women's Studies Quarterly,* vol. 17, nos. 1 & 2, Spring/ Summer 1989.

Zacur, Howard, M.D., and Blumenthal, Roger, M.D. *Estrogen Replacement Therapy: The Johns Hopkins Guide to Making an Informed Decision.* Baltimore: Johns Hopkins University, 1993.